18
SOULS
The Loss and Legacy of Cougar Flight 491

18
SOULS
The Loss and Legacy of Cougar Flight 491

Rod Etheridge

BOULDER
BOOKS

Library and Archives Canada Cataloguing in Publication

Etheridge, Rod, author
18 souls : the loss and legacy of Cougar flight 491 / Rod Etheridge.

ISBN 978-1-77523-450-0 (softcover)

1. Helicopters--Accidents--Newfoundland and Labrador.
2. Helicopters--Accidents--North Atlantic Ocean. I. Title.
II. Title: Eighteen souls.

TL553.53.C3E84 2019   363.12'46509718   C2018-905389-5

© 2019 Rod Etheridge
Design and layout: Tanya Montini
Cover photograph: Greg Locke
Editor: Stephanie Porter
Copy editor: Iona Bulgin
Printed in Canada

We acknowledge the financial support of the Government of Newfoundland and Labrador
through the Department of Tourism, Culture, Industry and Innovation.

We acknowledge the financial support for our publishing program
by the Government of Canada and the Department of Canadian Heritage
through the Canada Book Fund.

We acknowledge the financial support
of the Government of Canada.
Nous reconnaissons l'appui financier
du gouvernement du Canada.

Dedicated to my children
Jessica, Colton, and Rayanna

Where the seagull soars and the mighty ocean roars
When the wind from the North blows so frantic
On the banks of Newfoundland the oil rigs stand
In search of crude from the cold northwest Atlantic
—Bruce Moss, "Your Last Goodbye"

Contents

Foreword

The idea of writing this book came to me about a year and a half ago during a conversation with my wife. We were talking about the tragedy of Cougar Flight 491, and it occurred to me that, out of the darkness of that day, there has come a small beacon of light—a light that shines through the memorials and scholarships and fundraisers created by the families and friends of those who died, to help keep the memories of their loved ones alive.

It is in the spirit of exposing and spreading that light that I decided to delve into the lives and the legacies of those who lost their lives on Cougar Flight 491: Thomas Anwyll, Peter Breen, Gary Corbett, Matthew Davis, Wade Drake, Wade Duggan, Corey Eddy, Keith Escott, Colin Henley, Timothy Lanouette, Kenneth MacRae, Allison Maher, Gregory Morris, Derrick Mullowney, Burch Nash, John Pelley, and Paul Pike.

Each one of them had family, friends, a career, hobbies and interests, hopes and dreams, and no two were the same. As you read through these pages, you will get to know many of them and you will no doubt laugh and shed a tear as I have, but it would not be possible without the trust and support from the people closest to them. As you can imagine, some people find it too hard to speak about the person they lost on March 12, 2009. For those who spoke to me, I am truly humbled and appreciative. They opened up and spoke honestly and candidly, sharing a little piece of their broken hearts with me. I can only imagine how hard that must have been. That trust now stands as a collective testimony to keep the memories alive for all families who lost someone on Cougar Flight 491.

To tell the story of what happened that day, I relied heavily on the Transportation Safety Board's investigation into the crash and the testimony the lone survivor, Robert Decker, gave to the inquiry into offshore helicopter safety. This book would not have been possible were it not for the support and commitment of Gavin and Amanda Will at Boulder Books, along with the invaluable insight and unending reassurances from Stephanie Porter, Boulder's Managing Editor. Stephanie made the unfamiliar world of writing a book a lot less intimidating and for that I am truly thankful.

Rod Etheridge

The Flight
March 12, 2009

The flying.

He loved everything about his nursing job, except the flying.

But he had to do it every three weeks. In a loud, cramped helicopter buzzing high above the Atlantic Ocean, heading 350 kilometres from the nearest piece of land to the SeaRose.

The SeaRose is an FPSO—a floating production, storage, and offloading vessel—stationed in an area of the ocean called White Rose, one of the rich oil and gas fields off Newfoundland. The SeaRose processes and stores the crude that is taken from underneath the sea floor. The oil is later transferred to a tanker to be taken to a refinery or some other destination.

John Pelley loved being aboard "the rig," as the workers called the FPSO. The 41-year-old had met some of his best friends at sea, people who shared his love of music and hockey. He didn't mind the seven-hour drive from his home on the west coast of Newfoundland across the Trans-Canada Highway to the airport in St. John's. It was a commute during which he would sometimes see all four seasons through his windshield in one day.

He'd turn on Sirius XM satellite radio in his vehicle and tune in his treasured Toronto Maple Leafs. John was used to leaving home for work. He'd done it for many years, as had many of his friends and other generations of young Newfoundlanders who had come to depend on the lucrative jobs in the offshore oil industry. It was a chance to earn more money and help set up a good life for him and his wife, Lori Chynn.

But the flying?

"You know, John hated—hated, hated, hated—flying," Lori recalls. "I mean, we didn't travel because he didn't like to fly."

March 12, 2009, was a typical late winter, early spring day in Newfoundland. At 9 a.m., the St. John's weather station reported a mostly clear sky, some sun with light winds, but it was cold, with the temperature gauge hovering around -1° Celsius.

That morning, John and most of the other 15 passengers were preparing to start a three-week "hitch," as time at sea is referred to in the offshore industry. It's normally followed by three weeks at home. They, along with the pilot and the co-pilot, were heading out on Flight 491, also known as Flight 91, aboard the Sikorsky S-92A operated by Cougar Helicopters, part of its contract to transport offshore workers to and from oil rigs and platforms.

In a company brochure, Cougar referred to the S-92, a relatively new addition to its fleet of aircraft, as "tough, safe, reliable" and was configured to carry a total of 17 passengers and two flight crew.

The trip to the SeaRose from the airport in St. John's is routine, a 90-minute flight completed several times a day. Prior to passengers' boarding the helicopter they gather in a briefing room to watch a mandatory, 10-minute safety video.

When that's over, the passengers form a line to walk single file outside to the helicopter. On this morning, as during most trips, there's good-natured jostling to get to the front of the line in an attempt to claim the best seat. Few want to sit on the left side of the chopper facing forward, as that's where the double seats are and where a 150-gallon auxiliary fuel tank occupies the space of what normally would be three other seats. The right side is a line of single seats, which the workers prefer, as they can easily sit back and fall asleep.

The initial route plan would see them take off from Runway 20 and head to the SeaRose to drop off and pick up passengers, before the helicopter continued on to the nearby Hibernia oil platform, also on the Grand Banks. However, the crew decided shortly after they were in the air to reverse the order and head first to Hibernia, then to SeaRose.

There's not much room to move around or even talk once the chopper is airborne. It is almost overwhelmingly loud. The roar of the engines and the spinning of the main rotor blades that stretch about 20 metres across the top of the helicopter keeps conversations to a nod or a smile. Most passengers use the 90 minutes to nap or read a book.

John's good friend Mark Frost has spent many hours on choppers in his time working offshore. "A loud whine the whole time," Mark says, "a constant buzz and everyone has earmuffs on for ear protection ... earplugs in and earmuffs over them for protection. Lots of time you just point if you want to show someone something. If you're next to someone, you can hear a little, but normally you use hand signals."

Passengers are buckled in by a four-point harness seatbelt, which wraps around the large hooded survival suit that is mandatory for the start and finish of the flight. "Landing or takeoff you need your hood fully on and donned, so you have the suit fully on, but once you take off, you can have your hood unzipped a bit then, it's bunched up in the back so you can't incline your seat," Mark continues. "It's more military-like than it would be [on] a passenger flight like Air Canada. You sit down and you are just kind of stuck there for an hour and a half. The only thing you get up for is an emergency to talk to the pilot or something. There are small windows and they aren't perfectly aligned with the seats, so you might see a bird or whale or a boat sometimes, but otherwise it's pretty boring."

On this day, Mark was aboard the SeaRose waiting for his friend to arrive, anxious to meet up in the vessel's music room where they could often be seen playing guitar and singing songs, entertaining the other workers.

The two became friends in 2005. Mark was an instrumentation technician aboard the SeaRose; John, the nurse, or "the medic," as he was called. "I was on night shift, my first hitch, and I was in the music room when I came off shift in the morning," Mark remembers. "I was playing guitar and singing by myself, and the door pops open and he sticks his head in. This is John, he had heard the music and wondered who it was. And he came in and introduced himself. He was anxious to get together sometime when we were both off to play music."

The two moved quickly to create a music scene aboard the SeaRose. "The room was called the quiet room, actually," Mark says. "That was what it was listed as on the door and there were some books and stuff in there. And we had a social committee and we bought instruments. Like we had an electronic drum kit and guitar amp and bass amp and that kind of stuff. So, yeah, it was one of the more popular things to do in the evening."

Before long, John and Mark were singing and playing guitar together. They even convinced a bass player to join them. "We learned songs for something to do in our spare time. Eventually as we kept going, like Christmas time and different holidays, we'd have a little performance in the evening or day if they had an assembly to bring everyone together."

Heading out to sea the morning of March 12 alongside John was an offshore worker he had taken under his wing. Allison Maher, age 26, was the youngest person on board and the only female. She told her family that John was her best friend at sea. Marjorie Maher describes her daughter as having beautiful green eyes, auburn hair, a constant smile, and an insatiable love of jokes—so much so, that many days at home she wouldn't get off the couch for hours as she'd be in fits of laughter watching comedian after comedian on television.

Allison worked for East Coast Catering, a small company specializing in food and accommodation services to remote areas, such as the offshore. She was one of a small group of its workers—five were aboard the flight that day—whose job it was to ensure that rig workers had everything they needed. Her duties were mostly housekeeping: making sure beds were made and the linen clean and fresh.

Eighteen months earlier Allison had a blossoming career in graphic design, fuelled by a natural ability to draw. But, according to Marjorie, Allison grew frustrated with the low pay and lack of movement in her career and, out of the blue, decided to apply for a job in the offshore.

But to do that, Allison had to complete a mandatory Basic Survival Training course. "The phone rang this evening," Marjorie recalls, "and she just blurted out, 'Mom, I need $2,000!' And I said, 'Oh, do you? What for?' And she said, 'I'm going to do a course. I'm going to work offshore.' And I said, 'Oh, you're going to work offshore.' And I said, 'Wait now, I gets your father.' So anyway, she spoke to her father. And I said, 'Oh my God, Rick, she won't last out there 10 minutes and they'll have to bring her in out of it.'"

But Allison did last "out there" longer than 10 minutes. She borrowed the money from her father, completed the survival training, and landed a job on the SeaRose, quickly fitting in with her fellow employees. And, she quickly started earning the kind of money she needed to pay back her father and buy the house she always wanted. "Once she got on the offshore, she bounced onto her feet," Marjorie said. "She had a beautiful home."

While Allison seemed to be happy in her new job, after about a year and a half she started hinting to friends that she wanted to get out of that lifestyle— three weeks on and three weeks off—and was considering finding a new job. "She was kind of thinking about giving it up," Marjorie says. "Her friends told us. She never said anything to us."

But on this day and on this flight, Allison was heading back to work out on the water. She sat in what many seasoned offshore travellers consider the best seat in the helicopter, directly behind the co-pilot, facing down the fuselage toward the rows of passengers, similar to the seat a steward or stewardess occupies on a commercial airliner. All other seats faced forward. Marjorie says offering Allison that seat was her co-workers' way of showing her respect.

Also on board was Allison's boss, Greg Morris, age 40, a record-holding rower who also worked at East Coast Catering, as a chef. According to his father, Wayne, Greg never complained about having to fly to work every three weeks. "I asked him if he minded being in the chopper, and he said no. Same with the boat. He didn't mind that either. With the rowing he was used to the water. Rowing made him really strong."

Greg's only brother, Rick, agrees. "The only thing he ever complained about with the helicopters was that they were cold and they were noisy," he says. "He never had any concerns for safety. There were a bunch of times he mentioned that they'd be halfway out and that they'd have to turn around and fly back for some reason. The biggest pain in the ass he said was when it was really foggy and a couple of times the choppers couldn't fly and he'd have to take the supply boat in and that took 18 hours or something like that and it was a bumpy ride."

Rick especially remembers one time that Greg was forced to take the supply boat to get home for his three weeks off: "I went to pick him up at the wharf and he got off and he was beside himself because it chewed into a good day and a half of his time that he should have been home because he couldn't take the chopper in."

Someone who could've been on the chopper that morning but wasn't was Sheldon Langdon, another East Coast Catering employee. He and Greg were good friends who both had young children. "Me and Greg used to always say on the rig, 'You know, like if something happened to one of us, make sure the family is taken care of, you know, anything they need.' We'd talk about that kind of stuff because out there there's nothing else to talk about."

Sheldon was also friends with Allison and the others on the flight who worked for the catering company: Derek Mullowney, Keith Escott, and Peter Breen. Sheldon, who like Greg worked aboard the SeaRose as a chef, was supposed to be heading out to sea that morning with his co-workers. But their work schedules had been revamped. "I haven't told many people this," Sheldon says. "Greg and I used to travel the same day. And he said, 'Something gotta change here, because we both can't leave the galley the same time. Because if we get a chopper during lunchtime, then who's going to serve the line?' So, he said, 'I'm going to figure something out.' And I said, 'Well, you figure it out. It doesn't matter to me. You do whatever you have to do, and I'm good with it.'"

Sheldon wasn't too happy about not being on the same hitch as Greg, as they enjoyed working side by side. But he understood. Greg sat down with a pen and a piece of paper and drew up a new schedule. "So, he came up to me and said, 'What we're going to do is I'm going to change one Thursday and you change the other Thursday.' And I said, 'Yes, that's fine. We'll do one week apart. But that's not too bad, it's only one week.' And he said, 'Do you care if we change this week?' And I said, 'It's fine with me. Whatever's good with you.' So, he changed the schedule and, basically, I was off." That morning, while Greg and the others settled into their seats for the trip back to the SeaRose, Sheldon was at home with his family.

Tom Anwyll, age 46, was one of those passengers settling into his seat. As soon as the helicopter was airborne, Tom would often lean back, close his eyes, and nap, no matter how bumpy the ride. "He had no issues with flying," his wife, Brenda, says. "He would get into the seat and he would fall asleep. It did not matter if it was turbulence, it did not matter if there were air pockets, to him it was like a roller-coaster ride. He had no issues at all. And I guess if you're flying so much, you just become immune to that kind of stuff."

And Tom did fly a lot. He lived in British Columbia. But his specialty, inspecting and repairing lifeboats, often brought him to Newfoundland to work on the oil platforms at sea—as well as Australia and the exotic South Pacific island of Tahiti. But it was when he was first assigned to a job in Newfoundland to carry out a life-raft safety inspection that his heart found a second home. "He loved it," Brenda says. "He loved the people. He loved the scenery, you know, living by the ocean. He just thought that was the greatest thing. I think he just really had something in his heart that told him, you know, he just loved it there. Just about every time he came home from Newfoundland, he'd say, 'Are you sure you don't want to move there?'" When the call came that Tom's expertise was needed in the province again, he didn't hesitate.

Sitting nearby and also preparing to nap was Robert Decker of St. John's. Robert, age 27, had special training in tracking the weather, with an emphasis on ice conditions. Spring was his busy time of year, as massive icebergs slowly made their way down south from Greenland and the Arctic.

He wasn't supposed to be on the flight; he was actually expecting to fly to the offshore the next day, Friday, March 13. But he had received a call two days earlier asking if he could head out on Thursday instead. The ice conditions were more intense than anticipated and he was needed to spot any large chunks of ice floating too close to offshore platforms.

When he stepped onto the chopper, Robert headed straight to the mid-section of the passenger compartment to claim a much-coveted single seat on the right side. A Cougar worker went from row to row for a final check to make sure he and the others were strapped in properly with their shoulder straps pulled as tightly as possible over their bulky survival suits. Robert's routine once they were in the air would be to ease back into the seat to try to get some sleep, as he had done during the past 50 or more times he had made the trip.

The pilot was Matt Davis, a 34-year-old Newfoundlander considered to be a confident, skilful pilot with 13 years and almost 6,000 hours of flying experience. Matt lived for helicopters. He had dreamed of being in the pilot's seat ever since he was a child, when his father—a wildlife officer who often had to fly into the bush by helicopter—would let Matt accompany him on some of his trips. Matt would even draw helicopters whenever he picked up a pen or pencil.

When Matt finally became a pilot, he'd be up before the alarm went off, because he couldn't wait to get to work. He loved that his job took him places most people only dream of. It had taken him to Angola in southern Africa, where he flew government officials around the country; as far north as Ellesmere Island in Nunavut, where he looked down in pure bliss at scenes of ice-capped mountains and fjords; and to northern Labrador, where he was captivated by the ruggedness of the Torngat Mountains.

Matt loved talking about flying. If anyone had questions about his job, he could talk for hours. Shortly after going to work at Cougar, he was promoted to captain and started flying the S-92, a dream job. He also became the company's training officer for the chopper.

To Matt's left was his co-pilot, First Officer Tim Lanouette, who lived in British Columbia. Tim, age 47, was a former military man who had spent two decades in the Canadian Armed Forces. For more than 10 years of that time he flew the Navy's Sea King helicopters. He had accumulated nearly 3,000 total flying hours.

When he wasn't flying, Tim had another love: music. His military years had started at the Canadian Forces School of Music in western Canada, where he studied bass trombone. He also had an impressive command of bass and acoustic guitars.

At one point after military training, Tim was assigned to the base in Shearwater, Nova Scotia, where he met Kevin Lane. Kevin worked on the aircraft that Tim flew and they'd often be sent on missions together somewhere at sea in some part of the world. It was on the water that the two—pilot and technician, two worlds that rarely connect personally—realized that they shared a love of creating and playing music. Kevin fancied himself a singer/songwriter and Tim was intrigued one night when he heard Kevin's voice come from the ship's music room. "Want to play some music together?," Tim asked. As much as he loved singing, Kevin couldn't quite master harmony. He could hear it and he could understand it. But he couldn't reproduce it when he sang. Until he met Tim, who sat him down and showed him how to listen for the notes and sounds that combine to create harmony.

Before long, the two were jamming at sea and when they were onshore they formed a 1980s band. "We wrote a bunch of songs together," Kevin says. "What else do you do at sea? He wrote a lot. It's not something he shared with people … You could walk into a room and Tim would be playing, but you wouldn't know it was something he wrote."

The helicopter lifted off from St. John's airport at 9:17 a.m. local time. Less than two minutes into the flight the crew switched from communicating with the St. John's air tower to communicating with the air traffic control centre in Gander, which is normal procedure, as Gander controls all flights within Newfoundland and Labrador's airspace.

"Gander Centre, good day, it's, ah, Cougar 91 on the departure through 200 feet, for 9000, ah, IFT Sea Rose," was the flight's first communication with Gander, handled by Tim: the chopper was 200 feet in the air at the time and preparing to rise to 9,000 feet as it headed to the SeaRose. Ten minutes later he asked Gander tower for permission to change their flight plan.

"It's Cougar 91. Taking a look at the ops plan here," came the request. "Actually, we would like to amend our flight plan and we'd like to go Alpha routing, Hibernia, at this time, and then SeaRose."

Gander approved and confirmed the change with the Cougar crew. "Okay, Cougar 91 is cleared to Hibernia via the amended route."

Fifteen minutes into the flight the chopper levelled off at 9,000 feet. By then, the crew and passengers had settled in for the remaining one hour and eight minutes it would take to reach the Hibernia rig.

Less than 15 minutes later an amber caution message light flashed on the screen in front of the crew, flagging a drop in oil pressure in the helicopter's main gearbox. Almost immediately, that yellow light switched off and was replaced by a bright red warning message.

Matt and Tim shifted into emergency mode. The illumination of the red warning message was accompanied by a computer voice saying, "GEARBOX PRESSURE … GEARBOX PRESSURE."

The red light combined with a reading from the oil pressure gauge that the pressure had dropped to a dangerously low level created a condition in which the crew must "land immediately," according to the helicopter's flight manual. The pilot checklist advises that ditching or landing in hazardous terrain is preferable to staying in the air.

Matt, as captain, issued a mayday call to the air traffic control centre in Gander. He asked for—and received—immediate clearance to turn around and head back to land.

And so, less than 30 minutes after lifting off from St. John's airport, Cougar Flight 491 needed to get out of the air. The nearest land was the most easterly point of North America, Cape Spear—originally called Cabo da Esperança by the Portuguese, which translates to Cape of Hope—a National Historic Site where jagged rocks and cliffs hundreds of feet high are pounded by large and unpredictable waves, and where a lighthouse that provides comfort for seagoers still stands guard after nearly two centuries.

More than 50 nautical miles of ocean lay between Cape Spear and the helicopter.

The People

John Pelley, 41

He had her with his smile. They were 16 and still adjusting to life in high school. Their families were acquainted, but it wasn't until they hung out with the same group of friends in their junior high years that Lori Chynn really started to notice John Pelley. "Oh my God, he was a nice-looking boy. He was cute," she says. It sounds like she's still blushing more than three decades later. "John had a beautiful smile. Beautiful. Like, he had the most amazing smile and it was just his confidence and he was a smart boy. Confident but also very humble. Yeah, it was just—I don't know—we just fell in love."

They grew up in Deer Lake on Newfoundland's west coast, where the social scene for young people in the early 1980s consisted of a movie theatre, a pool hall, and the local stadium, Hodder Memorial.

John was heavily into hockey. Lori was a figure skater. Before long, they were the quintessential high school sweethearts. Many young people go their separate ways after high school, but John and Lori's relationship continued to grow. "I knew early on this was someone I wanted to spend time with," she says.

John's confidence impressed Lori, especially when he tackled something new. "John's brother played guitar right from birth. He had that natural talent. His dad was a musician too. But John never picked it up till he was 19. He was so into sports, hockey and softball. But let me tell you something about John, once he gets something in his mind, that's it. One of his friends was going to one of the colleges here and they kind of connected again. And they started strumming. So, he got this in his mind—he was going to learn to play guitar and that was it then. So, when he started, I thought, 'Oh no, here we go. I gotta listen to this!' But then people would say, 'Jeez, can you play at the Rod and Gun Club?' or 'My best friend is getting married, can you sing for them?' And he sang at their reception, sang a song for them, and I thought, 'Okay, he's not bad!'"

John also picked up the mandolin, but it was his voice that people especially wanted to hear: "He would also sing a cappella, and old traditional tunes like Sam Hall and Irish stuff. He'd just belt it out and people who knew him all his life were like, 'What? Where—where did this come from?' And the boys that went to school with him, when he went back for his reunion, they were like, 'What? You weren't in a band going to high school?' And he said, 'Nah, I just decided to pick up a guitar.'"

John went to university in St. John's for a few years after high school but realized he wasn't happy there; he headed back to Deer Lake, where he snagged a job working as an ambulance attendant. As his mother was a nurse, health care came naturally to him. "He loved not having a clue as to what to what he was going to come upon," says Lori. "I mean, he wasn't fazed by anything. [He was a] very calm person when it came to that kind of stuff." John stayed in that job for several years while Lori finished her education degree in St. John's, focusing on psychology and counselling. Before long she was back on the west coast working with the local school district.

John's job made for interesting discussions at meal time. "His stepfather is an anesthesiologist. And we'd be sitting around the table, you know, his mom the nurse, the doctor, and him, the paramedic, and they'd be talking about stories and situations and all that ... and here am I, you know, an educator and I'm like, 'Oh my God, this is gross, people, we're eating!'"

But she could tell from listening to them talk that he loved the work. So when, at age 27, John was trying to figure out what he wanted to do with his life and his mother suggested that he consider becoming a nurse, Lori knew it would be the right decision.

"It was kind of like 'apply to nursing school!' And he said, 'I'm too old for that.' And I said, 'No, you're not.'"

After some convincing, John headed to nursing school in 1994, the year they were married. "At that time there was a really tight group of guys that went into nursing," Lori recalls. "They were very big, burly men, so it was a nice image, me being a guidance counsellor in high school, it was nice for the image to have that. It was the '90s, and there was a bit of male stigma with the nurses and all that, so it was great, because at school even the teachers said it made a lot of people go, 'Oh, that is an option.'"

John became close friends with fellow student Shane Fudge. "At the time, there was eight or 10 guys and 40-plus girls in the class," Shane recalls. "So, most of the guys got to know each other fairly well and fairly quickly and most of our courses were together and as we grew that way, we started noticing there was two or three of us that had similar interests in regard to sports."

As Shane and John also shared a love of the outdoors, on weekends or holidays they'd gather a bunch of other friends and go moose hunting or fishing. John couldn't get enough of it. "If he was fly fishing, you would have to literally beg him to leave the river, and there were many nights I sat in my truck after dark waiting for him to call it a day."

When they graduated, few nursing jobs were available in the province.

Most graduates headed to other parts of Canada. But Shane accepted a job in the United States at a hospital in Portland, Maine. John followed a few weeks later. It was tough for Lori, working as an educational psychologist on Newfoundland's Northern Peninsula, to see her husband travel so far away for work. "But you know, you did what you had to do; jobs were hard to come by."

The quality of John's nursing work was noticed. "John was very confident in his abilities," Shane says, "and he was very keen and didn't miss much. In Maine, doctors said they usually don't bring in foreigners, but they always requested John to work with them."

They spent about two years away in the United States. "No matter how good it was, Newfoundland was still home," Shane says. "John was working down there and at the same time building a house back here, so we always had plans to return home. When we finished, I got offered a job in central Newfoundland and John got offered a job offshore. I went back to school for a short period and they persuaded me to go offshore as well. So, we ended up in the same field again."

Before long, they were working side by side on the SeaRose FPSO.

Offshore, when John wasn't working, he was usually in the music room with Mark Frost or watching hockey on television. Those two activities helped make being away from home and Lori for three weeks at a time bearable.

Saturday night in the theatre room, one door over from the music room, was always an extra special night on the SeaRose. "Because it was Hockey Night in Canada and Don Cherry," Mark explains. "No matter who was playing people would come in and the cooks would make wings and nachos to bring in for the first intermission. Lots of times during the week people would have movies on, but Saturday night they'd put hockey on."

The rivalry was so intense that they even created their own version of Hockey Night in Canada's *Hot Stove*, that part of the hockey broadcast where hosts and panelists would muse about players and hockey rumours during the second intermission of the televised game. "John was a big Toronto Maple Leafs fan and I was a Montreal Canadiens fan and Greg Morris was a Montreal Canadiens fan and Peter Breen was a Boston Bruins fan," Mark explains. "That was always fun, and then during our break times, John would come down in the cafeteria and Peter Breen would be there and Greg Morris, and the guys would be there with the cooks every morning at 9:15 and they'd talk hockey. So, they made up this little poster, one of the guys made it up with the Ron McLean *Satellite Hot Stove*, only they'd call it *The SeaRose Hot Stove* and it would have pictures on it with all the guys and saying that they were the panelists on the show." Mark still laughs, more than a decade later.

Their intense hockey interest extended from the offshore to their onshore time. Baker Hughes, an oilfield services company involved in lab testing offshore, held annual golf tournaments to raise money for charity, and one year, in 2008, hockey great Lanny McDonald was lined up to be their special guest for the event in St. John's.

Mark knew how much it would mean for John to meet a former star of the Toronto Maple Leafs and one of his childhood hockey heroes, so he hustled up three tickets for the tournament. "One of the guys who worked at Baker Hughes was able to take three guys with him to play at the golf tournament, so it was myself, John, and Greg Morris. Lanny McDonald ... was golfing at one of the holes and as you went around, you could shoot one hole against Lanny."

It was a great day for John because Lanny had played alongside Darryl Sittler, one of John's biggest hockey idols. "For him that was fabulous," Mark says. "I have pictures of Greg with Lanny's Stanley Cup ring on and the World Junior Championship Ring on and I got a picture with Lanny McDonald getting Greg in the headlock. Lanny made a point to talk to everyone, but we were probably talking to him the longest because he could tell we were more interested and stuff. Oh yeah, we had a great day that day!"

Lori too remembers how much that day meant to John. When he arrived home, he couldn't stop talking about it. "He came home, and he was so excited. He came home with everything signed by Lanny McDonald," she recalls, with laughter. "He kept showing me stuff and he said, 'This is the golf ball he signed,' and 'This is the hat he signed,' and 'This is the shirt he signed.'" Lori couldn't help but crack a joke. "And I said, 'John, did he sign your ass too, cause he signed everything else!' And he said, 'Lori, you don't understand ...'"

Only one other time had she seen him so excited about meeting someone—when Fergus O'Byrne, a legend in Newfoundland's traditional music scene, performed on the rig. During that trip John played and sang alongside one of his musical heroes. "He comes home at Christmastime and Fergus O'Byrne had been on the rig and he had a video, and he said, 'You gotta see this, Lori! You gotta watch this!' And he was like a child. He was like a child that had seen Santa Claus. So, we put the video on and, I mean, it's on YouTube, him singing 'Sonny's Dream' with Fergus. Oh my God, I gotta tell you that was the highlight of his life."

John and Lori had settled into a life of being apart for much of the year. When it was time for John to return to St. John's and the flight to the SeaRose, they had a routine. They'd take in some weekend hockey games at Hodder Memorial if it was during winter and, come Monday, she'd head back to high school in Deer Lake, where she worked as a guidance counsellor, and John would pack for his trip.

That's how it was in March 2009, when John finished his latest three weeks at home and was getting ready to head out to sea again. "We took in a Deer Lake Red Wings game because he left on the 11th and we were at the hockey games on Saturday night and Sunday before he left, the 7th and 8th of March. And then the ritual was that I would go back to work on Monday and John would leave to go back, to drive across the island on Wednesday."

And so it was, on the morning of March 12, 2009, that 41-year-old John Pelley, fresh from a trip home that included a week-long stint at the cabin with his buddies, stepped onto Cougar Flight 491 to head back to the SeaRose.

Lori was in school that day, as usual, and had just headed into the school office at the start of lunch, when one of the teachers spoke up: "Lori, you're wanted on the phone ..."

Allison Maher, 26

From an early age, Allison Maher showed two characteristics that astounded and confused her parents, because they had no idea of their origin. First: she had a natural flair for drawing. She would sit on the couch for hours drawing characters such as Mickey Mouse or Eeyore, filling the sheets with strokes and colours that looked like a trained professional had etched them. "She was a bit of an artist," her father, Richard, brags. "Even as a little girl, she'd be sitting there doodling. Very creative. And not only art, making things too. She'd make Christmas decorations. She'd spend hours on the chesterfield just at stuff like that. She could sit down with the pen and the pencil and she was unbelievable. I can't see how she could do it. It's amazing."

Then there was her entrepreneurial spirit. If there was a dollar to be made, Richard says, Allison, a teenager in the mid-1990s, would find a way to earn it. And that's exactly what she did with her artwork. "She was going into Grade 9 and she sat down one day, she was so bored and I said, 'Draw a nice picture.' And she said, 'What will I draw?' And a flower was blooming on the kitchen table, and I said, 'Draw this flower!' And that's what she done. The picture is beautiful. Filled with flowers.'"

Friends began asking Richard and Marjorie to get Allison to draw pictures for them. More and more requests came from relatives and friends and then a restaurant owner hired her to do a mural. As a teenager, Allison started her own tiny business doing just that—drawing murals on children's bedroom walls.

Her mother, Marjorie—Marge to family and friends—says people in Aquaforte, a tiny fishing community on the southern shore, where the family lives, loved her drawings of cartoon characters because of her attention to detail.

Richard and Marjorie's home is filled with Allison's pictures. On the walls. On the refrigerator. Dozens fill a large artist's binder. Allison loved drawing flowers, and two of the framed pictures on the wall are of bunches of brightly coloured daisies. Other drawings are of horses, or birds singing in trees. There's a pencil drawing of Jack Frost with swirling clouds of cold bursting from his mouth. And on every picture is Allison's signature mark: her name with a tiny daisy above the *I*. She signed it like that, Marjorie says, because of Allison's April birthday; the flower for that month is a daisy.

One of Marjorie and Richard's favourite pieces of her artwork is of a little boy in his bed at night. His blankets are all bunched up and there's a ball and a truck on the floor. The boy is lifting the edge of his quilt and peeking under the bed. Written in pencil above the picture is the question, "Is the Booggie man still under the bed?" They both crack up laughing at that pencil drawing. "I don't know where that came from." Richard laughs and explains that he has no-where near that kind of creativity. "I don't know where she got it, but it didn't come from us. I worked three jobs for most of my life. I was with Canada Post for 31 years. I fished besides that, and I worked with Revenue Canada besides that."

It was hard for Allison to understand why her father would head to work at the end of the workday. "I remember Allison was a little girl and I came home," Richard says, "and we lived in Mount Pearl at the time, and I was going back to work at the Post Office after punching in eight hours at Revenue Canada and as I was leaving to go to work Allison said, 'But, Daddy, you just came home from work!'" He laughs heartily as he tells the story.

Another side of Allison emerged as she grew up, a compassionate side. Both Marjorie and Richard agree she always favoured people who were down and out. "She loved the underdog. She always loved the underdog," her father says. "She was only a little girl and there was a guy who lived on the street downtown in St. John's and he was known as Hobo Bill and he always had a big parka on and he was always on a city bench. We were driving down there one day and she saw him, and she had to get out of the car and give him $2. That's the way she was. She always liked the children who were less fortunate in school, that's who she befriended. Like, that was her way."

Marjorie nods in agreement. "She had a cousin who had trouble with her back and her hands," she recalls. "And there was another kid who had something wrong with his lungs. And she'd come home from school and she'd be all upset and I'd say, 'Allison, what's wrong, honey?' And she'd say, 'Mom, some people are not very nice to those people.' She was so soft-hearted. She'd see people pick on them and she'd get so upset. She'd feel for them so much, she'd make them her friend."

She loved people, but she was very strong-willed and wouldn't back down from anyone or anything. Even though she was two years younger than her only brother, Brian, and they were like chalk and cheese, she was fiercely loyal and always stood up for him. "Some young fellow picked on Brian on the school bus one time, and Marge gets a phone call that she beat up someone on the bus!" As Richard laughs while telling the story, Marjorie chimes in. "And I said, 'What?' Apparently, he said something to Brian, and Allison turned on him!"

Marjorie says she could see Allison's independent spirit early on. "They'd get along here because there was only two of them," Marjorie says. "They played and played and played with blocks, those Lego blocks. They lived for putting them together. And they'd spend a lot of time out near the side of the road with the Tonka trucks in the sand. And there was a lot of sand and Brian would be digging and digging and you could barely see him in the sand. And Brian would have everything set up with the toys and the next thing you'd see Allison coming down and swinging her arms and this went here and that went there and it was clear she was the boss!"

As she grew, everyone quickly learned that Allison had little time for two things: school and mornings. "She was never too fussy about school," Marjorie remembers. "She wasn't a morning person. When she got up, she wouldn't have anything for breakfast. She'd open her bedroom door and she'd plow out through and she was gone! And she wouldn't speak. It wasn't a good thing to speak to her in the morning."

Like her father, she was a night owl. There are stories of her getting up at 3 a.m. and saying, "Come on, we're going to Walmart!"

Relatives describe Allison as a "spitfire." Her parents say that was because she was always bursting with energy and had a personality that "matched her flaming red hair, and her piercing green eyes."

Marjorie and Richard say people liked Allison for her infectious sense of humour. She would assign cute pet names to everything she owned, whether it was an ornamental turtle she called George—she bought it because it had a broken tail and she figured no one else would want it—or the trees, affectionately named Aloysius and Alphonsus, that she planted on each side of the door to her house.

Valerie Maher laughs when she recalls how Allison would come up with pet names for everything. She says that was all part of her big imagination. "I remember Allison being a small child on the school bus," Valerie says, "probably like six or seven years old, and she used to pretend that she was a cat or a bunny rabbit. She always had, like, such a sense of humour and such an imagination that she would literally jump around like a rabbit."

Valerie and Allison were cousins, and despite a few years difference in age—Valerie was the older one—they also became good friends. Sometimes they were mistaken for sisters because of the red hair and bubbly personality they shared. "The atmosphere was always very high when me and Allison were together. We always had like huge laughs and we would know what each other was talking about. I would say something like totally foolish and she would continue that. We had no filters."

When they were together, the conversation flowed seamlessly and usually it felt like they were the only two people in the room. "Me being an only girl in my family I looked at her as being a sister and that's why the friendship was so strong between us. I would say a sentence, she would finish it. She would say something, I would finish it. And it would just go on and on all night long. Literally, there was nights we were up all night just laughing and carrying on and just being totally foolish."

As Allison was growing up, she felt she could tackle anything, and she proved it when she put down laminate flooring in her bedroom. She was 13. "She did all the work in putting down the floor. She was real crafty. She gets that from her father," says Marjorie.

Richard laughs at that suggestion, but recalls how her craftiness often helped him. "I was out one day and I was at the cabin and I was building a door, and I couldn't get my hand plane working because it was too tight. I was screwing around with it and I took it apart a few times and I was getting frustrated and the next thing, she took it apart and fixed it and said, 'Here, Dad, try it now!' And it was perfect!"

Allison was interested in that kind of hands-on work, and being at home was more interesting to her than hanging out at the mall. "She'd always be out in the shed," Marjorie recalls. "Brian would be gone on his bike, he was at that age and everything was about his bike. But Allison was around. There were no girls here. And everyone who was in her class who was the same age as Allison was all about boys. So, she spent a lot of time around here. She was always with 'Mom,' right? Even when we'd go into town, she'd always say 'My God, Mom, this is some long drive.' She used to find the drive into St. John's some long. She'd be right delighted when she got home."

After high school, Brian went to work in the offshore. Allison didn't think that life was for her and, instead, she headed to college to study graphic design. She was soon earning a paycheque for her ability to draw and create. But the job at a small graphic design company in Mount Pearl, about an hour's drive from her hometown, didn't pay enough for her to live comfortably. She made new plans. She wanted her own house but she knew she would never afford it on her salary. "She said that to me one day when she was working at graphic design and not making a lot of money," Marjorie says, "and one time they gave her a 25-cent raise and she realized she wasn't going anywhere there ... She said, 'Mom, you wear a uniform working with ambulances and Dad has a uniform working with Canada Post, so I need a job with a uniform.'"

Allison could see the kind of money her brother was earning. In the spring of 2005, a call came out of the blue one night. Like many Newfoundlanders who wanted a better life, Allison, then 23, decided that she too would head offshore.

Her father loaned her the $2,000 she needed to do mandatory Basic Survival Training. Before long, she had completed the course and landed a full-time job at East Coast Catering. She even had to wear a uniform: matching shirts and pants. "The only reason she was there was to make more money because she wanted to buy a house," Richard says.

One day Allison went to a bank for a loan. "And she said to the bank manager that she had her own financial advisor," Marjorie remembers. "And he said, 'Oh really, who is that?' figuring he knew all the financial advisors in town. And she said, 'Oh, his name is Rick Maher.' And the manager said, 'I don't know him ...' And she said, 'Yeah, that's my dad!'"

Richard, the mailman–fish-plant worker–taxation office employee and, now, according to Allison, financial advisor, was also her banker, helping out when and where he could. "She phoned me one day and said, 'Dad, I want to get a house.' And she knew she didn't have a penny in the bank. So, I said, 'Yes, girl, if you want to get a house, go ahead.' And then the next day I got a call and she said, 'Dad, I need $10,000!'" he recalls with a hearty laugh. "I said I'll meet you at the bank when I get off work at three o'clock! And then the next day she said, 'Dad, I need another $2,000!' And this went on for awhile. But anyway, she got her house. And she paid me back all the money over time. She paid me back every cent."

To furnish her house, Allison put her entrepreneurial and negotiating skills to use in getting every deal she could. Richard says she had a knack for getting salespeople to lower their prices. "One day she was out buying a set of coffee and end tables," he says, "and I was telling her to go to different places because, I told her, 'The first place is not the last price.' And so this day she goes in and beat the salesman down and then she said, 'Now, are you going to deliver them for me?' And he said, 'We can't afford to deliver them for you, you're after beating us down so far in price!'"

Richard laughs so hard in retelling the story that his face turns red. "And she said, 'Well, throw them aboard the car, I'll bring them home myself!' And it took her three trips to get them home."

Along with her cousin Valerie, Allison had another close friend, Stephanie. Marjorie says it was a testament to Allison's kindness that she made sure never to hurt either one's feelings. "One day, Allison and Valerie went into a store and picked out all the light fixtures," Marjorie says. "Then Stephanie found out Allison was ready to install light fixtures in the house, so Stephanie said, 'Allison, me and you are going in to Kent Building Supplies and we're going to pick out the light fixtures.' So, here it was all the light fixtures were all picked out and ordered and everything and Allison said, 'What am I going to do now?' But she never said a word about it to Stephanie. She went in and picked out a whole new set of light fixtures. She never told Stephanie the difference. But they must have been similar because Stephanie went to her house later and never noticed anything different."

Marjorie still laughs when she recalls the fuss about the lights. "But she wouldn't tell Stephanie that she was in and had done this with Valerie. She didn't want to hurt her feelings. See, all her friends wanted to be part of it and they all wanted to do something for her."

Valerie remembers the trip to get the lights: the car she owned at the time—a little Mazda 3—was loaded down with all the lights and light fixtures and Allison had wrangled such a deal that when she got in the car she pretended she was the lady in a television commercial that was popular at the time. The customer runs out of the store yelling to her husband to "start the car!" because the furniture was so cheap she thought that the clerk had made a mistake.

Valerie says that's exactly how it played out when Allison got in the car after it was loaded down with the lights. "And she was hanging out the side of the door saying, 'Start the car, start the car!' You know, like that IKEA commercial. And here I am driving away and she's hanging out, singing out, 'Start the car,' and I don't know how someone didn't get hurt! But she had that type of personality."

Offshore, Allison settled in nicely to her new job and work routine. Three weeks on the rig. Three weeks at home. She liked the people she worked with and Marjorie says they felt the same about her. Sometimes the workers would find out at the last minute that their time at sea was being extended longer than the regular three-week hitch, or weather would keep flights grounded, meaning that they weren't getting home possibly for days. Allison would try to console them, Marjorie says. "I guess some of them would be in a foul mood after being offshore for 21 days, and then 22 days and then 23 days, and she'd be trying to say things to them, trying to cheer them up." One co-worker referred to her as "sunshine on foggy days," someone who "raised the spirits of all on board."

When the three-week hitch was over, Allison headed home to her cat, Skylar—her "little girl"—and her brand-new home in Mount Pearl. She was quick to tell everyone that it was the smallest house on the street. Her parents were quick to counter that she owned her own home at 25 and that is something she should be proud of. Allison's personal life was also going well. She was happily in a relationship and Marjorie says the two loved spending every minute they could together. They shared her home in Mount Pearl. "She liked fun but had no time for nightclubs. They would always be going through the door with a few slices of bread, heading to Bowring Park to feed the ducks. They spent an awful lot of time walking in that park. They were always laughing together."

When it was time to head back to sea, Marjorie says, Allison had a slight change in personality. Her mood darkened and she became a little uptight. She told her friends she was thinking about leaving the offshore to try to find work at one of the hospitals in the city. She'd hint at that sometimes when she spoke with her mother but she'd never come right out and say it.

Marjorie says that Allison became sentimental as her boyfriend drove her to the airport for the helicopter flight; he'd always reassure her by saying, "Now Allison, now Allison."

And so it was, on the morning of March 12, 2009, Allison Maher, 26 years old, excited about having her own home but considering a possible job change, stepped onto Cougar Flight 491 ready to head back to the SeaRose.

Her father, Richard, was on the road delivering the mail. Her mother, Marjorie, was at home in the kitchen studying. She worked with an ambulance service and was learning how to recognize symptoms of illnesses. For most of the morning she was concentrating on her notes and only half listening to the radio on in the background.

At one point, Marjorie heard something about a small plane and something about a crash, but that's all she heard as she was trying to concentrate on the information and medical terms that filled her head. Suddenly, the telephone rang.

Gregory Morris, 40

Paddy Dyer sighs deeply, closes his eyes, and pictures his childhood friend Greg Morris like it was yesterday. In his mind he can see the snowmobiles they spent hour after hour riding on, gliding from trail to trail in and out of the city of St. John's with nothing, only blinding white snow, in front of them.

It was the early 1980s and they weren't yet in their teens. "Back then Greg had an old Elan, twin cylinder. This is when we were kids, you know, like 10 years old at that time. And I had a 1976 Olympic 300, so I had the fast machine!" Paddy laughs.

The two would leave from their parents' homes in Logy Bay, a community on the edge of St. John's, and snowmobile on one of the many trails in the area, following the telephone pole lines and crisscrossing in and around the city. Often, they wouldn't stop until an engine conked out. "We'd break down and we'd walk back home again," he pauses and bursts into laughter while telling the story. "And we'd get our fathers to come up and get us going and we'd go on again! The two of us liked skidooing right from a young age and we liked the dirt bikes too and it was just a bond we had."

A bond born from a love of being outdoors made Paddy and Greg inseparable from the time Greg was in kindergarten and Paddy—the elder in the friendship—a year older and in Grade 1 at St. Francis of Assisi, an elementary school in Outer Cove, the community next door. Where you saw Greg, you saw Paddy. "We just had common interests," Paddy says. "It was different back then. You wouldn't do that now, let a 9- or 10-year-old take a Skidoo and go on by themselves."

Greg's parents, Wayne and Marie, remember those times well. After more than 50 years together, they can finish each other's sentences, especially when talking about Greg's childhood years. "I can look out the window now and I still see him coming down the road on his bike," Marie recalls wistfully, "with his blue sweater on, and he was probably only seven, and he'd take his bike and go down to Paddy Dyer's place or down around Poppy Dyer's Meadow, they used to call it. The young fellows would all hang out around there. He had friends coming out of his ears, no matter where he went."

Wayne nods as she speaks. "He was the life of the party," he chimes in. "That was the personality he had. He was that type. If someone was shy, he was the first person to talk to them. That was his nature."

Wayne and Marie, married in 1967, had two children, Greg and Rick. Greg was the older by four and a half years, and the two couldn't be more different. "Greg was very outgoing and social," Marie says. "Rick was quiet and into the books. If Greg got 55 or 60 in his test, he was delighted. If Rick came home with less than 90, he was disappointed."

Rick chuckles and agrees with that description of him and Greg. "He was the typical big brother," Rick says with a laugh. "If he broke something, he would make sure I would get blamed for it, or that we shared the blame. I was a bit more quiet and more academic type and he was very outgoing and very gregarious. He always had a bunch of people around. Had a big circle of friends. He very much enjoyed being social. I mean, even physically we were very different."

Standing about 6 feet tall, Greg was a big guy and always into sports. "I played stuff but not to the extent that he did," Rick says. "He enjoyed rowing and hockey and all that stuff, and softball in the summer, he was always really athletic."

As teenagers, Greg and Paddy discovered rowing, which was likely inevitable—Logy Bay was next to Outer Cove, a community known historically for the winning crews it entered into the St. John's Regatta, North America's oldest sporting event. Every year for two centuries, teams of rowers gather at Quidi Vidi Lake in the middle of St. John's in early August to compete for the coveted Regatta championship trophies. Nearly everyone in the city gets the day off work to celebrate the holiday.

Greg and Paddy heard that local rowing legend Mike Power wanted to bring together a team of young rowers to compete at an intermediate level in the 1985 Regatta. "He's a legend down at Quidi Vidi Lake," Paddy says of Mike Power. "He was steering the Senior Outer Cove men's crew at the time but Mike had the idea that he wanted to start up a junior age crew, which we were, all 16 and 17 years old, and it was the first year, the first time any of us ever rowed."

The crew of confident upstarts began working out early in the year and kept up a steady exercise regime, with their eye on turning heads come Regatta Day in August. "Mike trained us and steered us and we went down the pond and we ended up setting a record, which we didn't think was going to happen, but things started going well for us and we ended up setting an intermediate record that lasted for 15 years. The *Telegram* newspaper wrote an article that said we were the best first-year crew that ever rowed Quidi Vidi Lake," a beaming Paddy says.

The record books at the Regatta show the Men's Intermediate Race in 1985 was won by a team of first-year rowers, including Gregory Morris and

Patrick Dyer, whose names are among those gone down in Regatta history as setting a course race time of 9 minutes and 30 seconds.

Greg's father doesn't know where his son got his athletic side. He shakes his head and shrugs it off with a joke. "Hockey and rowing was his thing. I don't know where he got it. I had trouble just walking up the road!"

But another side of Greg developed as he got older. He enrolled at a local college in a three-year administration program and seemed to be heading into a career that involved sitting at a desk all day, when cooking caught his attention. "For some reason he ended up getting a job at a pizza place," his mother says. "Pizza Experts in St. John's. He picked up cooking there and then he went back to school and did marine cooking and went offshore." She believes his interest in being a chef came from his father's side of the family: "Wayne's father was a cook but we never made the connection until after Greg was into cooking."

Wayne agrees that his father may have been the inspiration. "He was on the boats for years during the war and then he was the head cook over at the old General Hospital on Forest Road. He must turn after Dad," he says about Greg, "because I burn water, I could never do anything like that!"

Paddy sums up Greg's talent in the kitchen by saying that, when Greg was around, "the food was always the best."

Soon, the friends started to get serious about life and responsibilities and Greg began his studies to become a chef. Paddy went into corrections and got a job as a Correctional Officer at Her Majesty's Penitentiary in St. John's.

They were hanging out the night Greg met the person he would eventually marry, Heather Warren. "I knew who Greg was," she says, "because my brother was friends with Paddy and Greg. I liked his personality. He was always happy. He was just a good guy. I guess we just had that connection, I suppose."

The cooking was a bonus. "His favourite thing to cook was meat. Greg loved cooking meat. He'd always do different things. Fajitas or wraps or Philly steaks. We'd always have these dinner parties and my favourite thing was seafood crepes. And they were so good. Even to this day my friend will call me and say, 'I just wish we could have those seafood crepes again!' Like, he'd come home and I'd try to make something and he'd say, 'No, you just go sit down.' He loved to eat. And he loved food."

And he loved football. Greg was addicted to the sport, according to Heather. Especially college football, and especially if it involved his beloved Michigan Wolverines. "He loved it. Loved it. Loved, loved it," Heather says. More than that, even: when it came to football and Greg, logic could easily go out the window. "Greg and my brother once travelled to Detroit to take in a football game," she recalls with a laugh, "and before they went to the game, they tried to concoct a plan. And they were saying, 'Now, we're going to streak across the football field. We're going to climb across the fence and streak across the football field.' And with that, I came down the stairs," Heather roars with laughter and raises her voice to a high-pitched fake yell, "and I said, 'You are not doing that! You are a responsible father!' That would be something he'd do. He'd do that in a heartbeat, just for a laugh, right? Just for a laugh."

Greg and Paddy's friendship remained strong even as life took them down different roads. "Greg was best man at my wedding and I was best man at his wedding," Paddy says. "Greg's son, Ian, is my godson and my daughter Brittany was Greg's goddaughter."

After cooking school, Greg took the East Coast Catering job offshore. He was part of a small team of people who prepared and served food to oil workers and ensured that their accommodations were taken care of, linen was fresh, and beds were made. By the time they were into their 30s, Greg and Heather were married and had two children, Ian and Erin (Erin is older by two years). Neither Heather nor Greg liked the idea of his leaving home to go to sea for work, but it gave them a salary they needed to raise a family. "It was either that or he's here earning piddly money," she says. "It was a sacrifice that he had to do."

When one parent works away from home, it's not easy for the other to run the household smoothly. Everything—cleaning dishes, doing laundry, paying bills, getting the children to and from school on time, and making sure homework is done every evening—falls to the parent at home, who often also has a full-time job. Becoming a part-time single parent is a heavy load and a big adjustment.

Heather admits that she sometimes found it tough; and it was also tough on offshore workers like Greg who had to leave their families, sometimes at crucial moments. "He was here for the birth of Erin," she says. "He wasn't here for the birth of Ian. My water broke like 4 in the morning and he was offshore and I called him and I told him my water had broke. And he tried to get in but it was a foggy day, the fog was really bad."

The doctors delayed the delivery as long as they could but baby Ian would only wait so long. "We tried to keep Ian from coming till Greg got in but 2 in the afternoon, it was like, 'Okay, he gotta come out now!' My sister was here and she came with me to the hospital and he was on the phone … she was holding the phone while I was giving birth."

Greg was able to get in later that day. "You can only imagine now the anxiety of being out there and trying to get in for that," Heather says. "It is sad that he couldn't be there. But that's it. That's the life of an offshore worker."

At sea, Greg met a kindred spirit in Sheldon Langdon, another young father working offshore to make a better life for him and his family. "Me and Greg just became buddies," Sheldon says. "I was working with him on days, so me and him was in the galley all the time together so you can get pretty close, pretty fast. You become a second family out on a rig. Especially on the SeaRose. You had a tighter core net of people you kinda got really close to. They were always on the same shifts and that created a tight bond."

In the kitchen hierarchy on the rig, Greg was called Camp Boss: he was in charge of the catering crew, he assigned rooms to the kitchen staff, and he ensured that everyone had what they needed. "We have a day shift and a night shift," Sheldon explains. "I'd start at 7:30 and do the lunch and supper and the night cook does the midnight meal and breakfast. So, when me and Greg were there, we used to work the 7:30 day shift till 7:30 in the night. We'd come in at 7:30 and start the soup right off the bat, whatever soup we'd decide to put on, and then we'd get into the meal for the 10:30 to 12:30." They would map out a seven-day meal plan to make food preparation easier. Depending on what day it was, they'd prepare salmon or cod or ribs, or steaks if it was a Friday night. In Newfoundland, says Sheldon, everyone likes pea soup, so on Saturdays they'd put on a pot of soup.

And just as Friday night was steak night, Greg and Sheldon decided Saturday would be finger food night, especially since just about everyone would be in the TV room glued to the NHL games. "Greg and I were both fanatical about hockey, so when we went to the SeaRose we said it'd be nice to make something for the boys during the hockey games in the nighttimes, just to make it more enjoyable, you know? You are so far away from home for three weeks, it gives you something to look forward to."

Word got around quickly about the Saturday night treats and it made for a fun-filled boisterous evening. "And it brought more people to the TV room in the nighttime to watch the game," Sheldon says, "which made it more enjoyable. I mean, you had 25 or 30 fellows there and everybody was chanting for different teams."

Greg and Sheldon had created more than just a night watching hockey— Greg cheering for his cherished Montreal Canadiens and Sheldon trying to yell over him, boasting about his Toronto Maple Leafs. It had become a much-anticipated event that kept the anguish of being away from their families half of the year at bay, if just for a short period of time.

Back home, Heather had adjusted to being the sole parent for six months of the year. She was a nurse in the Cardiac Care Unit of the Health Sciences Centre, the main health care centre in Newfoundland and Labrador. Often when the time neared for Greg to head out to sea, Heather would peek out the window at work, hoping that it would be foggy or that it would rain, that it would be messy enough to keep the helicopters grounded and flights cancelled. Just hoping he'd stay home a day or even a few hours longer.

And so it was, on the morning of March 12, 2009, that Greg Morris, 40 years old and well rested after three weeks at home with Heather and the children, headed to the airport to take Cougar Flight 491 to the SeaRose.

That day, Heather, scheduled to work the early morning shift, was up before anyone else and quietly scurried around the house, eating breakfast and getting ready for work, trying not to wake anyone. In their bed, Greg was cuddled snugly into four-year-old Ian. When she was ready to head out the door, Heather glanced into the bedroom and stood there and stared, deciding not to wake either of them to say goodbye. "Ian was in the bed with Greg and they were just tucked in and asleep and they were just so comfy, I said to myself, 'I'm not waking them up to just say goodbye.' So, I went in and I looked at them and I said, 'I'll talk to you later.' And I left."

At the hospital, the morning unfolded normally. Heather went through her routine of taking care of patients and sneaking a glance out the window every half hour or so in hopes that the weather had taken a turn for the worse and that Greg's flight would be delayed.

She had her fingers crossed as the morning hours passed, hoping that a fog bank would move in over the airport or maybe the March morning would bring freezing rain. "That day I kept looking out the window and I was always like, 'Oh, maybe he'll just stay home for another day. Maybe I'll get another day.' So, I used to be on the computer to see if the flight left. And I thought maybe he's not going to get out that day. So, I looked on the computer and it said the flight had gone."

Accepting that Greg had once again gone to sea, Heather busied herself with nursing duties. A short time later she was asked to come to the telephone.

Thomas Anwyll, 46

Mr. Mojo Rising.

Suzie Q.

American Woman.

Bang a Gong.

If there ever was an award for Best. Dog. Names. Ever., surely Tom Anwyll would've won it hands down.

He loved dogs and he loved music. It was only natural that he'd find a way to create a connection between them. "All of our dogs had musical names. It was either a line from a song or a name of a song, that kind of thing," his wife, Brenda, explains. "We had fun naming our dogs or any puppies we had. One of his favourites that he named was Mr. Mojo Rising because he liked the Doors."

That quirky sense of humour caught Brenda's attention when she first met Tom. It was at a drag-racing track in Mission, British Columbia, in the mid-1980s. "He was funny. He definitely made me laugh and he was a funny guy and he entertained me," she recalls.

Brenda lived in Coquitlam, about a 40-minute drive down the road, and it was her first time checking out "hot-rodding." Her cousin's boyfriend drove a rear-engine dragster, one of the long skinny race cars that helped propel racing legend Connie Kalitta into the Motorsports Hall of Fame of America.

As for Tom, he had never seen a drag-racing track that he could ignore. He travelled much of British Columbia and down into Washington to take in competitions. He loved race cars and engines and could often be seen tinkering with them.

A chance encounter brought him and Brenda together that day in Mission. She was 21 and, out of curiosity, decided to head to the track to watch her cousin's boyfriend race. Tom was several years older and knew her cousin through a friend of a friend. "So that was where I met him. And then it kind of just went on from there, you know. We hung out a little bit and did things in a group situation with friends and stuff like that. The two of us just hit it off because he made me laugh all the time."

And that wasn't the only reason they hit it off, she jokes. "He had sexy arms and I liked that. Big muscley arms. He lifted weights. He worked out at home at his gym with his weights, and he enjoyed keeping himself fit that way."

Soon, they were travelling the race-car circuit together. First, a road trip to Seattle, Washington, then south to Woodburn, Oregon. "Those were some neat trips and of course you're in a vehicle with a person so you're chatting and laughing and being entertained and that kind of thing, and that's where I guess I got an appreciation for his sense of humour. A very dry, British sense of humour."

British, because that's where his roots were laid down. Tom was born in Liverpool, England, hometown of the Beatles.

In the 1970s, when Tom was 12, his parents decided that it was time for the family to embark on a brand-new life in a brand-new country. "They just up and moved to Canada. Didn't know a single person here," Brenda says.

"Liverpool was not very prosperous at the time and his father wanted a better life ... So, he decided he was going to move his family to either Australia or Canada. His wife said no to Australia because they had snakes."

And so Tom grew up in the Vancouver and North Delta areas of British Columbia.

There was no trace of a British accent when Brenda met him about a decade later. "He said when you were 12 years old and you moved to a different country you lose your accent pretty quickly," she says. "There was not like a, you know, falling in love or love at first sight ... We became good friends and decided that this is it, we were going to date sort of thing. It was just a mutual attraction, I guess."

What people noticed most about their relationship was that Tom and Brenda really enjoyed being around each other. When her young niece once asked Brenda to name her best friend, she was surprised when Brenda replied, "Uncle Tom."

"We were very, very, very good friends and that was the big thing people would always say, you know. And that was the best thing, we had a wonderful friendship for sure as well as being partners."

Tom and Brenda married and moved to Surrey, about an hour's drive from Vancouver, and then to Aldergrove before settling in nearby Langley. "We bought a house in Langley and that was going to be our last home and it was a rancher style home ... he had a double car garage so he was happy and he loaded that thing with tools and car bits and old cars and all that kind of stuff and he, you know, was just in heaven. That was his kind of man cave."

And Tom did love cars. Especially antique vehicles. And *especially* antique vehicles from the United Kingdom. "He loved old British cars," Brenda says, ready to list his favourites. "The Austins, the Anglias, the Tens and little pickup trucks and stuff like that. Anything that was an old British car."

Any time the opportunity presented itself, Tom would buy an old car with a plan to rebuild it over time. But not to its original state, Brenda says. "He didn't put them back to original, he always hot-rodded them. So he would put bigger motors in. He was a steel fabricator by trade, so he would reinforce the chassis and he would change things out so he could put bigger motors in and fatter tires on and that kind of stuff."

Cars weren't his sole passion. Tom's love of music led him to collecting bass guitars: a total of 21 tucked in every imaginable space in the house—in his office, under the bed, in the closet. "He always used to say they're pretty," says Brenda. "For him, that was a piece of art, you know, beautiful wood or different colours or some have special meanings because he had to have the Beatles' Rickenbacker bass guitar and he had to have one of those because of course he was from Liverpool."

Tom didn't play in a band but instead picked at the guitar himself when he was home. "He would sit in his office with his little amplifier and plug one in and pluck away at it for an hour or so and that's what he enjoyed. He enjoyed doing that and teaching himself different things. He loved Flea, the musician from the Red Hot Chili Peppers, and his ultimate favourite band was Rush because they're Canadian, eh!," she jokes. "And then the Beatles, but he had a great appreciation for the bass player in bands."

And there was another love in Tom's life. Dogs. Especially bulldogs. "He liked the pushed-in faces. When I met him, he was like, 'Oh, I always wanted a bulldog!'" And that was fine with Brenda, because she too had a thing for bulldogs. "We found the French bulldog and that's kind of where our passion grew from there and we had frenchies from … well, 1989 we got our first French bulldog and we still have them today."

At one point, they had seven in their house.

And just as Tom would head out on the drag-racing circuit to check out different makes of cars, Brenda headed out on the dog show circuit, where her prize bulldogs often did well. "I went to California, Washington, Oregon, all over BC for dog shows. Pennsylvania, Minnesota, Colorado. It's kind of like an ongoing joke that if we go to a dog show everybody would know me and if we went to a drag car race everybody would know him. We were just the tag-alongs for each other!"

Over time, their dogs collected considerable hardware and a lot of prestige. Canadian championships, American championships, international championships. And although they had an appreciation for each other's hobbies—Tom with his cars, Brenda with her dogs—in all their years together, they only went on one vacation as a couple. "Because of the dogs and because of his travel, he preferred to stay home because he didn't really feel there were people who could take care of our dogs the way we did. So, we often took our holidays separate. He would go and stay on Gabriola Island and visit his parents and play golf and hang out with his dad and I would go up and do my dog shows."

However, in 2007, they decided to take in the Crufts' dog competition, billed as the "World's Greatest Dog Show," held in Birmingham, England, about two and a half hours from London. It was a chance for Tom to return to his boyhood country. Despite living his first 12 years in Liverpool, Tom had never actually been to London. "So it was nice to go and discover things, like Westminster Abbey and stuff like that, these things you see in books and on television.

"We were married in 1987 and in 2007 was the first time we ever actually went away on a holiday together," she laughs, "and I said, 'Well, I guess this is going to make us or break us. We'll find out if we like each other if we have to spend a whole week together!'"

When they first met, Tom was a delivery driver for a scrapyard. He knew all the local auto wreckers—and there were many in the Surrey-Delta area—and it was his job to make sure automobile parts were delivered. "It was a physical job, he was often on the back of the truck unloading pieces like transmissions or fenders. But he enjoyed it because he had that in with the cars … and it gave him connections in the car world and different auto dealers and mechanic shops."

Over time Tom became experienced in different types of welding and welding machinery. That's how he ended up working with a company called Engineering and Machinery System Inc., which fabricated steel conveyor systems for mines. The company also built Davit arms, the long, thin metal cranes that are used on ferries and cruise ships to lift or lower lifeboats.

Tom became so good at his job that he was scooped up by another company, Schat-Harding. "They hired him because he had this history of making these arms for the lifeboats. He kind of had that knowledge of how they worked. They hired him to do safety inspections and maintenance and repairs on these arms and then on the trolley systems that the lifeboats would hang from."

The job meant Tom had to travel a lot. "He worked on anything that had a lifeboat … the very first year that he worked for Schat-Harding he went to Tahiti four times working on their cruise ships. And I used to tease him that he had another family in Tahiti!"

Brenda says it took a while, but she became used to Tom's travelling. "Typically, he would be gone for a week to two weeks. He got to go to Australia, he got to work on a big cruise ship that circles Australia and goes to different ports there. He worked on some of the freighters in Vancouver … He worked on many, many of the BC ferries. And he was also called on to look after the lifeboats that are on oil rigs."

And that's how Tom's love affair with Newfoundland began. Flying to the province to repair or inspect lifeboats on offshore oil platforms, including Hibernia, the SeaRose, and the Terra Nova. He also helped maintain the lifeboat systems used at the offshore safety and survival centre just outside St. John's where rig workers underwent training.

Tom took his work very seriously. "I remember one time he had to put a lifeboat out of commission because it had a leak and of course you can't have a lifeboat with a leak … and it was quite the uproar because you can only have as many people on the rig as you have lifeboats for, this is a TSB [Transportation Safety Board] ruling or whatever it is, and of course that was quite the uproar because they had to get all these people off the oil rig."

Tom stood his ground. "He wasn't popular for a little while but he said, 'That's my job. I have to stand by it.' … He was very thorough at his job and he wasn't afraid to rock the boat. If it wasn't going to work, he would tell them it wasn't going to work."

During Tom's trips to St. John's he stayed at the Quality Hotel near the waterfront. A restaurant downstairs in the hotel, Rumpelstiltskin's, was his favourite place in the city because it was so close to the harbour.

Something about Newfoundland captured Tom's heart from the moment he arrived. When he would return to his home in British Columbia, he talked endlessly about the province and the people he met. "He asked me several times if I wanted to move to Newfoundland," says Brenda. Just about every time he came home from Newfoundland, he'd say, 'It's a great place. They are such nice people.'"

Brenda was interested in seeing St. John's, but not being particularly fond of winter or snow, she couldn't see herself relocating to the east coast. "I said to him, 'I don't want to live anywhere where they have to have poles to find the fire hydrants in the winter!' I live in BC, where we don't have a lot of snow. I'm sure I could get used to it, I'm sure I could learn how to drive in the snow, but do I want to? Not really!"

But Tom would have moved to the province in a heartbeat. "I think he loved the people. He loved the scenery, you know, living by the ocean. He just thought that was the greatest thing." As Brenda relays how much he talked about the island, she fights back the tears. "I think he just really had something in his heart that told him …" again, a long pause as she thinks about how Tom felt about Newfoundland, "you know, he just loved it there."

And so, whenever his bosses said there was a call to head to Newfoundland to work on a lifeboat, Tom jumped at the chance. Sometimes it was planned. Other times it was last minute. "We got to a point in our marriage where we didn't necessarily make plans. We did make plans but everybody knew that if I came without Tom it was because he got called out." They adjusted to the lifestyle, in part because Tom's work made him so happy. "He would've really preferred if he didn't travel as much, but he did really like his job and he really liked the company he worked for, so it was really important for him to do a good job and represent well."

A call to travel to Newfoundland came in around mid-March 2009. Tom, at home in Langley, wasn't feeling well. But work had to be done on the SeaRose. "I dropped him off at the airport on a Wednesday and I believe it was something that really couldn't wait. Because I remember he wasn't really feeling all that great. He had a little bit of a cold. I remember he had a little bit of a cough. I don't know if it was a service call that he had to do. I'm assuming it was something like a service call, something wasn't working properly or they came across something that had to be done right now. So, he was called and went out … it was rather a quick one, it wasn't planned I know that."

And so it was, on the morning of March 12, 2009, Tom Anwyll, 46 years old and back in St. John's, the place he considered his second home, was preparing to board Cougar Flight 491 to head to the offshore.

That Thursday morning Brenda arrived at Coastal Pacific Xpress, the trucking company where she worked, ready for another day at the office. She had just poured a cup of tea for herself and logged into her computer when she was told that someone at the front desk needed to speak with her.

Matthew Davis, 34

It was an idyllic childhood. Like something out of a child's adventure novel. Or like a childhood in the great outdoors of rural Newfoundland.

In the community of Holyrood, on the east coast of Newfoundland, Matt Davis considered the world around him as his very own playground. Every trail and every turn in the woods was an untold story waiting to be written.

His love of the outdoors came naturally. Both of his parents had jobs that kept them outside all day, and sometimes all night. Matt's father, Bill, was a well-known and respected wildlife officer. His mother, Jeane, worked in the same field. "The majority of our time was spent outdoors," she says, "in camps, out in the woods, wherever, and when most parents got up to go to work in their cars, lots of times his father would get picked up in a helicopter on a hill there in Holyrood because he was going back to do a caribou census or a moose census, or he was going to check on poachers and I could've been back there doing a beaver count."

For a few years, just after Matt was born in 1974, the family lived in

Clarenville, also on the east coast of the island. There, their home became a wild animal rescue centre. If an animal was injured, people often brought it to "the wildlife man's house."

"So in our basement or out in our backyard we could at any point in time [have] had maybe two great horned owls in cages or I often slept on the basement floor with a moose calf until we could get it out to the wildlife park the next day," says Jeane. "So, there was always animals coming and going, coming and going."

During those years Matt went everywhere with his father. If he could manage to climb up into the pickup truck, then his father couldn't leave home without him—even when he had dangerous work to attend to, such as checking bear traps.

One particular time when Matt was about four or five years old, he went with his father to check traps set up to catch a bear that was roaming the area. The traps, made of metal and mesh, looked like big culverts. Bill would place a piece of meat inside the cage so that when the bear stepped in and grabbed the food, a wire screen would be triggered to fall, trapping it inside.

That day it didn't quite work that way, Jeane says. "Bill and Matthew got in the truck to go check the bear traps, and of course Matthew jumps out of the truck and he's running ahead as fast as he can and he gets down to the bear trap and realizes that the screen is not down."

Little Matt had just turned to tell his father there was no bear to be seen, when the cage started shaking. As the bear, inside the trap, hadn't reached for the meat yet, the wire screen hadn't fallen. "So, Matthew goes running back to Dad, 'Daddy, Daddy, there's a bear in the cage, there's a bear in the cage! Quick, come see, there's a bear in the cage!' And Bill is saying, 'No hon,' you're just joshing me again, aren't ya? I know, because you're just trying to fool Daddy.' So, Bill walks right to the thing, not believing his son, and here he is face to face with a bear!"

Jeane laughs as she recalls how Bill sprang into action and quickly kicked the cage with his foot. The mesh fell, locking the bear inside. All was safe and sound, as another regular day unfolded in Matt's young life.

After a few years, the family was back in Holyrood and Matt made sure to make the most of the surroundings.

When his sister Amanda was born, Matt was five years old; he wanted a little brother but got a sister. "He turned me into a tomboy," she says. "I was basically his little brother whether I was a girl or not. He dragged me through the dirt. He dragged me everywhere. I was just his little shadow."

And then Amy came along, who quickly learned how much Matt loved exploring. "I don't know whether that came from my dad and him introducing him to it," Amy says, "or being in this playground. Like, Newfoundland is a beautiful place to live, and having everything readily accessible for you, you can go fishing, you can go snowmobiling, you can go up to the ice, whatever, not sure if it was one or the other but he just loved adventure."

Matt's older sister, Patricia, whom everyone calls PJ, says he also loved being on a dirt bike—he got his first one when he was only six—and there wasn't anything he wouldn't try. "He was definitely the leader in our pack of friends and cousins," she says. "We owned the woods, like little pioneers building forts and lean-tos."

One of those friends and cousins, Scott Parsons, remembers those days well. Scott and Matt, along with a handful of other cousins who lived in the area, were always together, from early morning until late at night. "I guess we were all sort of kindred spirits. It was that group of boys ... we were cousins and cousins are your first friends in the early years. It was just natural that we would hang out and boot around together. There were the rivers, there was the swimming," he reminisces. "There were campfires, building of forts, there were dirt bikes. Cruising the trails, up in the woods with the pellet guns."

It wasn't that long ago, just back to the 1980s, but for Scott—now in his

40s—it feels like a lifetime ago. "I guess it's a different time now, we weren't allowed indoors back then. I mean, we were pushed out of the house in the morning and allowed back when the street lights came on."

Amanda agrees. "You know, eight years old—if you think about it now, I would never do this with my kids, but my mom would drop us off at the gravel pit on the Trans-Canada Highway and my brother and I would hike into Blue Pond at Rocky Gully to go ice fishing for the day. To think, a 13-year-old and an eight-year-old on a frozen pond all day. I mean, I don't think I'd let my kids do that now but you know [Matt's] survival mode and what he had learned from our dad was key for him."

And that's what everyone believes it was all about for Matt: being like his father, whom he idolized.

Part of Bill Davis's job as wildlife officer for the region was to travel into the bush by helicopter. He didn't have to go to the airport to catch a flight; the pilot would swoop down into his neighbourhood and pick him up. When Matt heard the roar of the spinning blades and the pounding of the engine, he'd start running—not away from the loud noise, but toward it. The pilot would land on a hill next to their Nan's house, just across the street from where they lived, and then zip away once Matt's father was on board.

Jeane believes that watching his father step into a helicopter and seeing him disappear into the sky is where Matt's love of flying began. She has a picture of him from when he was four or five, dressed for bed and trying to crawl into a helicopter. "He was climbing up on the floats of the helicopter," she recalls, "with his pyjamas on at a time when little boy's pyjamas had those pebbled feet on the bottom and he was climbing up on the float of the helicopter, trying to go with Dad. He always said he was going to be a helicopter pilot."

Jeane and Bill had three girls and one boy, with 12 years between the youngest and oldest. Matt was funny and always playing pranks on the other children, but he didn't cause her any trouble, she insists, although she jokes that he was "one little antichrist," who always had a mischievous smile on his face that had people wondering what he was up to.

To PJ, that describes her brother perfectly. "Matt mellowed as he got older, but he was so mischievous as a kid," she says. "His acrobatic talents scaling kitchen drawers to climb on top of the fridge when he was three or attempting hitch-hiking with his buddy Tony at six. Mom and Dad gave him an electronics kit for Christmas to keep him occupied, well he wired up his bedroom and lights and sirens went off when you opened the door. He was eight. But Matt was a charmer with that smile and those dimples. Could get away with anything."

So, for Matt, life was one big adventure, much of it experienced with his father. But then it all changed.

Jeane lost her husband and the children lost their father to lung disease. Twelve-year-old Matt was shaken to his core. "When his father died, Matthew—I won't say he was in denial—but he found it very difficult to forgive," Jeane says. "Bill was a very staunch Catholic. And whenever we were near a Catholic church, we went on Sunday. Me and Bill and the kids. And Matthew found it very difficult."

Jeane often found Matt crying in his room at night. She would sit beside him to offer comfort. "And he would say, 'Mom, there is no God. Don't ask me to go to church anymore. There is no God. No God would take such a wonderful dad.'"

Three decades on, Amanda still recalls Matt's reaction the day their mother, broken-hearted herself, told them the news about their father. "[Matt] was devastated. I mean, I remember my mom coming into the living room and she gathered us in and she said I got something to tell you all. And I remember my brother just running for his bedroom."

Jeane says Matt understood the responsibility that came with being the only boy in a house of four children. If something was broken—a toilet or a light bulb—Matt was the one to fix it. Amanda believes that her brother felt that he had to become the protector of the family name. "He was basically running the household at 12," she recalls. "He took over for my dad. I was seven or eight years old when my dad passed away; he just took me under his wing and away we went. We cut wood. We had to bring it in for the winter. When I was eight, he taught me how to skin a rabbit." She laughs. "He taught me how to shoot a rifle. Showed me how to make sure I know gun safety, water safety, everything that was important to my dad growing up that he had taught him, Matt had made sure that myself and the rest of my siblings were very keen on."

Amy was only three when their father died. It was Matt who taught her how to tie her shoelaces and how to ride a bike, all while talking about their father. "And Matt would say, 'Dad used to do this and he used to have trapped animals and one time this and one time that,' so the stories that he told kind of kept it alive."

As hard it was, his father's death didn't break Matt's spirit. If anything, it made him stronger, more confident, and more certain than ever that he would follow his dream of being a pilot. "He wasn't the greatest math student," Amanda says, "and I remember one of his teachers at his high school told him that he could never be a helicopter pilot because his math was terrible, and he was like, 'Well, to hell with that, I'm going to be a helicopter pilot no matter what.' If he was going to do something, he was going to do it. He didn't care who told him what."

A love of helicopters and the dream of becoming a pilot stayed with Matt as he grew older. He was a talented artist—he even studied graphic design at one point—and when he sat down to draw, it was often a picture of a chopper that he'd outline on the paper.

By the early 1990s, Matt had a pilot's licence and was working at obtaining as much flying experience as he could. One of the places he was picking up that experience was Happy Valley-Goose Bay in Labrador, where he worked flying up and down the coast.

There, Matt met his future wife. Marsha Bragg was working at the local hospital as part of her nursing studies. She met him through a mutual friend. "It was a kiss on the cheek that first started a spark," she recalls of the moment she realized there was something between them. "He had asked me for a kiss because it was soon his birthday. A year later in 1998 we would still be going strong together and would make the plunge to move in together."

First came a pet dog, Tigger, who Matt called their "furry child." Next came their first house. And then came the Christmas when Matt popped the question by hiding an engagement ring in Marsha's stocking.

Jeane remembers the day Matt called from Labrador to say he had met someone whom he felt was *the one*. "He was looking at engagement rings, and he said, 'Mom, what do you think?' And I said, 'Well, sweetheart, you know this is one decision Mom can't make for you … But if you're happy with her, then we're all going to be happy with her.'"

Matt was indeed happy, and life was good. But even though they had plenty of friends and some of Marsha's family in Labrador, he wanted to be closer to his roots, in Holyrood. So, Matt took a job that allowed him to be home on the island for a month and then away for a month in northern Canada, flying out of Hall Beach, Nunavut. Matt and Marsha moved to Torbay, a small town outside St. John's, and bought their second home. "I have so many fond memories of Matt and I living on Birchy Nap Hill Road," Marsha recalls. "I often even to this day dream about the place. I guess because it was during a time of my life I was so happy."

Matt and Marsha married in 2002. As they both enjoyed a quiet life, instead of arranging a wedding at home and all the stresses that go with that, they opted for a vacation, just the two of them. "And that's exactly what we did. We eloped to the Dominican Republic. It really was the most relaxing day of our lives. Our wedding trip brought so many smiles and a few laughs."

One of the laughs from their vacation/honeymoon came while they were horseback riding. "The guide takes us off the resort to an area that looked a little sketchy," Marsha recalls. "He took us through a forest with no beaten horse path. That in itself felt a bit strange, we were the only two that went at that time."

The farther they rode, the scarier it became. "We were riding along through a forest while on horseback and jumping over trees that had blown down. We passed along a rundown home. In the front of this house on the porch deck sat a man in a rocking chair and in his hand he held a shotgun!"

Marsha yelled out to Matt so that they could turn around, but he was too far ahead and the noise of the horses' hooves drowned out her voice. When they finally emerged from the woods, they found themselves on a beautiful but deserted sandy beach. "And this is where it got even scarier for me," she says. "The horses start to trot along the beach. I sing out and tell the guide to make the horse slow down 'cause I felt like I was falling off."

However, the guide didn't speak English and he thought she was asking him to make the horse run faster. He whipped her horse and it raced away. Marsha was certain that she was going to go flying. "Meanwhile, Matt is still ahead of me going full trot," she says. "Loving every minute of it. Even with the stress I was feeling at that moment I had also loved that moment. Seeing Matt grinning from ear to ear 'cause he thought it was fun. Racing off into a sunset on horseback, something out of a movie."

The birth of their first child brought them even closer. Shannon was born on March 12, 2004. "Up until that point we were happy but nothing compared to the joy we felt when we welcomed Shannon. She was perfect in every sense of the way, healthy and so beautiful to us."

Matt called his mother to tell her the news. "He called me crying like a baby," Jeane recalls, "and he said, 'Mom, Mom, I just witnessed a miracle! We just got a little baby girl! And I was there and I helped her be born and, Mom, it was like a miracle.'"

Around that time, Matt took a new job with Great Slave Helicopters accompanying crews going up north on polar bear expeditions. He also flew out west and helped control forest fires with a group known as rapattack crews—those sent by helicopter to battle wildfires that are too difficult to drive or walk to. The pilot lowers the chopper as close as possible to the burning forest and a team of firefighters rappel out of the aircraft and tackle the fire once they hit the ground.

The work was exciting for someone who loved flying and loved being outdoors, but being away for long periods of time took its toll on Matt.

Searching for work closer to home, he was eventually hired as a pilot for Cougar Helicopters, flying out of St. John's. Matt finally had landed his dream job. He would fly every day and still be back home in Torbay for supper. Shortly after, he was upgraded to captain; he was later given the responsibility of training other pilots to fly Sikorsky's state-of-the-art aircraft.

As Matt's career grew, so did his family. Matt and Marsha had a second child in 2006, a boy Matt named William, after his father. The two children and one other addition—a dog named Frankie—made their family whole. "We were so over the moon in love with our little boy and girl. Our hearts were complete. Our world truly felt complete."

Marsha says that at times as the children grew it felt a little like a zoo at their house. Frankie seemed untrainable. "He just didn't get it at all," she says. "Matt ended up taking Frankie to obedience school and would come home feeling disappointed, saying he thought Frankie was going to fail doggie school." Marsha recalls a story about the time Matt took the dog duck hunting. Matt fired his gun and the bird went down, but the loud noise sent Frankie running in the opposite direction. Matt got his duck that day but lost his cellphone running to catch up with his terrified dog.

Matt enjoyed a close relationship with Marsha's family members who lived nearby, especially her sister Janis. Janis consulted Matt when she bought her first home, especially when she undertook extensive renovations. Matt had the attitude she needed to get through the stress of fixing up her first home. "'A few more coats of plaster,' he would say, knowing full well I was on the verge of tears! 'Hard work pays off in the end,' I can hear him say.... He wouldn't want you to just give up or settle. If I was to do these renos, then it needed to be done right."

Janis says Matt didn't mind standing up for himself when he strongly believed in something. Matt had a T-shirt with the sentence "If I agreed with you, we'd both be wrong" written across the front; Janis says it was perfect for him.

She delights in telling the story of getting one over on Matt by pulling off what she considers the perfect April Fool's joke. "I managed to trick him on April Fool's with a story of myself being pregnant out of wedlock. He believed it full heartedly and was so happy for me! He kept saying how great it was, and how happy Marsha will be when she finds out. That I'll make it work, and they'll help with whatever they could!" It was one of her proudest sister-in-law moments, as Matt wasn't easy to trick. Matt couldn't believe she had gotten one over on him—especially on April Fool's Day—and vowed to get her back.

Matt loved talking about his job. If someone asked him about flying, he would talk for hours. He also took the training aspect of flying seriously. "I guess that's why he decided to take on a training pilot role with Cougar," Marsha says. "He was so interested in his job and helping others."

Matt wrote short articles for the company's internal newspaper. He enjoyed his job so much that he didn't see it as work, according to Marsha. "When the alarm went off in the morning to get ready for work, well Matt would be up raring to go probably before the alarm even went off. Again, he just loved what he did. I always envied that about him 'cause I would be the one hitting snooze once or twice before rising for my day."

Matt's work took him to places most could only dream about, including

Labrador's rugged and beautiful Torngat Mountains, and Grise Fiord on Ellesmere Island in Nunavut with its amazing ice-capped mountains and fjords.

But flying also gave Matt an up-close view of disaster; at those times he was exhausted when he came home.

Marsha remembers the impact a work trip to Angola in western Africa in late 2008 had on Matt. The fallout from a long, drawn-out civil war still reverberated throughout the country. Cougar sent Matt and First Officer Tim Lanouette there as part of a contract to fly government officials around the region. Matt couldn't believe the beauty of Africa. He also saw the reality of what life could be like there.

"One day he was in a market and watched an infant crawl through the dirt," Marsha says, "while the mom was trying to sell pineapples in the street … he found that sad because it was so different from the way our little babies had been raised."

Another incident on that trip moved Matt and Tim so deeply they had to intervene. Several times they saw a child with Down Syndrome begging for food outside a café. Matt went over to him one day and gave him a new T-shirt, a pair of socks, and some energy bars.

As soon as Matt walked away, a security guard took the clothes and food from the child's hand. "Matt and Tim quickly turn around to the guard to explain," Marsha says. "The guard would not listen. So Matt and Tim found a guard they knew, asked him to talk with the other guard to make sure the child could keep the gift. The guard didn't dispute it further and Matt and Tim helped the boy put on his new shirt and socks."

Matt was happy for having made a difference. "Matt said the little boy was dancing around the street because he was so happy. It made him thankful for our family life and he missed us then more. He would ask me to go hold the children so tight he could feel it from there. It really made both Matt and I appreciate what we had in our life."

Hearing those stories makes Scott Parsons, Matt's cousin and friend, emotional. Scott lived near Matt and Marsha, and Matt would sometimes pop over during the day when he wasn't flying.

"It would be nothing for me to be in my office and I'd hear the door open and just by the sounds of the footsteps coming up the stairs I knew it was him," says Scott. "He'd skip the first one, hit the first landing and then bump, bump, it would take him four steps to get up over eight stairs. And every time he'd come up, it was so welcome, because it was a break for me."

Scott knew how much Matt loved flying but didn't like the risks that came with the job. One day in early March 2009 Scott broached the subject: "We were just chatting and I made a comment to him—we were talking about helicopters obviously and safety—and I said, 'Matt, b'y, you know, statistically speaking, it's only a matter of time till something goes wrong with one of these things, right?'" Scott pauses for a long time before he continues with Matt's response. "And he acknowledged it and brushed it off, and said, 'I understand the risks kind of thing' and that was toward the end of our conversation."

A few minutes later, Matt headed home to get ready to return to work.

And so it was, on March 12, 2009, 34-year-old Matt Davis, feeling blessed to have a family he cherished and a job he couldn't wait to go to every morning, was at St. John's airport, preparing to guide Cougar Flight 491 into the air and out over the ocean to offshore oil rigs and vessels.

Just before he boarded the helicopter, Matt called his little girl, Shannon, whom everyone called Sissy, to wish her a happy fifth birthday and to say that he'd be home right after work to spend the rest of the day with her. Three-year-old William said a quick hello and then handed the telephone to his mother. Matt had just enough time to tell Marsha that he was getting ready to board and that he would see them later to celebrate.

Mid-morning, Marsha's mother was in the kitchen of Matt and Marsha's home baking a cake. Marsha was nearby, watching Shannon open birthday presents. Just as she finished pulling off the wrapping paper, the laughter and happiness in the room was interrupted by the ringing of the telephone.

Timothy Lanouette, 47

Music has a magical ability to bring people together, no matter the language, the location, or other barriers in life.

And just as Mark Frost's and John Pelley's friendship can be traced to a chance music encounter, the same can be said of Tim Lanouette and Kevin Lane. It happened one night on the Canadian Forces ship HMCS *Provider*. In its heyday, the ship was a supply vessel that carried massive amounts of fuel and goods. Its main role was to refuel other Canadian naval ships at sea and stock them with food and supplies. The ship had a landing pad and a hangar large enough to accommodate a few Sea King helicopters, the military workhorse aircraft that carried out Canadian Forces missions all over the world and that Tim had spent more than a decade flying.

It was on board the *Provider* in the mid-to-late 1990s that Kevin first saw and heard of Tim. "He heard me playing up in the avionics room," Kevin recalls. "And he started talking to me and asking me if I'd like to play music with him."

That was all Kevin needed to hear. He was an electronics technician whose job it was to fix and maintain the electronic systems on the Sea King helicopters that Tim flew. But outside of work, music was his passion and an opportunity to jam with someone as interested as he was in playing was a no-brainer. Kevin knew Tim was a good musician because Tim had studied bass trombone at the Canadian Forces School of Music in British Columbia. And the military, according to Kevin, is serious about its band. "There's a weird thing that people don't know about band in the military," he explains. "That you actually have to have a degree in music. And to get into a military band, you have to be a ridiculous musician. There's tryouts. For every musical position you have tryouts. You basically study, study, study and then you are evaluated by a group of your peers and superiors and they decide whether or not you are good enough to get in. And they are looking for your ability to keep time, to understand music, to be expressive, to duplicate things. It's how good your ear is. You have to be very, very good."

Kevin, not a professional military musician, but who loved playing music, perked up when Tim walked into the ship's music room and showed interest in what he was doing.

They started playing music together in their spare time and Kevin quickly realized how much he could learn. "I really enjoy writing music and my ear was pretty good. I could understand what was happening but had a real hard time producing things ... He gave me the sense of confidence that wasn't really natural for me in music. So, that was the spark there."

Kevin appreciated that Tim didn't just say that he liked his playing but took the time to explain what he liked about it. "You know, there's lots of people will give you compliments," he says, "but it's a lot more meaningful when the person says something that's in context and what they're giving you praise for is something you can acknowledge and say, 'Yeah, I worked on that and I'm good at that.' And that was what Tim was like. He would affirm the things that you were good at."

For example, says Kevin, "I have a real hard time singing harmony. So, I can hear harmony and I can tell you what the harmony is. But I can't reproduce it for some reason. So, he's trying to teach me … he would make me stop and do it the way he knows it works. So, he's not blowing smoke and you can sort of—it was like an integrity and an honesty about him that I instantly liked."

In one way, Kevin is surprised that they became friends. Hierarchy is important in the military and it's not often that higher-ups mingle with lower ranks. As a pilot, Tim was on a much different military level than Kevin. "On the ship there's an interesting dynamic. At home, there's a real split between maintainers—which I was—and the air crew. And I think that's healthy for the way the military works. But when you're deployed, you're a lot more tight-knit group and you know there's far fewer people there. And the pilots have to depend on the individual maintainers a lot more. When we're home, there's a big system, but at sea we have 12 people that are maintaining your helicopter and you've got to know them and trust them. So, I had a little more access to him. He was a captain and I was a corporal. And so, it was sort of weird to hang out with him."

But they did hang out, and started performing together. At the time, Tim and Kevin were based in Nova Scotia at CFB Shearwater. Tim lived in Colby Village, about 10 minutes from the base; Kevin lived in an apartment in nearby Dartmouth. They sailed together for three years, mostly up and down the east coast to Boston, Norfolk, Virginia, and Puerto Rico.

Kevin was impressed with Tim's ability as a pilot and his commitment to be ready for anything that was thrown at him: "Tim approached everything the same way. You practice failures before they happen. This is the general way the Canadian Forces trains. But he took it very serious. And I think he just really saw the value in it."

Kevin recalls how Tim handled a relatively minor incident in 1999 when they were flying back from an air show in Muskoka, Ontario. "A bird flew under the rotor of the helicopter, so it just went right by us. And I didn't really think it was a big deal. But there was a French pilot and he was the aircraft commander and he seemed to be quite shaken by it. So, Tim went immediately into planning scenarios and that seemed to calm down the commander. And that's just how Tim did it."

The more time they spent together in an aircraft—electronics technicians often accompany the flight crew on assignments—the more Kevin respected Tim's abilities to fly. But one day he realized the reality of being a pilot and facing tough choices. "There was one day I got very, very mad at him," Kevin says. They were at sea and Kevin was on fire duty in the hangar area of the deck. Tim was bringing his helicopter in for a landing in rough seas. He eased the helicopter down slowly onto the unsteady ship, the rotor blades coming close to the deck, uncomfortably close for Kevin, who watched nervously from a short distance. "It was a manual landing. And I remember I got quite mad at him. And he said, 'Well, what do you do? I can't fly away. We're in the middle of the ocean. This is where I have to land. So, you know, I do it!' And that was a remarkable thing. He didn't seem to be freaked out at all. He seemed to be—he was sort of bothered that I was freaked out by having looked down at his rotor. But he was fine."

Before becoming a pilot, Tim studied music at the Canadian Forces School of Music near Victoria, British Columbia. That's where Pierre de Villers first met him. Pierre was a couple of years older and studying euphonium, a large brass instrument similar to a tuba. "We were young. I was one of the old guys," he jokes. "I was already in the Navy for three and a half years before I switched to music. So, when I got there, I was 20 or 21 but the majority of the people there were younger, they were 18 or 19."

Tim showed up at school just as Pierre was about to graduate. "I only had a few months left," Pierre says. "One of the things that impressed me musically was that he was there studying bass trombone, but he was also a great bass player and guitar player as well. So, it wasn't just the military brass instruments; he had other skills too."

Tim had transferred to the music school after working as a driver for the Department of National Defence. The two got to know each other some years later when they were both stationed in Moose Jaw, Saskatchewan. By then, Pierre was a professional musician with a job as bandmaster of the 15 Wing band at the air force base there. When Tim arrived, Pierre says, he was interested in becoming a military pilot. "Moose Jaw is where all the training was done for the entry level and he ended up being stuck in a big backlog of training and they were looking for places for the pilots who were waiting for training, because people get farmed out all over the place. And because he was a musician, he got farmed out to work with the band I was running. So, we would basically work together for—I don't know for how long it was—but it was probably a couple of years till his training started."

Pierre was impressed by Tim's drive. Tim already had his private flying licence, and while he was waiting to get into military flight training, he decided return to his old job as a driver to earn extra money. "He was delivering truckloads of fertilizer all over North Dakota and Saskatchewan and Alberta. And when he had enough money saved up from this truck driving, he took the training and he actually got his commercial pilot's licence ... before he was scheduled to get on his military training. But that's kind of what he did. He was always trying to stay one step ahead."

Pierre jokes that Tim always dressed impeccably, with not a hair out of place—even though Tim wasn't a serious guy. "He used to draw his cartoons," he remembers. "So, if something funny was to happen he would draw a cartoon about it."

Tim didn't want any publicity about his artwork, despite Pierre often trying to encourage him to do more of it. He persuaded Tim to design a special logo for his military band. "In the mid-'90s we were designing a crest for our band. We were doing shirts for when we did gigs that weren't big professional gigs, like street parades and stuff like that for the communities. So, we had this shirt done up and he designed this logo, this crest to put on the shirts and we started using it for other stuff like mugs.... He just whipped that up in no time at all. I always envy that because I can't draw a circle."

Training finished and, officially, a military pilot, Tim was transferred to Shearwater, where he flew Sea King helicopters—and played music with Kevin. One night Tim brought his bass to the music room, where Kevin was hanging out. "And he started playing something that he had been writing," Kevin says. "And I had never heard anybody play bass this way. He was using harmonics. You will hear harmonics in a guitar, these chiming sounds that almost sound like a bell. And he would do that on his bass. It was rhythmic and melodic at the same time, and it was just so much more complex than when I had heard anybody play bass before.... He was delighted that I recognized that this was unique."

They also played music together on land. They rounded up other musicians and formed a band called Big Johnson. Tim came up with the name, naming it for one of the guys in the band who had a guitar amplifier which Kevin says was basically a computer attached to a massive speaker. "And it was so loud! It was ridiculous." Kevin laughs. "When he was tuning his guitar, we'd all have to go outside. It's like the man was deaf. So, anyway we called the amp the Big Johnson and we decided that was a good name for a band."

Change is a fact of military life, with people often being uprooted after only a short time living in a particular place. Before long, Tim was posted out west, to Comox, British Columbia. Kevin says that Tim was excited to be moving back home to be near his family. The two kept in touch and around 2008 Tim was in Halifax and revealed to Kevin that he was retiring from the military after 24 years. He had taken a job as a pilot with Cougar Helicopters.

Tim would continue to live out west but would take on different travel assignments, including St. John's, where he'd be flying workers to the offshore.

Tim was extremely excited about the new job. The two talked about the intense training that comes with learning to fly a relatively new helicopter. "He said it was like drinking from a fire hose," Kevin says. "Because everything was so new. The technology between the Sea King and the S-92, they're light years apart. And that's what he said, it was like drinking from a fire hose in doing that course. As fast as he could learn stuff, things were coming at him. And he liked that, he was excited by that. But it was obviously a challenge he hadn't had to endure for quite a while. I think he outpaced anything the military could throw at him."

And so it was, on Thursday, March 12, 2009, that Tim Lanouette, about to turn 48, retired from the military, and less than 12 months into his new civilian job, lifted off from St. John's as first officer on Cougar Flight 491.

Hundreds of kilometres away in Nova Scotia, Kevin was sitting in an office at the base in Shearwater. He was on reassignment to a desk job. The news was on in the background. Around lunchtime, the announcer said something that caught Kevin's ear and gripped him with fear.

Peter Breen, 55

He had never met a *Seinfeld* episode he didn't like. He quoted lines from Jerry. He quoted lines from George. And he especially quoted lines from Kramer.

Peter Breen would sit in his den at home and roar with laughter at the television screen when his favourite show was on. He'd watch the episodes over and over. "Serenity now," he'd say, quoting Kramer at any sign of stress. "Serenity now."

Peter had such an obsession with the show that his oldest daughter, Janet Marie, bought him a 3-foot-tall framed picture of Kramer, exactly like the one used in one of the show's episodes, where the quirky character had his portrait drawn. Peter loved it and propped it up against the wall above his television. "It's huge, it's massive," Peter's wife, Janet, says. "He loved Kramer. Oh my God, he loved it. I'd be in the kitchen and Pete would be in the den, and you could hear him laughing. He lived in there; he had his chesterfield and his chair and his TV and whatever he wanted, and his Kramer picture and he loved it."

The *Seinfeld* collection was started by Janet Marie, who recorded the show for her father when he was offshore, working aboard the SeaRose. When they had almost every episode on VHS, they started collecting DVD versions, always giving them to him at Christmas or on his birthday.

Janet believes that her husband loved *Seinfeld* because he shared the comedian's dry sense of humour. Among Peter's friends, that sense of humour was legendary. Peter was considered the prankster, the guy always looking to have a laugh.

It didn't take long for Keith Normore to realize that this was true. Keith and Peter were roommates in a small trailer they shared with co-workers in the 1990s.

Back then, Keith and Peter worked at the construction site in Bull Arm, Trinity Bay, where Newfoundland's first offshore platform, the Hibernia Gravity-Basd Structure (GBS), was being built. Construction of the GBS was a massive undertaking. The site itself was basically a self-contained community, with some 5,000 employees working there at any given time. They all had to be fed, entertained, and given a place to sleep at the end of the day.

Keith and Peter worked for the on-site food and accommodations company Major Offshore Catering. Keith cleaned the rooms and Peter the pool and gymnasium. Peter, one of the older workers, in his late 30s, had been there for a while when Keith, 20 years old and hired for two weeks to replace someone who was serving a suspension, showed up.

That two-week stint turned into five and a half years. Part of the reason Keith stayed so long was because of his friendship with Peter. "We became instant buddies," he explains. "He was just so easy to get along with, easy to talk to. The first time you met him was like you knew him all your life." Keith was impressed that Peter could hold his own in a conversation with anyone: "He was a very intelligent man, there was nothing out of his league that he couldn't talk about. He was up on politics, up on sports, up on all the news. He was that way."

Initially, the two lived in the on-site camp, sharing food and accommodations with thousands of others. But as the project ramped up and the number of workers increased, employees were given a financial incentive to live off-site, in one of the nearby communities. "So, myself and Peter and couple of other fellers, that's what we ended up doing," Keith says. "We moved to Come By Chance and we lived together in Come By Chance for five years while we worked at Hibernia."

They worked long hours and Peter only got home to see his wife and family on weekends. Often Janet and the children—Shannon, Janet Marie, Noelle, and Andrew—made the trek over the highway to visit him and his friends at their trailer. There, Keith realized how much of a prankster Peter really was—usually at the expense of their younger, naive roommate, Scotty. "He was really gullible, he'd believe anything. He used to go to bed early and we never went to bed early. We were always having a drink and watching the game or something like that."

One night when they were particularly bored, Peter started a water fight that quickly got out of control. "It started off with someone just flicking water at you and a laugh and then it escalated into whatever you could get your hands on, like rubber boots, and you fill them up with water and throw them at each other." Before long the trailer was soaked. Peter even dragged Scotty, who was asleep in his bed, into it. "Peter and Scott stayed in the same room in the back of the trailer, and Scotty was in bed asleep and Peter said, 'I'm going in and getting Scotty now!' And I said, 'No!'"

But there was no stopping Peter, according to Keith. "So, anyway he filled up a big old bucket of water, went in and opened the door and said, 'Scotty!' And Scotty sat up in the bed and Peter threw the bucket of water at him. And he drowned Scotty and soaked the bed and Scotty got up and went off his head and said, 'Okay, Peter, f— you!' And he said, 'I'm getting in your bed!' And Peter said 'Yes, buddy, you go ahead and get in my bed, don't worry about me. I'll sleep in the chair.'"

But the tomfoolery wasn't over. "Peter left the room for about 45 minutes and then he came back with another bucket of water and threw it over him again, in the other bed." Keith can't hold back the laughter as he tells the story. By then much of the trailer was soaked, but none of that mattered. For Peter, it was all about the fun. "He was always there to make you laugh or smile with a prank and that sort of thing," Keith says. "He was a really easy fella to get along with and you know he was just a genuine soul."

Keith also quickly learned that there was no more committed Boston Bruins fan than Peter. Hockey was everything to him. Win or lose, it was all about his team. "He'd be always tormenting everybody about their team, you know," Keith says. "He'd be making little digs at them. But he didn't care and if somebody said something about the Bruins, he'd say, 'yeah, sure, we'll get the next one.' Nothing ever fazed him."

People tried to get him to give up on his beloved Bruins when they were going through a bad season. "You could not turn him against the Bruins, he was never ever disgusted or upset with them," Keith says. "People would try to get to him because he was such a torment about the other teams, but people used to get right disgusted because they could never get Peter mad about the Bruins!"

His love for the Bruins can be traced to his childhood on Prospect Street in downtown St. John's. Peter came from a family of five boys and two girls, with 18 years between the youngest and the oldest. Their father, Peter Sr., married when he was 40, and then along came the seven children. Peter's older sister, Judy, says it makes for an interesting family dynamic. "Kevin, John, and I are two years apart and the rest are like a second family," she says.

Peter was closest in age and relationship to his brother Noel, just two years older. Noel still remembers how Peter's love for the Bruins began. Growing up, all their friends either had a Montreal or a Toronto hockey jersey, two of the most cherished teams in Canada in the 1950s and 1960s. One Christmas their aunt gave Peter and Noel knitted turtleneck sweaters. One had the

Chicago Blackhawks logo; the other, the Boston Bruins logo. Being children on a Christmas morning, Peter and Noel dove for the gifts, each grabbing one and ripping open the wrapping paper. "Of course, I got the Blackhawks one and he got the Bruins," Noel recalls. "That's how we became Blackhawks and Bruins fans. And it was just the luck of the draw that, when he unwrapped that Christmas present, he got the Bruins."

There were enough boys in the Breen household that they could head down to the basement, dress up in their hockey gear, and pretend that they were on the ice. Peter's younger brother Danny remembers it mostly being about the contact part of the sport, with Danny always on the receiving end of the action. "They used to dress me up in all my hockey gear and bring me down to the basement and check me, and I was only about four or five years old. That would be until Dad came down and caught them, and they scattered then."

Kevin, one of Peter's other brothers, laughs when he recalls those basement competitions. "Danny would come up over the stairs and he'd be as a red as a beet!"

Despite being used as a punching bag, Danny remembers the compassionate side of Peter. "Pete used to be responsible for taking me to school. He took me to my first movie, to my first hockey game," he says.

Peter was named for his father. He even looked like him. Peter Sr., a longshoreman and an athlete, played soccer and he rowed, and his ability to manoeuvre a paddle through the water landed his team in the record books at the Royal St. John's Regatta, a rowing record that stood for more than 80 years. There's even a bench in the name of Peter Sr. at Quidi Vidi Lake, where the Regatta has been held almost annually since 1816.

Peter Jr. excelled in softball and basketball. "Pete played on championship teams; his athleticism comes from our dad," Noel says. Judy says young Peter inherited many of his father's traits. "His mannerisms, everything," she says. "He was quick and you couldn't get much past him. He had a great sense of humour. Very dry. And humble. He didn't like to be in the spotlight. But he knew everyone. And everyone knew him."

So it should come as no surprise that Peter had the ability to turn a young girl's head. Janet and Peter, 17 or 18 years old in the early 1970s, met one night at a local bus stop in St. John's, near a popular place where their friends hung out, sneaking a beer or two when no one was looking. "And Pete and two or three of the other guys came over talking to us," Janet says, "and then the guys said 'come on Pete, we're leaving.' And he said 'no I'm not, I'm staying here to talk to the girls.' And anyway, he did stay and that was it!"

Janet fell for him that evening. "It was just like bang! It just took off. He was just a really nice guy. Super, super nice. Oh my God, he was handsome," she explains, while blushing. "He had hair right down to his shoulders, I can see it now, he had some long hair! My dad used to say, 'I don't know which one of you is the woman!'" Janet laughs.

They started seeing each other as often as they could, even for the few minutes between their last class and when Peter had to report to work at his part-time job. "When he was in high school, he worked in Ayres downtown," says Janet. "There was two Ayres. There was the big one on the corner and there was a smaller one joined to Bowring's there. And that's the one he worked at, in the shoe department. And I remember I'd go down and we'd meet after school and we'd go into Shelley's restaurant, which was across the street. And we'd go in there and have a bite to eat and then he'd go to work and I'd get the bus home."

The romance blossomed and within three years—barely out of their teens—Janet and Peter married. "They say when you meet somebody, you know. That's just the way it was. I mean, it was crazy. He didn't drive a car. I didn't drive a car. I remember my mom and dad, every time he was at the house they'd drive him home; they wouldn't dare let him walk home or get a bus."

Some of other Breen boys showed an interest in politics as they grew older. Danny and Kevin are in the St. John's municipal record books as being the only two brothers ever elected to city council. Danny was elected mayor in 2017. But Peter showed no interest in politics, despite spending much of his time talking to people. "If he was walking down one side of Water Street. and he saw someone coming up the other side, he'd cross the street to talk with them," Danny says. "He was very sociable."

But Peter was happier in a volunteer role, helping out behind the scenes. Peter was what people in St. John's, a city steeped in religion, tradition, and history, called a "St. Bon's boy." In its heyday in the early 1900s, St. Bonaventure's College—adjacent to the towering Roman Catholic Basilica Cathedral—was one of the more prestigious schools in the province and even had its own ice rink. The young people enrolled there were considered the cream of the crop, the future leaders, some of whom would be named Rhodes Scholars, who would travel to study at Oxford University in the UK.

But in the 1960s, during a school reorganization throughout the city, St. Bon's was downgraded to an elementary school. Peter, a student there from Grades 1 to 8, moved to a different school. In 1998, St. Bon's closed.

But those St. Bon's years were formative, and when plans were developed to reopen St. Bon's within a year as a private school, Peter jumped in to help. "He cleaned the place, he painted the place," Kevin says. Judy clearly remembers the amount of work her brother did getting the school ready for occupancy: "In fact, the chapel was closed and he was the one who made it possible to have it ready for the first graduating class of the new St. Bon's."

Peter always looked to help others, Janet says. "Nobody knows what Pete did for other people. In a snowstorm, he would go out and he would shovel our driveway and then he'd shovel others," she says. "Then he'd leave and go in and shovel his mom's, and then he'd go to my mom and dad's and he'd shovel them. And then he'd go to my aunt and uncles and shovel them! And the kids used to say, 'Mom, Dad is going to have a heart attack.' He did so much for other people. Oh my God."

Peter also helped others when there was no snow on the ground. "We have Icelandic friends who moved in next door … and Pete would go out and cut their grass for them. And their back gardens were huge. And every time he mowed ours, he mowed theirs without fail. That was Pete."

Family and friends were always central to Peter's life, even when he was young. Danny remembers Peter's first job after high school, at A. Harvey and Company, a long-time St. John's waterfront business that specialized in marine services. Their father worked just down the road as the secretary-treasurer of the Longshoremen's Protective Union, known locally as the LSPU. Every day, Danny says, Peter made the five-minute walk down the road to sit in their father's office and have lunch with him.

The job at Harvey's eventually led Peter to Bull Arm and the Hibernia construction site. Janet says she and the four children spent many a weekend on the road driving to see Peter in Come By Chance.

Telling stories about the years their father spent living in a rural town about an hour and a half outside the city makes Janet and the children laugh. Noelle, showing her father's sense of humour, has a different take on those weekends around the bay. "That was our vacation. We didn't go to Florida. We went to Come By Chance," she says, laughing.

After nearly six years of working and living together, Peter and Keith Normore realized that they'd be soon looking for new jobs as construction of the Hibernia rig was coming to an end. Deciding to stay in the same line of work, they took jobs in the offshore. They went to work for East Coast Catering, which had the contract to clean rooms and provide food to oil workers.

The rigs Peter and Keith worked on are well known in the Newfoundland offshore. Billy Shoemaker. Glomar Grand Banks. Henry Goodrich. For nine years, the two worked side by side and built friendships with other rig workers such as Greg Morris and Derek Mullowney.

For the most part, Keith enjoyed the work environment. "Once it gets in your bones, like, I don't know what it is but it's a whole new family," he explains, "because when you're offshore it's a family type of thing and you have to take care of each other because you don't know if something is going to go wrong or who's going to be pulling your ass out of the fire."

But after nine years, Keith had had enough. The company he and Peter worked for snagged a huge contract to provide cafeteria and housekeeping services to the SeaRose FPSO, and while it meant double the pay, Keith decided it was time to start his own business.

It wasn't long after Peter started working on the SeaRose that Danny started hearing stories about the friendly hockey rivalry developing between his brother and his offshore friends. "The only thing he loved more than cheering for the Bruins was hating the Canadiens. And I think Greg Morris was a Habs fan and they'd be at it constantly. And there was another guy, Derek Mullowney. And Derek hated hockey. So he'd be in the middle of the two of them and they'd be fighting." Danny laughs.

"The big joke out there was that they knew Pete was after cleaning up their room because when they went in, TSN was on, on the TV. Because he would go down and do the rooms and he'd turn on the TV and watch the sports scores from the night before."

Danny laughs about one particular story. Peter was cleaning the room of a person who was into only his second day ever at sea. After starting his shift, the new hire realized that he needed something from his room. "And when he opened the door," Danny says, "there was a fellow sitting there in the chair watching TV and on the phone. Because not all the rooms had the phones. So he went back upstairs and he said, 'There's somebody in my room!' And they said, 'Oh, that's Pete. He does that every morning.'"

In this case, Peter wasn't just watching the sports scores from the night before. "He'd be calling our mother," says Danny. "He'd call [our] mother every morning when he was offshore. He would go down to the rooms and he'd find one that had a phone and that would be the first room he'd do, and he'd phone Mom from the room.

"He was devoted to our mother. He'd visit her all the time. And he'd be offshore and he'd call her every morning because she was worried about him. God, did she ever worry. He'd phone to let her know he was okay." When he was onshore, Peter frequently visited his elderly mother.

And so it was, on the morning of March 12, 2009, Peter Breen, the 55-year-old practical joker who loved to laugh and to make people laugh, was back at St. John's airport, ready to step onto Cougar Flight 491 and head to the SeaRose for three more weeks.

The night before, he dropped over to his brother John's house with a surprise gift. John had always been involved in martial arts and Peter had phoned him that day to say he had something for him and would be over later to drop it off. "And he came over with a martial arts sword," John recalls. "I don't know where he got it. And when he came to the front door he came in and we chatted for a few minutes and then he went."

As Peter walked down the driveway, John closed the door, turned to his wife, Eleanor, and said, "That's really strange that Pete would come to the front door." Strange, because they had grown up in a home where their mother always told them to use the back door, and that stayed with Peter all his life, according to John. "He had never walked in the front door of my house. He'd always come in the backyard and come in through the back door."

The next morning, something else unusual happened. Peter had to be at the airport an hour or two before the 9 a.m. flight to go through the normal safety session and pre-boarding screening. Because he was up so early, and his three-week-on, three-week-off schedule was such a routine in the Breen household, it was common for 17-year-old Andrew to sleep through his father's departure, and not say goodbye. Other times Andrew would be up and getting ready for school, but he would be in the shower, so he'd just yell out "Dad, love you, goodbye" from behind the shower curtain.

This particular morning, when Peter was all packed up, he yelled out, "I'm leaving, Andrew, I'm going." Peter then turned to his wife. "And he looked at me," Janet says, "and I'll never forget this, he said, 'I'm not leaving until Andrew is out of the shower and I can give him a hug and a kiss goodbye.'"

Andrew also recalls the unusual moment. "I had a head full of shampoo, and rinsed my hair," he says. "I wasn't done with the shower, got out, put a towel around me and went and said goodbye, and went and got back in. Never once had I done that, not once. It was just the weirdest thing."

Janet gave Peter a ride to the airport, as she always did. She then headed home and, for the next few hours, puttered around the house with the radio on in the background. At one point, Janet Marie arrived to have breakfast with her.

They were in the kitchen together when the announcer suddenly said something that threw their minds and lives into chaos.

Gary Corbett, 46

"Now, we didn't build anything that NASA was looking for, just hobby stuff around the house," Jack Walsh, age 65, says with a laugh.

Jack is all smiles when he talks about his exploits in the shed with his buddy Gary Corbett. Both mechanically minded, they were always tinkering with new inventions on a Friday night as they played a game of darts and enjoyed a beer or two.

As Jack was a marine engineer, his mind leaned toward design. Gary was more into mechanics and hydraulics and how to turn those designs into something physical. As Jack puts it: "We were good at making stuff look good and work good." They spent time together dreaming up ideas and then working to make them become reality. "We did a lot of projects together," Jack says. "We could size something up and between the two of us, with my knowledge of mechanics and engineering and his of welding and hydraulics, we could come up with anything."

The collaboration Jack remembers most clearly is the time they created a contraption to feed a local softball team. No one in the league had ever seen the likes of it.

It came about when one of the teams playing in a tournament wanted to treat the players to Jiggs' dinner, a traditional Newfoundland meal of potatoes, carrots, cabbage, salt beef, turnip, pease pudding, and, of course, turkey. The team had to feed about three dozen players but didn't have a large enough pot in which to boil all the ingredients.

That's when Jack and Gary got to work in the shed. "We made a big pot out of a triple kitchen sink that came out of an industrial kitchen," Jack explains. "We cut it up in three pieces. We used one sink for the pot, and the other sink we connected with a piano hinge to make a cover and we made a propane burner out of an axle stand for a car. And we hooked it all up to the propane bottle."

When it was all welded together, they had a giant stainless steel pot and makeshift propane stove that could handle all the team's cooking needs during local ball tournaments—not just for one meal but for years to come. The team, in fact the entire league, was very impressed. "We cooked enough Jiggs' dinner at their ball tournaments for about 30 people. And we made that and it's still going after about 25 years."

Jack and Gary met by happenstance. Jack grew up a mile or two from Gary's family in Kelligrews, one of a string of communities along the shoreline of Conception Bay that amalgamated in the 1970s to become Conception Bay South. "I used to hang around with his brother first," Jack recalls. "His brother Roger was a couple of years older than Gary. But me and Gary connected mostly when we used to do a lot of hunting and fishing, a lot of outdoor things. He was more into that than Roger."

Despite nearly a decade difference in age, the two fast became close friends. "He was always in a good mood. He was always happy. We went moose hunting and bird hunting, because he had a setter, and trouting. We did a lot of fishing in Cape Shore, Branch, Salmonier Line, Witless Bay Line, even out as far as central Newfoundland."

Gary loved any outdoor activity from a young age. "He enjoyed hunting with his friends," says his sister Debbie. "Every weekend Gary and two of his best friends and his dog would go into the woods around home and set the rabbit snares. As they got older and learned to fire a gun, one of the friends' dad would take them up to the country hunting. Moose, rabbits, birds, fishing, he loved it all!"

They grew up in a busy home. Mother, father, five children, and Nan and Pop all under one roof. Gary was the second youngest. "Outside the home he was a shy, quiet little boy, but when he was at home we all knew it," Debbie says. "He wasn't going to be left out of anything that was happening. And with so many people, he always had someone's attention."

Debbie says Gary knew early on what career he wanted after he graduated from his high school, Queen Elizabeth High in nearby Foxtrap. "He knew that getting an education was the way to get what he wanted, needed out of life," she says. "He finished high school and then attended the College of North Atlantic. He received his diploma in welding."

As a teenager and young adult, Debbie says, sports and hunting took up all of Gary's time when he wasn't in school or working. Until he met Cecilia Myers.

That changed everything. Cecilia lived about 20 minutes away in a town located along the same stretch of highway. "Girlfriends weren't high on his list at that time," Debbie says, "then he met a young woman from Chapel's Cove. She stole his heart and so began the next phase of his life."

The first thing Cecilia—or Ceily, as she's known—noticed about Gary was his laughter. "He had a unique hearty laugh," she recalls, "which could be heard everywhere."

They were just hitting their 20s and the place for the 20-something crowd to hang out at that time in the 1980s was The Hat Lounge in Holyrood, which was about halfway between her home and Gary's. The live music was the drawing card, especially on weekends, when the club was usually packed. "Gary was at a table with six or seven of his friends," she recalls, "and I was with a few of mine at a table nearby. Nothing overly exciting. The usual, had a few dances, met his friends, etc. We talked and got along well and I guess it was his good looks and yes, his laughter, that initially caught my eye.

"Gary was actually very shy and quiet back then," Ceily says, "until you got to know him and he was comfortable around you. We got along so well and began seeing each other on a regular basis."

They found that they had common interests. "We enjoyed spending time together, having fun with friends, camping, hiking." She quickly realized how much he loved the outdoors. "He owned a Skidoo, a canoe, and an ATV. He loved to hunt and always managed to get his moose, very quickly I might add. I remember a couple of times he was only gone an hour or so and he'd call saying he had his moose."

But while Gary loved being in the outdoors or heading to Jack's shed on a weekend night for a game of darts and a few beers, Ceily says he was very focused when it came to plans for his future. "Gary was a very strong-willed and determined man. He was a hard worker, very loyal, and also very stubborn! Gary always had goals and was determined to meet them."

One of those goals was to get a job that paid enough for him to buy his own home. "His family had never owned their own home," Ceily explains, "and they had rented and lived in a couple of different places."

After graduating from college with a welding certificate, Gary spent the next years working and training in the field and soon became certified as a journeyman welder. In the late 1980s, he went to work at Hyflodraulic Limited, a company owned by his friend. The industrial business specializes in keeping mechanical systems running smoothly. Gary transitioned from welding into the hydraulics side of the business and soon became a certified hydraulic mechanic;

he was considered to be one of the best around. "Gary ... positioned himself high amongst the best mechanical and hydraulic experts in North America," his company's website brags; he "was called upon by many engineers in the oil and gas industry to assist them in their modifications and refits."

Ceily says Gary did well because he cared deeply about his work. "Gary worked hard to get ahead in his career. He loved his work and hardly ever missed a day. He would always arrive early."

But there was one part of the job he didn't like. As the offshore oil industry expanded in the province, much of his company's work evolved into contracts with companies working offshore. That meant that Gary had to leave his office at the facility in Mount Pearl—a city that borders St. John's—and head out to the rigs to do hydraulics repair or maintenance work. "He went offshore several times a year but not on a regular basis," Ceily says. "The one thing he hated about going offshore was the helicopter ride. He hated flying over the water."

But as it was part of the job, he accepted the risk. "When Gary was offshore, he would telephone home every night," she says.

While his career was on the upturn, so was his family life. Gary had found everything he wanted—especially the love of his life, Ceily—and he didn't even have to leave the town where he was born. "We got married ... And the love we shared was special; it was ours to share with each other and our children when they came along."

In 1987, Gary got what he always wanted when he and Ceily bought their first home. Before long they had a family of three children: Stacey, and twins Chad and Chelsea, two years younger.

The children were Gary's pride and joy and he went everywhere with them. "His family was everything to him and him to us," Ceily says. "Gary encouraged them so much in school ... he would always stress to the kids the importance of getting a good education and working hard. Every report card left him beaming and he attended everything he could possibly attend with the children, whether it be school concerts, soccer, tae kwon do, ballet recitals."

Some of the family's best times were during the summers when they'd either head to a friend's cabin for a weekend or a week or hit the road visiting parks. "Gary loved taking us to the cabins," she says, "and having a great time with the kids—seadooing, kayaking, ATV trails, campfires."

Their favourite spots were Gros Morne and Terra Nova national parks. Chelsea and her sister and brother remember those trips well. "He was always an outdoors person. Taking us for hikes, fishing, or out on the ATV," she says. "We would always take a vacation in the summer somewhere around the island. Terra Nova or a friend's cabin. An especially memorable and exciting vacation was a trip to Prince Edward Island and New Brunswick."

Those long trips in the vehicle also turned into much family teasing. Chelsea says that her father excelled at it, recounting a running joke from when she was younger and he tried to convince her she wasn't human. "He loved to tell me that I was a monkey," Chelsea recalls. "When I would protest and say, 'Am not!' he would explain that, yes, I was, because when I was born I had a tail that the doctors had to remove. As if this was a fact! He thought he was hilarious."

And then there was the say-my-name joke, as the children dubbed it. "On any given day, if any of us children were silently sitting near each other he would whisper our names," Chelsea says. "We would look up, look around and Dad would be minding his own business. A few seconds later, we would hear him whisper our names again. We would say 'What?' He would look at us confused and surprised, and say 'What? I didn't say anything.'" They'd go back to doing whatever they were doing, and he'd start whispering their names again. "And again we would hear our name. 'Dad, stop!' 'Stop what?,' he'd say. 'You keep saying my name!'" This is when Gary would break out into the Destiny's Child song "Say My Name." "Except he didn't know all of the words, so he would just repeat the same lyrics, getting gradually louder, 'Say my name, say my name, say my name, SAY MY NAME!' And he would laugh and laugh."

Chelsea and the others would retaliate by poking fun at his "growing" bald spot.

But over the years, going offshore took its toll. By 2009, Gary told Ceily that he was no longer interested in leaving her and the children to fly out to sea for a week or longer at a time, and when his Basic Survival Training certificate expired—in about three years—he wasn't going to renew it.

Then new contract work came up for the Hibernia platform in spring 2009. A handful of people from Gary's office, Gary included, had to fly out to the rig. The plan was for them to head out there on the morning of Friday, March 13. However, on March 11, Gary received a call about the possibility of leaving that Thursday instead of on Friday.

Gary agreed to go early, telling Ceily that the earlier he left the earlier he would return. It was decided that his co-worker Wade Duggan would head out with Gary on the earlier flight.

The night before leaving, Gary visited his friend Jack Walsh. Gary and Jack always helped each other out. "We became best friends. We used to do everything on Saturdays, like I would help him with work on his house, he'd help me and we just did everything together. And when he got married, I was at his wedding and he had three kids and I stood up to [be godfather to] one of his kids, so we just kept getting closer and closer over time."

Jack, who lived on his own, says that he liked going to Gary's home because of the laughter he'd hear from Gary and the children. "He was always really, really good with his kids. And that is what drew me. And when you'd go down into his house, there was always a good feeling in the house. Well, it was just—it just felt good being around all his family."

Gary decided to visit that night because Jack had just been released from hospital after suffering a broken leg, and he was having a rough time trying to get around and fend for himself.

Jack was home on the couch unable to move around. "I slipped on ice and I broke the two bones in my lower right leg and I was really incapacitated for about six months. Gary had cooked a pork chop dinner with all the fixings and he had brought it up, you know, and we had talked for a long time and I had a prescription to get some painkillers and I couldn't get there to get it, and he offered to go get them. That was the way he was."

And so it was, on March 12, 2009, Gary Corbett, 46 years old and thinking that he would soon stop travelling to the offshore, was at St. John's airport and ready to step on board Cougar Flight 491.

Before he left, he told his 14-year-old son, Chad, he'd take him fishing as soon as he got back home.

Later that morning, Ceily was at work in a government building just a few doors down from Gary's company, when Gary's boss and his wife walked into her office. He mentioned something about a helicopter. Ceily, confused by what he was saying, was hit by a wave of panic and fear.

Around the same time, Jack was at home sitting on the couch watching television when a news bulletin flashed on the screen.

Wade Duggan, 32

When it came to hockey, Wade Duggan's appetite for the sport was like his father's: insatiable.

From the time his parents helped him wiggle his feet into a pair of skates and lace them up, Wade was out the door and on one of two frozen ponds, either Brigus Pond or Island Pond. Both were just down the road from his home in Brigus South on Newfoundland's southern shore. The tiny fishing community on the Avalon Peninsula is a 50-minute drive from St. John's, according to the map, but it usually takes almost twice that time because of the twisting and narrow two-lane highway that winds up and down the shore, jutting close to the edge of the Atlantic Ocean.

Wade wasn't alone on the ice. The town, like many rural Newfoundland communities in the early to mid-1980s, was filled with children, and most of them rushed home to get their skates and sticks as soon as school let them out in the winter time.

Wade, a big boy with a big smile stretching across his freckled face, led the way. "He was on the ponds every evening after he come out of school," Kevin recalls. "I mean, he was on the ponds every weekday and Saturday and Sundays. He loved it so much. He'd get to school and write different things about hockey. He was all hockey."

Kevin and his wife, Mary, had two children: Wade and Greg. "We grew up on the ponds, skating and stuff," Greg says. "I was five years older, so I was running with a different crowd."

For the first five years of his life, Greg had his mother all to himself. He jokes that they basically grew up together as she was only 20 when he was born.

But suddenly Wade came along and, as they got older, Greg had a new best friend. "Me and Wade, we were really close, b'y," Greg says. "Oh Jesus, we were more than brothers, we were best friends too. I mean, I remembers picking on each other when we were younger and hitting him and telling him [I was] toughening him up for life, and all this sort of thing."

Back then, there was no organized hockey on the southern shore, so the children were left to rustle up an even number of friends to be divvied up into teams for their own street or pond games.

Then Wade heard that the nearest large community was willing to accept players from Brigus South. "He came home one day," his father recalls, "and said, 'We're allowed to join the Goulds hockey league!' And I said, 'go for it, no problem!'"

Kevin didn't need much convincing. He was as much a hockey fan as his son. Perhaps even more, says Greg, who believes it was their father who got Wade hooked on hockey in the first place, especially his favourite team, the Toronto Maple Leafs. "Father loved hockey," he says. "Wade was more like Father. Father has a quiet demeanour, but when he speaks, you listen. That's the way it is. I was more like me mother for being outgoing, I'm not shy. I wouldn't say Wade was shy. He just—he wasn't like me, you know what I mean? It's like Father, Father is happy enough just sitting down and watching a hockey game by himself. And that's the way Wade was. He wasn't a loner or anything; he was just happy enough sitting down by himself."

Kevin worked at a brewery in St. John's, which meant many mornings he was on the road before daylight. When the boys signed up for minor hockey and Kevin agreed to coach them, he started logging even more miles. That's when he decided he needed a larger vehicle, one that accommodated the children and the hockey gear he would be carting around.

Wade made the final decision that he go with a Chevy Astro van, a vehicle with plenty of room. "The Astro, she was brand new when I bought it. We had two picked out, and Wade said, 'Father, I'll pick the one,' and he picked the Astro."

It was perfect for what they needed, Kevin says. "I was coaching and I had more than Wade with me. Seven or eight young fellows. And that one had two seats in the back and two seats in the front. And we were on the road all the time, I mean I was driving back and forth to work at Labatt Brewery in St. John's too and that put extra miles on it. I worked for Labatt Brewery for 27 or 29 years, something like that. And it's a good thing I had a half decent job, because I did an awful lot of overtime to get Greg and Wade on the road. I mean, hockey wasn't as expensive then but it's the same amount of money, a dollar now was 50 cents back then."

By the middle of that first season with the Goulds minor hockey, Wade had made the all-star team. "He loved it, he loved it, he loved it," Kevin emphasizes. "A lot of times I didn't have to get him out of bed, I mean he had to get me out of bed to get to hockey. We were down in Baie Verte playing hockey, La Scie playing hockey, Bishop's Falls playing hockey, Grand Falls playing hockey, and we'd come back to Springdale, tournaments down there. And we played down in Whitbourne too."

Greg shakes his head in admiration at what his father did to make sure that he and Wade and all the other children got to their games. "He was the fellow that drove everyone around, he was the parent who did all that."

They travelled through snowstorms that sometimes left them on the road waiting out the weather. Those unintentional long weekends often made for fun nights, despite the harrowing weather. "We were coming in from Whitbourne one night," Kevin recalls. "And a big huge storm hit us and we got into the Bluefin Motel and there were four or five hockey teams stuck there that night and they all had to stay the night. The owner opened the garage and we put five or six cars in there and I put the van in and half the teams were in the van carrying on and whatever and sleeping and we never got through till six o'clock the next morning."

Greg didn't go up through the minor hockey system—he was a teenager by the time the boys could get into organized hockey—but Wade went through the various levels.

As a father and coach, Kevin was impressed with Wade's commitment to the sport. He became known as a dedicated player and as he rose through atom, peewee, bantam, and all the other levels of hockey, he was noticed for his playing and for his size. He played defence, and by the time he was in his late teens, he had grown into a big, solid player—about 6 feet 3 without skates, and 220 pounds.

Greg says that his brother's strength and size helped him create a presence on the ice. "He was a good strong defenceman. He was a better player than I was," Greg says. "Oh yeah, he was a good hockey player. Strong. And he could fight too, right? But regards to fighting off the ice, he'd never think about it. It's just the emotion of the game. What happens on the ice stays on the ice, right?"

Wade was picked up by a junior team in Conception Bay South and Kevin loved his son's blossoming hockey career. "When Wade went playing hockey, I used to go with him too. See, when he'd go out to Conception Bay South, he'd drive, he had his licence then, and I'd sit back and relax. And when he'd go to practice, I'd go with him. Wherever he'd play."

In 1994 Wade had an opportunity to play outside the province in

Buckingham, a small town just across the river from Ottawa, inside the Quebec border.

Kevin says the team heard of Wade's abilities through one of his teammates in Conception Bay South who was going to Quebec to play.

Then one day his telephone rang. It was the Quebec Provincial Junior A Hockey League asking Wade and his family if he wanted a shot at playing with the Buckingham Castors. He was 17. "It was right after Christmas," Kevin says. "It was unreal, you know? He couldn't believe it, just couldn't fathom it. He wanted to go so bad you know, he had no problem."

Back then making a long-distance call was a huge deal, and Kevin knew that when the monthly bill came in. He jokes that it cost him a small fortune in telephone calls to talk to his son every night. While Wade was in Buckingham, Kevin flew up to watch him play. He loves to tell the story about how starry-eyed Wade was when he got to play in the same stadium in Quebec City where the former Quebec Nordiques played when they were in the NHL: "He was down in the Colisée in Quebec and he said he was looking up at the different lights and he couldn't get over it. They played there in a tournament. He told me it was the highlight. He said he'd never give it up for the world, the experience he had."

Another once-in-a-lifetime experience came when he had a chance to rub shoulders with, and learn from, NHL Hall-of-Famer Steve Shutt, who played with the Montreal Canadiens for 13 years, and nabbed five Stanley Cups along the way in the 1970s.

Shutt's son Jason was a goalie on Wade's team. "Well, they got to be real great friends," Kevin recalls. "Steve Shutt used to come down and practice with them ... and I was talking to Wade and I said, 'What's he like, what's Steve Shutt like as a human being?' And he said, 'Father, he's that good he could be a Newfoundlander!'" Kevin bursts out laughing. "You know, that's what he said, right?"

That was a good year for Wade, although he was a teen who was living away from home for the first time. He enjoyed himself and wanted to stay there, and the team wanted to keep him in the lineup, but Buckingham folded from the league after that season.

Wade returned home, where he quickly resumed playing hockey locally, showing more confidence than ever on the ice. "When he started first," his father, ever the coach, says, "he was lacking a bit of confidence, but when that confidence came, he was all go. He was all go, no doubt about it. Confidence is 50 per cent of the battle, right? You got to have confidence, even in your work."

Wade was about to join the Bell Island Juniors team after he returned home, but one day he caught someone else's eye while he was on the ice. "They were practicing in August see, and he went out and he was sure he would've made the team, the coach there said so. And there was a guy there in the arena, the Prince of Wales arena in St. John's, and there was a guy there in the arena from Dartmouth, Nova Scotia. And he wanted him to go up there and try out. And he went on up there."

Wade made the team and moved away again. But this time was different. No bright lights or legendary coliseums, only more time away from his family and friends. Wade was lonely. He put in his year and came back to Brigus South, this time for good. "He was pretty lonely, I must say," Kevin says. "He was 19 then ... he spent a year with Amherst. When he came home after that, he was satisfied with what he had done."

Any thoughts to a possible pro hockey career had ended. Greg believes that his kid brother could've gone much further in hockey if he had been picked up at an earlier age. "He was kind of too old when he got discovered, like that is as far as he went. It was too late in the game then. Wade was a little too late when he got discovered."

With the boys grown and finished with their minor hockey years, it was time to retire the Astro van that had seen just about every stadium parking lot in the province. When Kevin parked it in his driveway that final time—the motor still running fine, he happily points out—it had an amazing 535,000 kilometres on it, according to Greg. Eventually, they found someone who carted it away to use it for parts.

For Wade, about to enter his 20s, it was time to focus on his education and career. He took a course in the trades at a college about an hour and a half from his hometown and graduated as a millwright. He also studied hydraulics, which helped him land a job at Hyflodraulics Limited in Mount Pearl. The company specializes in mechanical systems and at the time was positioning itself to supply services to the burgeoning offshore. Wade finished his apprenticeship and became a qualified journeyman millwright.

He didn't give up on hockey though. He continued playing in local rec leagues and in senior hockey. He even helped his hometown Southern Shore Breakers snag a Herder championship—the cherished trophy of Newfoundland Senior Hockey League that still brings thousands of fans out to local stadiums every winter—in the late 1990s. His father easily lists the senior teams Wade played for over the years. "He was with the Goulds, he was on the southern shore and won the Herder, and he played with Conception Bay South Senior."

Grownups now and both married, Wade and Greg stayed close. "Wade never did nothing in his life without running it by me first," Greg says. "Like Wade, if he was stuck for $20, he'd phone me. That's the way we are. That's the way we operated. Whatever he needed or any decision, if he was buying something or whatever, whatever he had on the go, he'd phone me and run it by me. He'd ask what my opinion was first. Always. Because I was the older brother. And I'd always talk back and forth with him. I talked to him every day, every single day. It's just the way we were."

Wade enjoyed working at Hyflodraulics. The company treated him well and he was good at what he did. Before long, he and a co-worker, welder Gary

Corbett, became known for having two of the best mechanical minds around.

Kevin says that a friend of his from the Coast Guard told him the organization was working on a project one time and had telephoned around looking for the best two mechanics in town. Wade and Gary were sent to the wharf to help out that day.

As the oil industry continued to grow, Hyflodraulics was getting more contract work offshore and that meant that the company relied heavily on Wade's and Gary's abilities. "When Husky Energy needed specialty workers out there," Greg says, "they'd phone Hyflo and Hyflo would send out their men, and Wade and Gary would be their main fellows, they were who they wanted all the time. They were their main two men."

Greg knew most of the people who were flying back and forth to the various rigs and platforms because he was already working at Hibernia, but he was always surprised to learn how many of them mentioned knowing Wade.

While he loved the work he did, and went where he was asked to go, Wade didn't like the offshore, according to Greg: "I'll say this, he didn't want to go offshore. I'll tell you that right now. No sir, he hated it. He didn't like it at all. He could've had a job offshore if he wanted, but he didn't want to be out there all the time. He just wanted to go out and do his thing and be home, more so."

In the spring of 2009, Wade was lined up to do a job on the Hibernia platform. He and Gary were booked to fly out on Friday, March 13. "That was the original plan," Greg says, "that they'd leave Friday morning. And all that week before, he was at the house every day of the week and he was going Friday and I said I'm going out the following Tuesday."

Then Wade called to say there was a last-minute change in plans. "He called me Wednesday night and said, 'I just got a call to go tomorrow instead of Friday.' So, I said, 'All right, I'll see you when I gets out Tuesday, and have a good trip.'"

Wade called his parents next, as he always did before leaving for the offshore. "He phoned about eight o'clock," Kevin says. "He said, 'Father, I'm going out tomorrow morning now.'"

Kevin never worried about his two sons travelling to the offshore, but he did worry about the kind of work they did on the rigs. "The last time Wade was out he was working on the big cranes, you know, and he was telling me about it. And I had said to him, 'Now, b'y, don't you be doing stuff that you— that is dangerous, you know? Whatever you do, don't—say you're not going to do it. That it can't be done.'"

It never crossed his mind to worry about the helicopter flight to the rig. "As far as I was concerned, they were safe. I was sure they were, you know. Accidents will happen, you know, but other than that, no, it didn't bother me. Nothing else went through my mind, right? I drove back and forth from the southern shore for more than 25 years, I mean I was on the road in storms after storm after storm and I was in more danger as far as I was concerned, you know what I mean?"

And so it was, on the morning of March 12, 2009, 32-year-old Wade Duggan, at the top of his trade and in demand, was back at St. John's airport and preparing to board Cougar Flight 491 to head to Hibernia.

Later that morning, Greg was at his home keeping an eye on a ham he had boiling on the stove. He had just finished chatting with a friend who had dropped by, when the telephone rang.

Wade Drake, 42

The way Wade Drake's family saw it, Wade had always loved anything that involved speed. In living his life, they say, there was one gear: overdrive.

Whether it was on a snowmobile riding the groomed trails of western Newfoundland or popping into his sister's house for a visit, everything was at full tilt. "Oh my God, larger than life" is how Gertie describes Wade, who was three years younger. "He'd come into my home and there was no such thing as knocking, he'd just walk in. He would always fly in through the door with his cowboy boots on, stamping his feet. It didn't matter if the kids were asleep. He'd go right in and take them right out of the crib."

Wade would yell out to Gertie by the nickname he had tagged her with long ago. "He always called me Weezie. I'm not sure why!" she says, laughing. But her brother Peter knows the origin: Wade nicknamed Gertie after Louise Jefferson in the television sitcom *The Jeffersons*. "He used to say Gertie had big boobs just like Weezie!" Peter laughs.

Gertie says Wade's entrance into her house with his big smile and gregarious personality was always a spectacle. "He'd come in and no matter where I was, he'd yell, 'Weezie, where you to?' And he'd just roar it out. And I'd say, 'Wade, take off the boots.' That would drive me! And he'd grab you and pick you up in his arms! You wouldn't know what he'd do."

Peter, known as Junior because he was named after his father, says that "even as a child Wade was always full of energy. If Wade walked into a room, he always had to be the centre of attention. You knew he was here. Wade didn't come in and shy away or anything like that. If he didn't know you, he'd say, 'Now, who's you?'"

When Wade was in a crowd, people hung on to his every word. Gertie nods in agreement as she listens to her brother describe Wade. "That's right," she says, "and he always had everyone in stitches laughing. He was a charmer. That's what he was."

Wade was born into a big family. His parents, Peter and Adelaide, had nine children—Evelina, Peter, Wanda, Derrick, Gertie, Ronald, Wade, Lucille, Ken—in a 10-year span during the 1960s, making the Drake household in Lord's Cove on Newfoundland's Burin Peninsula a busy spot. "There was a big crowd of us and I wouldn't want it any other way," says Peter, the oldest boy. "Looking back now, it was so nice to have that big family."

The population of Lord's Cove was just a few hundred and the Drakes were no different than their neighbours when it came to the size of their family. Gertie says that having so many young people around taught them a sense of family and community: "We had it good. But everyone was the same. There was no one better than anyone else. We all had to work, and we had to work around the house."

Lord's Cove is one of those tiny communities on the island of Newfoundland that most people would have troubling locating on a map. It's about as far south as it is possible to travel on the south coast of the province. Perhaps the only time it has ever received any public attention was in 1929 when a tsunami and tidal wave ravaged a string of communities in the area, Lord's Cove being one of them. More than 24 people died. Houses and fishing wharves were destroyed. Tens of thousands of kilograms of salt cod—a staple for survival—were washed out to sea. Many families lost their livelihoods.

In later years, those who weren't employed in the fishery found work at the nearby fluorspar mine in St. Lawrence, an operation with a history of industrial disease. That's where Peter Sr. worked.

The Drakes suffered two near tragedies related to the mine, which their father, who worked there as a driller, often referred to as a "death hole." In the mid-1960s a large load of stone struck him in the jaw, nearly crushing his face. Then, in the early 1970s a small cave-in occurred near where he was working. "A chunk of clay fell from above and it buried him," Peter recalls. "Only his head was sticking out. But they dug all around him and got him out." His father suffered a broken back and his leg was crushed. Peter wasn't yet 10 when he had to take on responsibility, because his father wasn't mobile.

Tragedy struck again some years later. Their mother died suddenly at the age of 41 from a massive heart attack, leaving their father to try to keep working while running a household and raising nine children.

The loss of their mother hit them all hard, especially their father, Peter says. He feels his father gave up after Adelaide died, as he seemed to slip into depression. Peter spent even more time helping raise his younger brothers and sisters then, especially Wade, who was seven years younger.

Despite his high energy and bubbly personality, another side of Wade emerged before their mother had passed and their father had become sick. "How I would describe Wade as a child—we'd always say he was stubborn," Peter sums up. "If he wanted something or if he wanted to do something, then he was going to do it. He was that stubborn. It was hard to tell him no. It was no good to say, 'Wade, no you can't do it.'"

Gertie recounts a family story of one of those times when Wade wouldn't take no for an answer. With nine children, family road trips weren't an option. About the only time the family vehicle moved was if their parents went out to run errands such as buying groceries, often on their own—it was usually their only time alone together. But one day Wade wasn't having any of that. "When that car moved, he wanted to be in it," Gertie recalls. "And this day, Father said, 'No you're not going, we're going out. We have business to do.'"

Gertie says that her parents started to drive away, but Wade was adamant. "They started down the path in the car and he chased behind the car. And they were going up the road, and my father was driving slowly because Wade was running alongside the car and my father didn't want to run him over."

She laughs hysterically as she remembers the details. "But Wade caught a hold of the car door and my father put down the window and said, 'Let go of that door!' And Wade said, 'No, I want to go!' And Father yelled out, 'Let go of that door!' And Father kept going a little faster and faster, but Wade would not let go of that door!"

Wade was barely the height of the car door. He was only 10 or 11 years old. Finally, their father gave in and stopped, letting Wade get in the back seat.

Stories like that about Wade as a child are plentiful. "Another time they got in the car—it was a Valiant they had—and went on," Peter remembers. "They were going to Lamaline, which was a little ways away. And when they got in Lamaline, he popped up in the back seat. They didn't see him there because he got tight in to the back of the seat so they couldn't see him." Peter again roars with laughter.

But Wade, they say, was very kind and soft-hearted, without a mean bone in his body.

Wanda Parsons cherished that soft-heartedness from the moment she met Wade. Wanda was friends with Wade's sister growing up, and was a frequent visitor to his house. They lived in different communities, but by the time she was 16 and he was 18, they attended the same high school, St. Joseph's

Academy in Lamaline. Wanda lived about 10 minutes to the left of the school in Point May; Wade, about 10 minutes to the right.

One night they were all at a dance together and Bryan Adams's big hit at the time, "Heaven," came blasting over the loudspeaker in the high school gym. Wade approached a surprised Wanda. "He just asked me to dance," she says, "and I couldn't believe he even asked me because I always thought of him like a family member. And I think it's because I was friends with his sister and his whole family really. So, I was like … I never thought he'd want to dance with me. He was a different personality and he seemed older than me. I mean, I was two years younger."

But, a few months later they were dating and were soon seen together at all the high school dances at St. Joseph's. While Wade had a vibrant and outgoing personality that matched his big face-covering grin, Wanda was quiet and shy. "It's like opposites attract," she says. "And I guess it just happens. It'd be a boring old world if everyone was the same."

She liked being around Wade and soon began to see him as her protector. "It wasn't only attraction, it was like he always took care of me. He made friends wherever he went. If we went into a room, he'd be the first one to say, 'Hey everybody!' He liked the attention and he was always a very happy-go-lucky, happy person."

But, like magnets, once Wade and Wanda were together it was tough to separate them. Also, Wanda's family enjoyed having Wade around. They thought of him as one of their own.

After high school, Wade took a job in a fish plant for a year while waiting for Wanda to graduate so that they could go to community college together in nearby Burin. When they enrolled, she signed up for a secretarial course and he studied carpentry. After graduating and working in that field for a few years, the industry entered a downturn. Wade signed up for a scaffolding course being offered to help people get ready to enter the oil industry.

Then came his big break. He was hired to work at Bull Arm on the Hibernia construction project; he and Wanda couldn't believe it. "Here we are, a young couple," she recalls, "we were like, you're getting the chance at this start-up operation with Hibernia and you never know, it may turn into something else."

It did turn into something else—10 years of steady, full-time employment. Wanda worked at a local nursing home and, along the way, they got married, bought a house in nearby Fortune, and had two girls, Taylor and Jenna-Wade. "We kind of had it all, you know," Wanda says.

Wade was nervous about being a parent, but he adjusted easily, and he joked about expecting to have his hands full keeping the boys away when the girls got older.

When the Hibernia work ended, Wade switched to the SeaRose, where he put his scaffolding experience to use, becoming maintenance lead on the vessel. Wade loved the work. "I guess it's a very intricate thing to do," Wanda says of Wade's job. "It's a big skill to have … and he was the one who made sure it was safe before people used that scaffolding. And from what I can understand from the guys is that he was a guy who knew his work."

At sea Wade concentrated on his job. But when he was home for those three-week stints, being on the water was the furthest thing from his mind. "One thing I couldn't get him on was a boat or a cruise ship or anything like that," Wanda recalls. "He'd say, 'I'm not doing that. I'm on an oil rig for three weeks looking at water, I'm not going on a trip where I'm going to be on a boat to look at water.'"

Instead they took annual vacations to other provinces and even went on the quintessential Newfoundland family trip to Disneyland when the girls were young.

Wanda says Wade's being away half the year was the only lifestyle they knew. Wade realized how tough it was for her to work full-time and be the sole caregiver for six months of the year, so when he was at home the children were his priority.

Wade loved to shower the girls with gifts. He bought them musical instruments, including a guitar and an accordion. He loved music and he instilled that love in his daughters. Taylor had a knack for playing guitar and they both had sweet voices. Their love of music grew and it brought them closer to their father. When he was home, he'd take them to music lessons and to the local concerts so that they could show off their abilities.

Whenever Wade would take the girls somewhere, he'd also include the family dog, a small Shih Tzu named Kandi. She became so attached to Wade and enjoyed going for a drive so much that he just had to rattle the truck keys and Kandi would come running.

Wanda admits she wasn't in favour of getting a dog at first. She felt that the family was busy enough without having to worry about taking care of a pet. But before long, Wade and Kandi were a team not often seen apart. "He had always said that when he seen other people talk to their pets, that he would never be one of them," Wanda says. "It didn't take long for that to change and when he would catch himself doing it, he would laughingly say, 'I am one of them!'"

The salary of an offshore worker also allowed Wade to have the toys he loved so much: snowmobiles, ATVs, motorbikes. His sister Gertie says that Wade liked having the financial freedom to make those purchases. "He had all the toys. He had the best Skidoo and it was the fastest. He bought a motorcycle and I thought, 'That's the end of it, he's going to be killed.' Sure he got one picture of the Skidoo going right up in the air."

Peter tells the story about the time Wade bought one of the more powerful snowmobiles money could buy. "He bought a Skidoo and the engine was 1200 cc. And someone said to him one day, 'How come you got a Skidoo that's a 1200?' And Wade said, 'Because I couldn't get her in a 1300!'"

Wade was also smart and careful and knew his way around the big machines. Wanda says her husband always put safety first, as he did on the job—but she admits his love for travelling fast wasn't always easy for her. "He liked going up the hills on the Skidoo," she says. "Stuff where I'd be there saying, 'Don't do that! You shouldn't be doing that!' You're going to hurt yourself.' I used to worry about him, like if he went on the Skidoo, like any wife would worry."

Wade also spent time golfing and playing soccer; soccer was a spillover from his youth and from growing up on the south coast of the province, which is renowned for championship soccer teams.

Stories about Wade were legendary within the family, according to Gertie. "Sure the day of our father's funeral," she says, "he got up on the roof of the house and here he is with a suit on! We buried our father and we came back to the house, of course, for an Irish wake, a few drinks and something to eat. Wade was trying to call his wife but he couldn't get any reception on his cellphone. So, he climbed up on to our porch door with his suit on and climbed on to the roof of the porch and then he went from there and got up on the roof of the house. Now, our father's house was a high house … a two-storey saltbox house. Then, someone called me out and said, 'Look at Wade—he's on top of the house leaning on the chimney and talking on the cellphone!' Oh my God, he'd do anything for a laugh."

More than brothers, Wade and Peter were close friends, connected by their love of the outdoors. "Especially winter time," Peter says. "Skidoos was a big thing for us. He loved it and I loved it. He'd come home and he had his Skidoo and his quad and where I had the cabin, he'd be back and forth to the cabin with me. I have a cabin in Grand Bank, and then of course he decided to build his own cabin right next to me."

Every winter Wade would go on one multi-day snowmobile adventure with his friends, including medic John Pelley, whom he met on the SeaRose.

John lived on the west coast of the province, known for its incredible cabin country and legendary trails. Wade would go there for yearly snowmobile trips. "Wade would come in and he would do his stuff with the children but in winter time he'd set up a trip and head out to the west coast with friends of his and mine," Peter says.

In mid-February 2009, the trip was in Gros Morne National Park area, where he met up with John and the others. For a week they stayed in a cabin from which they could go on long daily snowmobile trips. Wade was adamant that Peter join them that year, and he did.

During the daylight hours they'd take to their snowmobiles and travel for hours, allowing Wade to go as far and as fast as he wanted. "He liked high marking," Peter recalls. "Which is seeing how far you can get up a mountain before turning to come back down. That's the kind of stuff he'd do. And we all sat back, me and John Pelley included, we were all sat back on our Skidoos near the bottom of a mountain. And John would say, 'Now Drakey, try that one!' And that's all he needed. He was gone!"

In the evenings they'd wind down after a long day outdoors. John would take out his guitar and entertain them while they sat around drinking beer or rum and eating chicken or fish.

One night Wade and John told a story about being on the helicopter for the 90-minute trip, with no washroom. Wade said he had to go so bad his whole body tensed up, but John couldn't figure out what was wrong. When he couldn't take it anymore, Wade whipped off his seatbelt, unzipped his survival suit, grabbed a barf bag, and hunched down in the corner to pee. Peter says John didn't know what to think of what he was seeing. "And then John said, 'I was just looking at Drakey from the other end of the helicopter and I said, 'Well, holy Christ, he's gone off the head! He's finally flipped out. He's gone off the head for sure!'" Peter says everyone was in stitches listening to them tell the story.

When the week in Gros Morne ended, everyone went their own way. John headed home to Deer Lake to spend time with his wife, Lori, before leaving for his next hitch on the SeaRose. Peter and Wade headed back to their homes and families on the Burin Peninsula.

Peter had to get back to his job, which also involved working on the water. He was employed on the pilot boats that guide the big ships into Placentia Bay and into the shoreline community of Come By Chance, where they'd pick up crude to deliver to other parts of the world. Peter's work also kept him away from home—two weeks on and two weeks off. The company had him set up in an apartment in nearby Arnold's Cove, a two-and-a-half-hour drive from his home.

Before Peter said goodbye to Wade, they talked about Wade's plan to build a cabin next to his brother. The materials were stored at Peter's cabin. "We had everything cut out and ready to go and before he went out, we did the foundation and we had that ready to go. And we had all the material that we'd need for when he'd come in the next time. We were going to go in and start the deck and the foundation."

Wade had a busy two weeks back at home before heading out to sea. The children were growing up fast—Jenna-Wade was 7; Taylor, 11—and they needed to be shuttled around to activities such as figure skating. He took Taylor to an ice show three hours away in Placentia, where he beamed with pride when she was handed a medal for her performance.

The girls also wanted to go to St. John's to try out for a national TV talent show similar to *Canadian Idol*. They were treated like stars at the auditions. They were interviewed by the show hosts and got to perform. When little Jenna-Wade walked out on the stage, Wade sat there with a huge smile on his face as she sang all the words of a Taylor Swift song without missing a beat.

When they returned home, the girls performed in another concert. For that one, they received a standing ovation. Wanda says Wade was really pleased with the confidence building in the children. "If you speak to anyone who was at those places, the concert or who seen them on TV or seen Wade there during the skate, they would say to you, yes he was so proud of those girls. You could tell because you could see it in his face. He only got a short time home but he did all this stuff. If there's anything, it's the look on his face, the pride for Jenna-Wade and Taylor; he lived for his kids."

But then it was time to go back to work. Whenever his three weeks at home were up, things always felt a little tense around their home. Wanda says they tried to keep everything in perspective: that leaving for a short period of time was better than leaving the island permanently for work.

They usually said their goodbyes the day or evening before the flight out— the drive to St. John's took more than four hours and Wade would always leave home the previous day to make sure that he didn't miss the morning flight. But Wanda says for some reason, in March 2009, he kept putting off the trip.

First, he planned to leave home at noon. Then he decided to wait until the girls got home from school at 3 p.m. Then he delayed it further and waited for Wanda to get off work at 4 p.m. About an hour after that Wade stopped putting off the inevitable: "He finally got everything ready and said his goodbyes to everybody in the porch and he looked at the girls and he says, 'Take care of Mom.'"

Eventually, Wade headed out the door, but Wanda says he seemed to be looking for any reason he could find not to get into the truck and drive away. "And I still see him walking to the truck, then getting out of the truck and going and picking up something that blew from behind our garage and, like, I'm, 'What are you doing?' And he says, 'I'm picking this up.' He picked it up and carried it back and put it back behind the garage and got in the truck and left."

It became clear that Wade didn't want to leave. "Here he was, he was putting off that trip to St. John's as long as he could because he left, it must've been at least five o'clock on March 11 when he left here and he had to drive to St. John's."

When he arrived at his brother's house in St. John's, Wade called Wanda to say that he made it safely and to say good night. "He calls me and he says, 'I'm thinking I'm getting the flu so I think I'll have a cup of tea now.' And he said, 'Loves you!' And I said, 'Good night, loves you!' and hung up."

And so it was on the morning of March 12, 2009, that Wade Drake, age 42, and squeezing every possible ounce of enjoyment out of life, was back in St. John's and preparing to step aboard Cougar Flight 491 to head back to the SeaRose.

For Wanda, it was back to the routine of dropping the children off at school and heading to her job at the nursing home.

Peter spent that morning on the water. An oil tanker would be arriving and Peter was part of the crew taking a pilot boat out to pull alongside the vessel and help guide it into port. It wasn't easy. The weather was nasty and miserable. Peter couldn't wait to get off work later that morning and head back to his apartment. As soon as he stepped inside the door, the telephone started ringing.

Burch Nash, 44

For Burch Nash, life started with a helicopter ride.

His parents, Marjorie and Harold, lived in Gaultois, a tiny fishing community on the south coast of Newfoundland. The nearest hospital was in Harbour Breton, a 20-minute ferry ride followed by a 90-minute drive.

In the mid-1960s travelling long distances for medical services was a troublesome but accepted way of life in rural Newfoundland. Most people in Gaultois who needed to go to the hospital sailed on the ferry and then travelled the bumpy road to their destination. By air it was only a 15- to 20-minute flight, but those were usually reserved for the well-to-do and government charters.

Harold worked for many years at the fish plant in Gaultois. He was a fish cutter for nearly two decades before putting in another 18 years in the cold storage room, where it was his job to pack the fish snugly into boxes for shipping. "Night and day I worked, Sundays and all," Harold recalls. In those days, the men worked at the plant, while the women stayed home raising the children.

When Burch was born, the wife of the plant manager also happened to be in Harbour Breton delivering a baby. The plant manager had arranged a helicopter flight to get his wife and son home, and when he learned that Marjorie was also about to be released from hospital with her newborn, he suggested to Harold that they join them on the helicopter.

Marjorie and Harold struggled to choose a name for their baby boy. Two days before the christening they still hadn't settled on what to name him. "I just couldn't think of a name," Marjorie says. Then it dawned on her. "The manager of the plant, Spencer Lake, had his son and he called him Burch. And that's what we called our son."

It was an unusual name, but Harold had no problem with it, as he worked for the Lake Group of Companies which ran the plant "for a good many years," as he puts it. "And I said yes, call him Burch," Harold says. After a while, everyone started calling him Burchy. Marjorie and Harold already had a four-year-old daughter, Glenda.

Life in rural Newfoundland in those days, especially for those trying to make a living from the ocean, wasn't easy. And Harold had known his share of pain. He was only two years old when his father drowned off Rose Blanche, another community along the south coast. His body was never recovered. "I lost my dad at sea, and that's all I know. That's all we know about him."

Within a year of Burch's birth, Marjorie and Harold's family of four expanded to a household of nine. Marjorie's sister-in-law died suddenly at the age of 29. She suffered an aneurysm one morning and was immediately put on a trawler and rushed to hospital across the bay. She didn't survive. Later that same day her body was returned to the community in a coffin. Marjorie's brother was left to raise two children on his own.

Without a second thought, Marjorie and Harold took him and his two children in, and also Marjorie's mother and father, who by then were quite elderly. "And we looked after them," Harold says. "So it was the nine of us."

With their own children, 11 months and five years old, Marjorie's brother, his two children who were about the same ages as Burch and Glenda, and Marjorie's parents, life was suddenly very busy. "Marjorie was an angel to everybody," Harold says. "She didn't have no education at all. But she could work and cook and clean. And I never had none either. My wife, she never went to a school—in little places and outports they taught in porches and living rooms and that kind of stuff. You never got no education. I don't have any education. We just know right from wrong."

Marjorie cooked the meals and kept everyone fed and clothed and the place clean. "I'll tell you," she says, "I knew what work was because there were no washers and dryers, if you were lucky you had a spin washer and then you had to put it through the ringer and rollers and stuff like that."

Her elderly mother would often try to get out of bed at night. Marjorie slept in a rocking chair in the room alongside her most nights with her feet up on the bed so that she'd wake up when her mother moved. She became so exhausted caring for everyone that she once went to the outport doctor and asked if her mother could be admitted to the hospital for a weekend, long enough to give her a break. The answer: no.

Glenda recalls the strain on her family back then. But not caring for others, she says, wasn't an option. "Well, the thing is, back then, and you don't see it so much today, but you looked out to the extended family. It just seemed to be something you had to do. You had to look out to your mother and father. You had to look out to others, you know."

After about a year Marjorie and Harold packed everyone up and moved farther east along the south coast to Fortune, where Harold once again worked in the local fish plant.

It's against this backdrop of caring for one another and putting family first that the Nash children grew up in their new hometown. Burch was an altar boy. Glenda sang in the Sunday choir. Like most families of a girl and a boy, Glenda was her father's girl, and Burch his mother's boy. But as they grew older, Glenda saw her father's characteristics in her brother.

From an early age, Burch treasured father-and-son moments. "I used to go fishing with him when he was a kid," Harold recalls. "We had a cabin and a trailer in the country and we used to go in there."

Summer days were spent at nearby Fortune Brook. After they'd bait their hooks and cast their lines into the water, Burch would beg his father to sing him his favourite song, Dick Nolan's Newfoundland classic about a stolen sheep. "And when he'd get up there and get settled down, he'd say 'Dad, sing me "Aunt Martha's Sheep!"' He loved that song. I don't know any more than the man in the moon why, but that's what he'd ask me to do. And I would do it. He was about six or seven years old then."

Around that time, Burch got his first haircut. No one can remember why it didn't happen earlier, but they remember clearly that he wanted long hair. "You look at his [school] picture, you might think he was a girl because he had long hair right down his back," Harold says with a laugh. When his parents finally marched him to the barber shop, Burch was not pleased. "I remember he cried," Harold recalls. "We told him he had to get it cut, but he didn't want to."

Burch went back to letting it grow long after that; he put it in a ponytail, and that's the way it stayed for years. "He was at a softball tournament in Marystown," Glenda reminisces, and laughs, "and a Larry Mullins was on his team and someone said to Larry, 'What, do you have a girl playing on your team?' And he said, 'No, we don't have no girls! That's not a girl, that's Burch!'"

Burch loved any sport: softball, hockey, soccer. Harold says his son excelled at most, which made Burch popular around town. "My God, man, he was liked by everybody. He was well liked, I tell you that. Not because he was my boy. He was a good soccer player and a good hockey player. He was in good shape. He had a lot of medals, a lot of them. For hockey and soccer and baseball. You name it. I don't know where he got the love for sports, but soccer was his favourite."

Marjorie believes that he was good at sports because he spent so much time at it, especially street hockey. There wasn't much else for children to do in a small town, so they'd spend hours in the laneway outside Burch's house. A bunch of them would gather round, string together makeshift nets, and host a neighbourhood tournament.

Burch loved practical jokes. He was often considered the life of the party, entertaining people with stories and his favourite saying: "If you can't convince them, confuse them." He loved music—especially Pink Floyd—and when he was old enough to get his driver's licence, he loved getting behind the steering wheel of any fast machine he could get his hands on.

He longed to have a motorbike, but his mother said she'd worry too much about him getting hurt; out of respect for her, he agreed not to buy one until he could get her blessing. "I'd say 'my darling, I don't want you to have a motorcycle because too many people get killed on them,'" Marjorie explains. "And after a while he said, 'Mom, I really want one,' and I said, 'All right, if you want her, you have her.'" Burch was 43 when he finally earned her approval and got his motorbike.

Burch also loved playing cards. Especially 45s, which is a shortened version of the popular card game 120s. His failed attempts to win were legendary in the family and a running joke: Burch desperately wanted to beat his father at the game but never could.

When Burch was in high school, Glenda started dating the person she'd eventually marry, Claude Rose, who also became friends with her brother. Claude even taught Burch how to drive a standard and later on they went on moose hunting trips together. "I know it was his brother-in-law," Glenda says, "but I just think that he looked up to Claude as a brother."

When he graduated, Burch, like many of his friends, went to work in the local fish plant, loading boats. But he wasn't there long before he decided to go back to school to study accounting. He even tried university.

Around that time, in the mid-1980s, he met Marilyn Walsh, who lived 45 minutes down the road in Marystown. Marilyn was smitten with Burch from the moment she met him. She was out dancing with friends one night and Burch and his buddies happened to be at the same club. "So, we were just standing next to them and then we just started dancing. He was a good dancer and he liked to have a good time," she says. "That's what got me was that even when he didn't know people, he was just as nice to them as what he was to the people that he knew. And that was it, we were with each other from that night on."

Eventually Burch returned to the fishing industry. He took a job at the fish plant in Marystown, a job he secured with the help of Marilyn's father, who was the plant's production manager.

Back home, his mother would make his lunches for the week. She'd cook chicken or a roast or make a dozen hamburgers at one time. She'd then make gravy, put that and the meat in separate Ziploc bags and freeze it all for Burch to take to work each day.

In his day, Harold was one of the top fish cutters at the Gaultois plant. Burch was the same in his job. The company rewarded cutters on the assembly line for reaching a certain quota. Every year, Burch was one who would receive the extra money.

Having a steady paycheque gave Burch and Marilyn a chance to plan their life. They got married, built their own home, and soon had three girls: Alicia, Allison, and Alexandria.

Harold says Burch loved being a father, although he was extremely nervous when Allison was born, because she was so tiny. He refused to leave the hospital while she was still there. "And he wanted me to go out to the chapel in the hospital with him," his father says, "and he wanted me to go out and kneel down and say a prayer for her. She was just a little small baby and it kind of scared him."

Before starting a family, Burch enjoyed fast vehicles and even had his own sports car, a Chevrolet Camaro. He treated the car like it was gold and put it in storage every winter. But when he and Marilyn were expecting their first child, he went to his mother and reluctantly said, "the car has to go."

"Yep, he really changed 180 degrees," Claude says. "I mean, I'll never forget it. Marilyn was pregnant and he knew he had to sell that car; it broke his heart because he knew he now needed something for his family, right?"

So, he traded his beloved Camaro for a family car. He and Marilyn bought their first brand-new vehicle together, a Chevy Corsica. "He grew up," Marilyn laughs. "He was responsible. That's the way he was. He didn't leave us standing for anything. Like, when he'd get paid, it was the family first. There was no such thing as going out and partying and this kind of stuff. He was a homebody … He did go play darts on Sunday nights with his friends and he liked to go out on the Skidoo in the winter and stuff."

Glenda agrees that parenthood changed her brother. "It's funny because, as a young fellow, when he was going to school, out to university and trade school and all that," she says, "every cent he made he spent. That's the way that he was. When he became a father and started working, oh man, you couldn't get five cents out of him! It was like chalk and cheese from when I knew my brother when he was a young lad and working like you would in the summertime with the jobs and that. Oh, he liked to spend his money. But when he became a parent, when he became a dad, that changed totally. It's like he just took on the responsibilities of being a father, making sure that the kids had everything."

Burch loved spending time with his daughters when he wasn't working. After Glenda and Claude married, they moved to Paradise, just outside St. John's. They bought a large sailboat, and on the weekends Burch and his family often travelled to Paradise to go sailing on Conception Bay.

Those visits made for some of their best memories, Glenda says. "He used to come in and we'd put on the music and me and Burch would get out and dance and then we'd get the kids involved and we'd be dancing all around. Burch loved music and he'd always be dancing and that's one thing the girls loved about their dad, you know, he could be cooking and he'd be dancing and singing and he'd want the girls to dance with him."

She remembers that breakfast would always be a blast when he came by on the weekends with Marilyn and the children. The three girls gave him the nickname "The Cool Dad."

Marilyn says it was the same when they were at home in Marystown. Burch would jump around singing his favourite song, "Sweet Caroline," with the children, and they'd all join in when it came time to yell out the chorus line "Bomp, bom bom!"

When they were a little older, the girls would record videos of their father and themselves dancing around the kitchen table belting out the words of the hit song of the day, "You're a Rockstar" by Smash Mouth.

His nickname stuck and even caught on with Alicia's friends when she was a teenager. "All of Alicia's friends called him the cool teen dad," Marilyn recalls. "If she had friends over, it was like he wanted to be their age again. He was there with them and talking with them and swapping stories with them and playing cards. I was the mean mom and he was the cool dad," she jokes.

For about seven consecutive years the two families, along with Burch and Glenda's parents, would pack up their vehicles and spend long weekends in Kilmory Resort in Swift Current, about two hours outside St. John's. They all looked forward to these gatherings. "Every long weekend we got together," says Claude. "We were in three different places, we used to call their mother and father in Fortune and say 'don't forget the lobster.' And then Burchy would load up the van where he lived in Marystown, he'd get everything ready and he'd get the girls and Marilyn and we'd leave here in Paradise and say, 'We're going to meet you in Kilmory!'"

"We'd always book the biggest cabin there," Glenda recalls. "We loved it and the kids loved it."

Then the fishery stumbled and Burch could see that things weren't looking good for a future in that industry. "He was smart enough to see that you ain't going to get rich at a fish plant, cutting fish," Claude says. "I mean, it's good jobs for some people but you're not gonna get rich and as times got tougher with the fishery ... I think he got the message because he was smart."

When the cod fishery eventually collapsed, Burch put down his filleting knife and looked for a new opportunity. He faced the same worrisome choice as many other young Newfoundland men: stay at home and cross his fingers in hopes of getting hired on make-work projects, leave the province to find a paycheque, or take advantage of a federal government program that helped people switch to a new career.

Burch opted for the latter. "I know a lot of people that just waited around for the governments to give them handouts and projects," Claude says. "But he took the initiative and said to the government, 'Okay, you give us a few dollars and I'll go back to school' ... He was ready to move on and he took advantage of that, you know."

Burch talked with one of Marilyn's in-laws who owned a fleet of offshore support vessels and asked what he needed to do to work on the big boats. "So, he gave him a list of stuff and you know he came home with that list and he set it in his mind and he went out to the school and he done every one of those courses that he was told he had to do."

For a while he got work on the factory freezer trawlers run by the big fishing companies. From there he went to work aboard the vessels that provide service to the oil industry and eventually accepted a job with Canship Ugland and Husky Energy working as a deck operator on the SeaRose.

Glenda says the reason he went offshore was simple: to earn money for the benefit of his family: "He was going to do his damnedest to make sure the three kids did well, and for him and Marilyn to have a nice home, vacations, and have some toys. And that's what he was working for."

Because their oldest daughter was getting ready to go to university, Burch and Marilyn sold their home in Marystown and moved to Paradise. Not only were they nearby as she did her studies, but it brought them closer to Glenda and Claude, and Burch didn't have to travel as far to get home when he got off the helicopter.

Marilyn says that Burch would tell people he loved everything about his job except the 90-minute flight to and from the rig. "He absolutely hated flying out there," she says. "He told my mother that ... she would always ask him, 'how's work?' And he'd say, 'I love my job but I hate how I get there.'" But Burch would never ever explain to Marilyn why he disliked the helicopter flight so much.

One night he and other workers were late getting in from the SeaRose for their three-week hitch. When Marilyn picked him up at the heliport, Burch gave a cryptic answer when she asked why they hadn't landed on time. "He said, 'Well, you're some lucky to see me tonight.' And I said, 'Why, were you guys going to be cancelled?' And he said, 'Nope. I thought we were gone tonight.' And that was all; he wouldn't tell me anything else."

And so it was, on the morning of March 12, 2009, Burch Nash, age 44, and working at a job that allowed him to give his family the life he felt they deserved, was back at St. John's airport.

The previous evening he popped over to his sister's for a game of 45s with his father. That night, for the first time ever, the cards were all working in Burch's favour. "I remember he had the five of diamonds and we was having the slammer round," Marjorie recalls. "And he kept his five of diamonds till the last. And he had the slam!" With a big grin on his face, Burch slapped the winning card down on the table. He had finally beaten his father at 45s.

It was early in the evening, about 8:30, and Burch had to get home, but

Harold asked his son to stay a little longer. "You gonna have a little drop of whiskey before you goes?" Burch turned it down, saying he couldn't have any alcohol as he was flying out on the helicopter in the morning and offshore rules forbade workers from drinking the night before a flight.

Before he left, Marjorie slipped a $20 bill into his coat pocket, which she often did over the years so her son would always have a little cash on hand. "When I put it in his pocket, I said, 'You go to Tim Hortons tomorrow morning and get a coffee.'"

Glenda's husband, Claude, arrived home just as Burch was leaving. "You're going again," he said as he walked up to the side door, where Burch stood with his mother's arm wrapped around his waist. "I'll see you the next time."

Burch headed home to Paradise and, a short time later, already missing him, Marjorie telephoned her son to say goodbye again. "I said, 'Mom loves you,'" Marjorie recalls. "And he said, 'Love you too, Mom.' And that was the last words out of his mouth."

The next morning, Marilyn drove Burch to the airport as she always did when he had to return to work. She told him she loved him and wished him a good flight. He smiled and while walking toward the heliport he started calling out and reminding her of things she had to do while he was gone. He kept returning to the truck to tell her one more thing. Finally, Marilyn laughed and said, "Get out of the truck!" She had to return home because their 14- and 15-year-old girls had to get to school. She told him to call her that night.

Burch smiled, waved his hand, and said, "I'll see ya when I see ya," and he turned to walk over to where the helicopter and the others were waiting.

A few hours later, Marilyn was at home alone when her telephone rang.

Kenneth MacRae, 47

Michelle MacRae's memories of growing up aren't totally clear, but she remembers her father with full clarity: "He was fun-loving. He was just a very easy going and fun-loving guy. He was very permissive. He would say, 'Don't make a mess,' but he would never be mad if we did. And we did!"

Ken MacRae was born in Halifax, into a military family of five boys, and spent many of his teenage years in Trenton, Ontario. It wasn't a surprise that he chose that kind of life when he grew up. Through his military career, Ken was posted to various bases around the country: Cold Lake, Greenwood, Edmonton, Trenton. He even did a stint in Italy. Michelle and her family moved around so often while she was growing up that she believes it was inevitable that it rubbed off on her. "I never stay in one place too long," she says. "I moved around a lot as a kid and now even as an adult I go a little stir crazy if I'm in one place longer than a couple of months."

Lee-Ann Brubacher met Ken in Trenton. She says Ken was "that dreamboat guy that girls fawned over." He seemed to have it all: "He was very handsome, beaming smile, perfect teeth, tall, and nice hair. He was a good-looking fellow. I mean, he was genuinely nice and kind. He was well known that way."

Lee-Ann got to know Ken better after she married his brother. "He wasn't a jokester," she explains. "He would talk very seriously but then he would throw in something that was kind of funny to kind of—if it was getting a little tense, it would lighten the mood. I'm thinking of family dynamics when there would be a little bit of tension because of brothers annoying each other. He was that kind of person. He was the peacemaker ... the middle kid ... he was the fourth of five boys, so he was in that middle ground where he would sort of lighten the mood. And then he'd say something for everybody to crack up and then everyone would forget why they were annoyed."

Lee-Ann learned the rules of poker from Ken. He also taught her how to play crib. But sometimes when the husbands and wives got together for a game, they wouldn't get far tallying up their points and moving their pegs along the scoreboard because, right in the middle of a hand, Ken would haul out his collection of cassette tapes and start playing them. "He pulled out this cassette tape and put it in one of those portable recorders," she recalls, "and he played all these old skits from radio times. So, there was Abbott and Costello and George Burns and Gracie Allen and Jack Lemmon and all these skits that they did. And it was all on this tape and I remember us sitting there at a table trying to play cribbage, but we had to stop because we were listening to this old tape and all these old recordings. It was a lot of fun. He would always bring in stuff like that and lighten the mood."

Just as they'd laugh and joke around, Ken and Lee-Ann often got caught up in spirited political debates—with Ken leaning toward the conservative side with his opinions, while Lee-Ann's views were more liberal. "I remember him accusing the *Ottawa Citizen*, which I always thought was very balanced in their reporting, but he thought it so liberal and he just cracked me up. It was too funny."

But they were always on the same side when it came to their love of Canada. "We always found common ground when it came to human rights and dignity and anything to do with protection of our country because I'm patriotic, especially being in the Armed Forces. His father was Navy, my father was Air Force. We had a lot of common ground because of that."

Ken's oldest brother served in many missions with the United Nations, as did Ken. "He was in Italy during Kosovo ... when the former Yugoslavia was being torn apart. The Air Force was based [in Italy], the UN Air Force and he was ground support for the CF-18s."

When Ken's and Lee-Ann's children played together, Ken became one of them. If they were going to get all dirtied up in the mud and rain—as they did one particular time when the children were all under five—then so was he. Lee-Ann says it got out of hand, very fast. "The [kiddie] pool got filled with warm water and rainwater and leaves and all kinds of stuff," she recalls. "It finally stopped raining and the kids went out back to start playing ... and decided that it would be a good idea to drain the little kiddie pool ... it made a lot of muck and there they were sliding in this muck. He thought this was great fun. And I remember just being aghast. It was awful; muck was everywhere, their boots were ruined, the backyard was a disaster, every blade of glass was gone."

"They had a blast I got to tell you and Ken was saying, 'Let kids be kids!'"

There was such a mess that they had to line the children up to clean them. "It was just crazy. We had an assembly line. He would hose them down outside, I would yank off their boots, and then they'd come in and I'd sort of pass them to my husband and then when they'd run upstairs Ken would throw them in the tub."

Lee-Ann bursts into laughter. "They had muck everywhere! I mean, I remember my son went head first into it and there was nothing left of his face, it was just—there was muck everywhere. In his eyelashes, in his ears, up his nose, and he started crying and I was trying to stop laughing."

That was long before Michelle was born, but she remembers her father doing similar crazy, fun things like that with her when he wasn't on the road. "My dad and I were super close. He had a picture of me on his phone and it was me holding a deer skull. And I was this, like, super angsty teenager, I had this really weird-like T-shirt hoodie on and my bangs were over my eyes, and that was his good luck charm for hunting."

Ken loved being in the woods, especially to chase big game. Everyone in the family was exposed to that passion—even the children. A prized animal trophy is mounted in his garage in Auburn, Nova Scotia. "There is still to this day, a 10-point buck in the garage that my sister shot," Michelle says. "It was her first year and it's mounted in the garage … She got it on her own, I mean, she went with our dad but she got it on her own."

They lived in Alberta at the time. Michelle also went hunting with her father, but she refused to kill a deer. She even went out of her way to dissuade him from using his gun. "I would never shoot anything. I remember I would sit in the blind and never let him shoot them."

But Michelle's older sister, Alyssa, saw it differently. She's the one who shot that buck when she was only about 15. "I showed the most interest out of all four children," Alyssa says of hunting. She remembers that particular hunting trip. "I named him Ralph," she says, with a laugh. "Dad said that's why you don't bring girls hunting, because they name it."

Alyssa and Michelle are sisters by way of a blended family. Ken came into Alyssa's life when she was five years old. "I'm not his daughter biologically but in every other way I was. He embraced me, he cared for me. I latched on to him and he held me right back."

Alyssa loved being in the woods with her father so much that she sometimes skipped school to go with him. "You know, at home, not that you're competing for attention," she explains, "but there's chores that have to be done, there's other siblings that need time with Dad, and Mom and the dog, and there's all sorts of stuff going on at home. It was our time to be away from it."

Their outings would always start the same way—at Tim Hortons, with a coffee for him and a hot chocolate and bagel for her. "On some level, that was his Zen. That was his time for him to be outside … and to sit in that glen and it didn't matter if the deer comes along or not, it's about being in the woods and being in nature and celebrating it," she says. "He hated going to shopping malls. The only place he'd ever go shopping [was] Canadian Tire or a hunting and fishing store because there are less people."

Alyssa believes that her father loved hunting for much more than just the stalking of the big animal and the eventual kill. "I believe in respecting animals and that's what he taught me," she says. "It's not for the sport of it, I mean you can enjoy that part of it but you respect the animal. These are the things he taught me … he'd go hunting and sometimes a group of hunters would have one tag … and they would split the meat because that's what it was about. It's about being outside in nature with your friends and providing food for your family."

Unlike many girls her own age, she was interested in hockey and signed up to play. Ken would take her to the practices and games. In one of her favourite photos, Alyssa is wearing a dress and hockey gloves and she's landing a good-natured hockey punch on her father. Her passion for the game continued as she grew older. "He bought me Oilers tickets for my birthday one year, and we drove down to Edmonton and I think we were on a bit of a timeline because we had to drive down, go to the hockey game, sleep a few hours, and then drive back early the next morning and we were both tired and my job was to keep him awake; it was a dangerous drive home!"

Alyssa and Ken enjoyed their father-daughter time. "He was just like, very chill. He was just a very patient, kind, genuine human being. He put other people before himself, a lot of the times. He wanted to encourage us to do our best. He didn't judge what that was or what it wasn't. I don't know, he was just—he was funny, he had the best sense of humour, he was a very relaxed individual, supportive in everything."

Sometimes he supported her without her actually realizing it. For example, she found it hard to lose weight as a child. "I struggled with my weight for a good chunk of my childhood and he never pushed me to be athletic. But he'd involve me in something he was doing so that I would. Or he would say, 'Hey, do you want to play soccer?' He wouldn't shove it down my throat, he'd encourage me the right way to go do something athletic."

After more than two decades in the military, Ken retired and went to work for a private company. But his job still involved considerable travel. He worked as a senior analyst at FGG Inspections, a company based out of Edmonton, and his specialty was electrical inspections involving non-destructive testing (NDT). In layman's terms, Ken tested material such as the tubing used in drilling oil wells offshore to determine the pressure it could withstand. The work was very specialized and FGG's employees were sent all around the world because of their expertise.

Michelle tried to convince her father to leave Alberta and move the family back to Nova Scotia. She used that extensive travel as her argument to convince him to leave western Canada. "He travelled to work all the time anyway with his company, whether it was Holland or Texas or LA or anywhere, so I said, 'If you really need to go to the office, you can just fly there. It's not a big deal. Let's just move back to Nova Scotia.'"

From there he continued to go on various work assignments—to other countries or out west again, where he'd fit in another hunting trip with his old mates, including Jason Gulliver.

Ken and Jason had met in the mid-to-late 1990s in northern Alberta. Ken was still in the military and Jason an employee at FGG, which his brother owned. From the moment they met, Jason knew that he and Ken were kindred spirits.

Jason had moved to Alberta from his hometown of St. John's, and he realized that the pair shared a love of the outdoors and an even greater love of hunting. "I don't think there was anything to dislike about Ken," he says. "He was so easy to talk to. I don't think that man got upset at anything. He was so laid back. We were both avid outdoors people."

They'd often go ice fishing in Cold Lake. Then they got into deer hunting, and Jason recalls how Ken could tolerate even the coldest days. "Ken liked to be in the bush fairly early, before first light," he says. "This one morning I dropped him off and it was -30. And so I go and get my spot I'd sit in for a couple of hours. And I'd come out and I'm literally freezing cold. I go pick up Kenny … and of course I see him trotting across the field and at that time he had a beard and he had more frost on his face than anything. You know what I mean? And he gets in and I said, 'You cold?' And he said, 'Nah, it's a little balmy!' … Like it didn't faze him at all. And we all got a good crack out of that because we were all freezing and I don't think he was even cold, to be honest."

Shortly after Jason met Ken, Ken started talking about leaving the military, saying that he was thinking about taking a job in the private sector, part-time, at FGG. "I was one of the key people he talked to, to see what it would be like and how everything was. I couldn't recommend a better place to be at the time. That kind of made his decision when he was leaving the military and where to go and what to do."

FGG's services were in demand, and Jason says that led to them being a tight-knit group. "When we were all there at that time when Kenny was with the company," he says, "I bet we spent more time as a group than we did with our own families. We worked together. We partied together. We hunted together. It was a pretty tight group. … Most of the guys that worked for the company all lived in the same area outside of Edmonton in the Fort Saskatchewan area and we all had the same or similar interests between work and hunting and fishing and all that kind of stuff. So, the group just kind of clicked."

The family eventually moved back to Nova Scotia, but Ken remained working at FGG despite moving thousands of kilometres across the country. And he also didn't give up his hunting time with his friends in Alberta. "He would come out here for hunting season," Jason says. "He'd come out and stay with me or he'd stay with my brother. So, most of the work we'd just fly him out and he'd come out here and stay a few days on either end. He was pretty much like a brother. You always had a spot for Kenny to stay if he came out this way, right? So, that's kind of the way it was for everybody."

Their favourite hunting spot was in Smoky Lake County, Alberta, in a tiny village called Waskatenau, a 45-minute drive north of Fort Saskatchewan. "We'd leave here in the mornings, you know, like 5:30. And we'd drive out there and we'd hunt all day and we'd drive home at the end of the day. We'd go back to probably my brother's shop and hang out there and have a couple of ryes and talk about the day and make out the game plan for the next day and do it all again. And we'd do that for all of the month of November."

One of the jobs the company managed to snag involved the testing of tubing on the SeaRose FPSO. Jason made the trip to the rig twice but quickly realized it wasn't his thing. "After my second one, I pretty much told them I didn't enjoy it. I don't like it. I don't like being offshore. I don't like anything about it."

When an assignment came up in the spring of 2009 to work offshore Newfoundland, Ken wanted to go. "Because Kenny was ex-military and he worked on these helicopters all the time, his comfort level was 10-fold what my comfort level was," Jason says. "So then the next job came up and Kenny was pretty much the first one to volunteer himself to go."

The flight was leaving on the morning of March 12. To be there on time, Ken left his home in Nova Scotia on March 11 and flew to St. John's. Alyssa was away at university, working on a degree in Human Resources. Michelle still lived at home. "I remember hugging him in the driveway," she says. "And he left and drove to the airport." The next morning she was in a hurry to get to school, so she didn't have time to talk for long when he called to check in a few hours before takeoff.

And so it was, on the morning of March 12, 2009, Ken MacRae, age 47, and once again working away from home, was at St. John's airport and preparing to take Cougar Flight 491 to an offshore platform.

Later that day, Michelle, 14 years old and in Grade 9, was at school, out of breath from dancing her heart out during a rehearsal of West Kings High School's production of *Footloose*. She had a small role as a chorus dancer in the theatre production but secretly wished she had lines to deliver. Her teacher suddenly asked to speak with her privately, outside the classroom in the hallway. Michelle's heart skipped a beat. She was certain he was about to reward her efforts with that longed-for speaking part.

The Crash

"Gander Centre, Cougar 91 Mayday."

Captain Matt Davis calmly alerted the air traffic control centre in Gander at 9:45 a.m. to a problem with Flight 491. The helicopter had been in the air for about 30 minutes and, until that transmission, First Officer Tim Lanouette had been handling the communications.

The helicopter was cruising at an altitude of 9,000 feet, 54 nautical miles off St. John's when that first sign of trouble came. "We have main gearbox oil pressure problems, request immediate, ah, clearance back to St. John's," Matt stated. He was reacting to the illumination of an amber caution light, which had quickly switched to a red warning light in the cockpit that indicated the oil pressure in the main gearbox was dangerously low. The light was accompanied by a verbal message: "GEARBOX PRESSURE."

Gander granted the request to return to St. John's and advised the pilot to make a right turn and head back to the airport. The controller then asked which runway Matt would prefer to land on. "Ah, I'm going to be going for the nearest piece of terra, terra firma I can get to," Matt replied. He explained that he had the helicopter in a descent, headed toward the surface of the ocean. Matt was advised that if he could see the shoreline then he could start toward the nearest piece of land. He agreed and reiterated the seriousness of the problem: "Whatever I see first, I say. If it's Cape Spear or a parking lot, we've lost all main gearbox oil pressure at this time."

The air traffic controller calculated the distance from the flight's location over the ocean to Cape Spear and informed Matt that the distance was 42 miles. "You're unable to maintain altitude, is that correct?," the controller then asked. "In this condition, we have to be down as close to the surface as possible in case we have a catastrophic failure," Matt replied, explaining why he was in a descent.

The controller said that he understood and let him know that the Joint Rescue Coordination Centre in Halifax, which is responsible for search and rescue in the region, had been notified. Likewise, Matt said he had also brought Cougar Helicopters in the loop. "They're getting another aircraft ready, for ah, just in case ..." The air traffic controller again replied, "Understood."

Normally, three CH-149 Cormorant helicopters, the Canadian Forces' Search and Rescue aircraft in Newfoundland and Labrador, are stationed in Gander, a three-and-a-half-hour drive from St. John's. But that day they were all in Nova Scotia, along with multiple Search and Rescue units from across Canada taking part in a joint rescue training exercise off Cape Breton. Cougar Helicopters was the backup when Search and Rescue couldn't respond.

As Flight 491 continued to descend, Matt and Tim were troubleshooting. They ran through the emergency procedures and checklist to determine if they could narrow down what had gone wrong: a faulty sensor, a failed oil pump, or an actual massive oil leak?

The two talked about getting their immersion suits ready and whether the landing gear should be extended. They also talked about the possibility of unusual smells or vibrations, which their training had taught them was another indication that the main gearbox was failing. There was neither, and no abnormal sounds were coming from the back of the helicopter.

Shortly after letting the crew know that Search and Rescue was aware of the developing situation, the air traffic controller in Gander asked how much fuel and the number of people the helicopter had on board. "We have about three hours fuel on board and it's, ah, 18 persons on board," Matt says. The controller acknowledged, "18 souls on board."

The Cougar dispatcher informed Matt that the rescue centre in Halifax was asking if ditching was imminent, probable, or possible. Both Matt and Tim agreed that ditching had become a possibility. Matt also told the company dispatcher that they suspected that the helicopter was experiencing an oil pump or an oil pressure sensor problem, since the oil temperature gauge remained in the normal range.

Pilots watch that gauge closely for guidance as to whether a problem with the oil pressure is more serious than a faulty sensor. The expectation is that the temperature would rise if there is an actual loss of oil. With the temperature still indicating that it was in the normal range, Matt told Cougar that he didn't believe they had lost all of the oil from the main gearbox.

Many of the 16 passengers were sleeping until Matt announced over the PA system that there was a major problem and that they were heading to the closest piece of land. The passengers were asked to zip up their survival suits.

A short time later, they were advised that the aircraft would be ditching in the ocean. The pilots' voices came over the PA: "Brace. Brace. Brace."

Passengers know the safety command from their training. It alerts everyone to prepare for an emergency landing by putting their feet flat on the floor and leaning forward and downward as far as possible, with their heads close to their knees and their hands on their head.

Shortly after the brace call, the helicopter started moving erratically from left to right. A high-pitched squeal was emitted, stopping for a short period when the helicopter started to lift again and resuming when it went back into a descent.

Matt radioed St. John's: "Ah, we are getting prepared to ditch, please dispatch …" The controller replied that he had marked their position.

The pilots then announced over the loudspeaker: "Ditching. Ditching. Ditching."

A few seconds later, Tim inadvertently turned on a microphone switch—likely while helping Matt with the controls—that allowed air traffic control in Gander to briefly hear the conversation in the cockpit. Tim could be heard offering encouragement as Matt tried to gain some control over the big machine during the high-speed descent. "There you go, you got it, you got it, you got it," Tim said repeatedly. "Okay, it's, it's all right, you're doing good, you're …"

His transmission suddenly cut off. At that exact moment, the flight data recorder lost power and stopped recording. The crew said nothing prior to losing power that would indicate why they were suddenly ditching.

At 9:56 a.m., less than one minute after Matt had advised officials on land that the helicopter was going into the water, 11 minutes after that initial yellow light of caution flashed on, and not yet 40 minutes since the helicopter's wheels had lifted off the ground at St. John's airport, Flight 491 struck the water 35 nautical miles out to sea.

Its large fuselage, tilted right, nose slightly up in the air, struck hard. The force was so great that the entire airframe was severely damaged and the emergency flotation system, which would have allowed the chopper to float long enough for people to possibly escape from the aircraft, didn't deploy. The helicopter sank fast.

In Gander, the air traffic controller was trying to find an aircraft close to latitude-longitude 47°26'03"N, 51°56'35"W, the last reported geographical location of Flight 491.

The communication between the controller and the crew of other aircraft that were either flying through the province's airspace or in the vicinity of the crash location was a series of questions and answers between the controller and other pilots to determine which aircraft could get to the area as fast as possible.

In the moments after Flight 491 stopped communicating, the air traffic controller appeared to be already thinking about the complication involving the Cormorant Search and Rescue helicopters. "All the rescue helicopters are over in Sydney somewhere and they're all dispatched, but they're a ways away now," he reported to the tower controller in St. John's, who requested an update after hearing of trouble with the flight.

One of the planes in the vicinity was a Provincial Airlines patrol aircraft. The small fixed-wing plane had just taken off and was on its way to carry out ice surveillance off the east coast. The crew reported to Gander that it had been following the situation and could be over the site within nine minutes.

When radar showed that the fixed-wing was getting close, the controller asked if they were picking up a distress signal from the helicopter's emergency locator transmitter. The pilot replied that they were not. Seconds later— approximately 17 minutes after Flight 491 reported that it was ditching— Gander informed the pilot that the plane should be right over the location and asked if the crew had any luck spotting anything.

The reply was immediate. "Okay, we got one raft, people in the water," the pilot said. "We got people in the water, sir, and debris." The controller reaffirmed their position and the pilot reiterated what they were seeing less than 800 feet below. "Looks like she went down there, we got debris all over the place."

About 40 seconds after reporting seeing debris, the pilot asked the controller how many people were on board Cougar 491: "18 souls on board" was the reply.

Another 45 seconds passed and then the pilot stated, "Time is of the essence." He was asked to repeat his last message, and said, "Time is critical."

The air traffic controller immediately advised another aircraft heading to the scene that the first plane on-site was reporting "time is of the essence." That pilot responded that the aircraft was travelling at maximum speed toward the location.

The pilot of the Provincial Airlines plane reported again that a raft could be seen in the water near the crash site and that there were people in the water waving.

The controller continued speaking with the crew of other aircraft to confirm their altitude and distance from the site, and he then asked the patrol aircraft on-site again for a head count of the people in the water. The pilot replied, "As of right now, sir, we've only got two. There's supposed to be two life rafts and we've only got one found."

The pilot offered to fly over a wider area to see if there was another life raft floating farther away. The controller was asked again when the rescue aircraft would arrive. The answer: "Eight minutes to nine minutes."

At 10:37 a.m., more than 40 minutes after Flight 491 struck water, a Cougar rescue helicopter left St. John's airport. It took 18 minutes for it to reach the crash site, where the crew spotted two people in the water. A man was waving, while the other person appeared to be face down in the water. The man waving was Robert Decker, a 27-year-old offshore ice and weather specialist. The downdraft of the helicopter's rotor blades just metres above him churned the ocean water, tossing him up and down with the waves.

A rescue basket was lowered to the surface but Robert didn't have the strength to haul himself up over the edge of the wire cage to climb in, despite trying repeatedly. Cougar rescue specialist Ian Wheeler was lowered down on a hoist. After Ian reached Robert and was in the water beside him, Robert—who by then could barely see—thought that he heard Ian say he was going back up to the chopper to get another piece of equipment. That's when Robert mustered up what little strength he had and grabbed at Ian's shoulder. He barely got his words out. "Please don't leave me here," Robert pleaded, before passing out.

Ian stayed with him in the water. With the 2.5-metre waves crashing all around him, he hooked a cable onto Robert and had the crew above slowly reel the cable in, hoisting him out of the water. Ian remained in the water until the hoist was lowered again to lift him back into the helicopter.

It took 20 minutes to complete, but Robert was finally out of the water, nearly one hour and 20 minutes after the crash. By then, he was in a hypothermic state and could not see. The cold water had numbed his hands and legs to the point that he couldn't feel them. His injuries were severe: a ruptured vertebra in his back, a broken sternum, a broken ankle, and a dislocated ankle. Robert was flown to the Health Sciences Centre in St. John's and rushed to the intensive care unit.

Another 25 minutes passed before a second Cougar rescue helicopter arrived, at 11:40 a.m., at the same spot and hoisted the second person from the water. This time, there were no vital signs.

Twenty-six-year-old Allison Maher had not survived.

As rescue specialists and other crewmembers of the planes and helicopters that were arriving scanned the ocean below them, they saw no sign of the other 16 who were aboard the flight, and no sign of the helicopter itself. No distress signals were detected from the chopper's emergency locator transmitter or from the personal locator beacons worn by the passengers and crew.

On land, telephone calls started going out to mothers and fathers, sisters, brothers, and wives to tell them of the major emergency involving their loved ones unfolding 35 miles out to sea. A conference room at the Comfort Inn, a hotel next door to Cougar's offices, also known as the Airport Inn, was booked so that family members could head there to meet with company officials and investigators who hoped to provide up-to-date information.

As so it was on March 12, 2009, in a province known for its unique time zone, time was about to stand still. Again. Still wounded by the heartbreak of a previous mass offshore tragedy, the sinking of the Ocean Ranger and the loss of 84 lives nearly three decades earlier, the people of Newfoundland and Labrador would soon be shaking their heads and holding their collective breath, not believing that it was possible that another offshore nightmare could revisit and re-haunt the population of half a million.

The Loss

John Pelley

It was lunchtime at Elwood Regional High School in Deer Lake and guidance counsellor Lori Chynn, like many of the students, was heading down the hall to get some food. As she entered the staff office, one of the teachers told her that she was wanted on the telephone. Lori took the call, but with so many children in the area she couldn't hear clearly what the person on the other end of the line was saying. She put the caller on hold while she went to her own office, where she could close the door.

As she walked down the corridor, Lori realized that the woman on the telephone had said something about calling from Atlantic Offshore Medical Services (AOMS). That was her husband, John Pelley's, employer. AOMS provides medical services and staff, including nurses such as John, to companies operating in remote environments.

Lori entered her office and picked up the telephone, thinking that she was going to hear that John had possibly reinjured the shoulder he had earlier dislocated while playing softball. Or worse still, she thought perhaps he was in a car accident on the way to the airport that morning for the flight back to the offshore.

The possibility of his being in a highway crash was always on Lori's mind because he spent so many hours driving to and from St. John's to catch the flight to the SeaRose. The idea of something going wrong during the helicopter flight never entered her mind. "When you live on the west coast of the island," she says, "you don't really understand the offshore. My biggest concern, my fear was the highways. I didn't see these choppers. I didn't see people getting on these choppers. I knew he had to go for survival training and all that but I had no visual of what this looked like. It was the highway that was the worry."

When the woman from AOMS explained why she was calling, Lori struggled to grasp what she was being told. "She said that the chopper had gone down. And I said, 'Is everybody all right?' And she kind of avoided the question."

Lori remembers the woman saying something about her flying to St. John's. But not fully understanding, Lori said she would instead head to her parents' house next door to the school. "I went into my vice-principal's office and he looked at me, and again I didn't clue in and I said, 'John's chopper went down.' And he said, 'Yeah, I know. I just had a call that it's on the news.' And I said, 'I probably shouldn't drive. Can you bring me to my mom's?' So, we got over to my mom and dad's and they had the news on."

Lori called the company spokesperson back, who again suggested that she fly to St. John's. This time, Lori agreed, and the woman told her that they'd arrange for her to get on the next plane. Before leaving her parent's house she noticed that the TV news special was showing a shot of an ambulance parked near a helicopter. The chopper was on a landing pad located in the parking lot of the Health Sciences Centre in St. John's.

The news footage showed someone being taken out of the helicopter, placed on a stretcher, and eased into an ambulance. Catching that one brief scene assured Lori that everyone must be okay and were being taken to the hospital to be treated. She still didn't realize the seriousness of the situation, even after the company official asked if anyone was travelling with her on the plane for support. Instead, Lori was thinking that she'd arrive in St. John's to face a frustrated John, who would not be happy with all the attention he was getting. "I thought, 'Okay, I'm going in there and he's going to be at the Health Sciences. He's going to be pissed off that all this is happening.' Because I'm not seeing the enormity of this, you know, I'm saying 'Okay, he's going to be thinking, Oh my, now I gotta get checked out and stuff.'"

Lori's father travelled with her to St. John's. They were greeted at the airport by several people, including one who held up a piece of paper with Lori's name on it. They identified themselves, and Lori was again confused. "So we get there and we are met by some people who say they are with AOMS and a psychologist and I still didn't clue in, I'm thinking 'What's she doing here?'"

Onboard the SeaRose, Mark Frost was preparing for bed. Mark worked in the maintenance department, and his routine after working all night was to go to the music room for a few hours by himself to unwind by singing and playing guitar instead of heading straight to bed.

Mid-morning he headed to his room and was getting ready to go to sleep when he heard someone announce over the vessel's loudspeaker that Cougar Flight 491 was en route. That meant his friend John was on the way and would be there in about an hour and a half.

Mark didn't wake until just before supper. After showering and getting dressed, he headed downstairs to the food area. That's when he noticed that something was amiss. "When I got down to the stairs to go into the galley," he says, "I noticed there was a whole bunch of flight suits all over the hall and all laid out, and there were some people going around that were supposed to go in on the flight that day and I thought that was strange, because I looked outside and it was a beautiful day, and it was a beautiful day when I went to bed as well. Like, clear, which usually means no problem. Usually if it's foggy that's when you have issues with flights and stuff."

Mark asked a woman walking toward him if there was a problem. "Flights didn't get in today?" he asked. "And she gave me this funny look. She was just looking at me like she just didn't know what to say. And, actually, she never did say anything. I asked as I was walking by and I kept walking, and she never did respond."

Mark thought that her reaction was strange, but he shrugged it off and kept walking toward the kitchen. "I walked a little farther and I ran into another girl from the galley who was supposed to leave that day too, and she must've overheard me because she said, 'You didn't hear what happened?'" Mark said he didn't, and that's when she told him. "She said, 'Well, the helicopter crashed and they don't know where everyone is, and there's one guy—one survivor and the other guys are missing.'" She blurted it out. Mark was momentarily shocked, grasping to digest what he had just heard: "It was a lot for me to take in. I don't know if I heard it all or stopped listening. And then as I kept walking, I didn't know whether to believe it or not."

Mark went to the food line and filled up the plate on his tray. At that time of day there are few people in the galley because it's before all the day-shift people get off work and the people who are there are preparing for the night shift. "So, I went over to this one table with a bunch of people and sat down and everyone was really quiet. Usually people are joking around and talking and stuff. And I sat down and the OIM, who is the offshore installation manager, was sat right across from me and he just said something like 'In times like these, you need to be strong.' And that's when it hit me that this is real, they're not joking. Something happened."

Someone switched on the television in the galley and there, staring Mark in the face, was confirmation that the chopper carrying his good friend had indeed crashed into the ocean. There was still no word if any of the missing passengers and crew had made it safely into a lifeboat.

On the SeaRose, just about everything except for critical work had come to a halt. Managers, recognizing that employees likely couldn't concentrate on their jobs, told everyone that if they didn't want to work—if they felt that their mind wasn't on what they were supposed to be doing and felt they couldn't do it safely—then they didn't have to.

Everyone had the same question. "I mean, it didn't make sense," says Mark. "Like, how could a whole helicopter go missing on a nice day? And all those brightly coloured suits and stuff, like, you know, the number of planes and helicopters looking for the chopper. There's no way that it could blow or drift far enough away that you wouldn't find it … so, we kinda knew that it must be under the water."

Not knowing what was going on and whether his friend was alive sent Mark into a tailspin. He spent that first night searching his computer's hard drive, digging out pictures of him and the others from when they were going through training, and pictures they had taken during Christmas parties on board the vessel. Pictures of his workmates sitting around laughing and enjoying each other's company.

The next day everyone on board the rig was close to accepting that the helicopter was underwater and there probably wouldn't be any survivors. Mark slipped deeper and deeper into overwhelming sadness.

That night, instead of reporting for work, he headed to the music room. Within minutes of picking up his guitar, he started writing and recording a song about John. "I just wrote the song as quick as that," he recalls. "It probably only took, I don't know, an hour maybe, just playing chords and writing down lyrics. And then I recorded it myself, playing and singing. I had my own laptop out there at the time. I used to bring it out because I had some recording software and I had recorded some other things in my spare time. Anyway, I just recorded the song that night."

As I look back on the things I felt that day,
I went to bed knowing you were on your way,
I had no way of knowing what had happened to you,
And when I awoke, I could not believe it was true.

That you could fall into the ocean,
That you could fall into the sea,
That you could fall into the ocean,
That you'd be taken away from me.

As I look back on all the good times spent together,
I knew we had a friendship to last forever,
We would sing and play and laugh our cares away,
And never a thought of what could happen any day.

And now that you're gone, this place just seems so bare,
And that it's happened to you, my friend, just doesn't seem fair,
But you've touched my life and everyone's you've known,
And you'll never be forgotten, but now I sing alone.

That you could fall into the ocean,
That you could fall into the sea,
That you could fall into the ocean,
That you'd be taken away from me.

Mark couldn't hold back his tears. "As much hurt as I was feeling, when I was putting my emotions to work I didn't think about anything else only getting that done, getting it written, getting it recorded, and it just seemed really important to me that 'I gotta do this, I gotta do this tonight,' and there was times I had to stop and cry."

Lori was accompanied to the Comfort Inn Airport, where a command headquarters had been set up to brief the families and the media. But suddenly everyone was redirected to another location, the Capital Hotel, about 15 minutes away.

There were questions from people who were as confused as Lori and few answers, only a long, frustrating wait. "I didn't know any of these families," she says, "so I wasn't talking to them. I was two days thinking, 'He's coming home.' I guess my brain was doing what it had to do to not lose my mind at the time. And knowing the person John was, he would come home from hunting and fishing with stories and I'm like, 'Oh my God, you did what? And what happened? And how are you still alive?' So all I was thinking was, 'This is going to be some story when we are out on a Saturday night with our friends.'"

Lori was startled by the questions some family members were firing at Cougar and TSB officials. "I remember being in the briefing thinking, 'My God, these people are asking questions, how do they get the courage—how do they know what to ask?' Like I felt—I just didn't know what to ask. Didn't know what to say. Didn't know what to think. I don't know if I was naive. I would hear stories after about how he would tell people how he hated to fly or stuff that went on with the chopper. I didn't know any of this, probably because he didn't want to frighten the life out of me. He didn't want to worry me. I knew his dread of flying was not just helicopters, it was planes. And even when he had to go on the boat, he didn't mind it. He'd rather 18 hours on the boat than two hours on the chopper. So I heard all these stories after that he would tell his uncles and people like that. But my mind did not go there. My mind didn't even go to that he was still under the water until somebody said, 'It's now a recovery and not a rescue.'"

Those eight words catapulted Lori into reality. She was familiar with the phrase because of a recent experience at her school. "A year before we had lost a former student in a drowning and he was missing for 70-something days and it was on the news. And I could remember those words being used. 'It's now a recovery and not a rescue.' And that's when I knew John wasn't coming home. When I heard that ..."

Lori's voice trails off as she remembers another horrible moment in the meeting room with other wives and family members as officials explained the fate of John and the 15 others who were missing. It was certain they were inside the helicopter, which was nearly 200 metres underwater. "One of the wives said, 'Are you going to go down and get them?' And I'm like, 'Go down and get them?' And then it hit me where he was."

All the confusion and shock that had strained Lori's mind suddenly evaporated. So did the denial that had crept into her head and stayed there hour after hour, filling her with the hope that John was strong enough to get out of the sinking helicopter and climb into a lifeboat. She finally knew this was much more than John re-injuring his shoulder or being banged up in a car accident. His greatest fear had come true.

Allison Maher

Richard Maher was delivering mail in the east end of St. John's near the airport on the morning of March 12, 2009, when he heard a helicopter overhead. He looked up because he knew that his daughter, Allison, was leaving on Cougar Flight 491 that morning. "And the helicopter flew over my head, and I said to myself, 'There she goes …'"

At their home in Aquaforte, his wife, Marjorie, spent much of the morning in her kitchen studying for an exam that was part of her job at a local ambulance service. A radio was on in the living room. She thought that she heard something about a small plane crashing offshore. "But I was so involved in the studying," she says, "that I was really only half listening."

A short time later the telephone rang. She turned her attention from the books to pick up the receiver. A man identified himself and said something about a problem offshore and that the helicopter was in the water. Marjorie remembers only one other detail about the call. "They just said, 'Don't be worried now; it was a controlled landing.' And I think I just went blank because I didn't know what I said to him. Nothing registered with me. And the next thing, I turned on the TV with the 12 o'clock news and they showed Robert Decker being took off the stretcher and took away in the ambulance."

Richard continued on his mail delivery route. A little while later, his cellphone rang. It was his brother-in-law with news that the helicopter had crashed. A frantic Richard made some telephone calls, trying to get more information, but had a tough time finding out anything specific. "First, they told me it was a controlled landing," he says—the same words used by the person who had called Marjorie. "So it didn't really bother me. It did bother me," he corrects, "but I got myself back together and went on. I said I'd give it to her and finish my route and that's what I did. And I went back out and waited for the call to come that she'd be in, because it was a controlled landing. And time went on and went on, and I thought, 'That's not a controlled landing. That's a fucking crash!'"

Richard knew that something very serious had happened offshore, as the company was now asking families to gather at a nearby hotel. "So, I called Marjorie and said, 'Get someone to bring you toward St. John's, I'm coming to get you, and make sure you get Brian,'" he says, referring to their son. "And by that time we knew then—well, we didn't know—but I knew. And we were all meeting at the Airport Inn and I even got lost going to the Airport Inn because I was so screwed up—and I used to deliver mail down around there."

Brian was at college preparing to write an exam. That's where Marjorie reached him. Marjorie knew that Allison's boyfriend had dropped her off at the airport and was planning to head out over the highway. "I knew he was going away from St. John's and I had to stop him. And I had to get him to come back. And I called him and I said, 'Where are you to now?' And he must've been between communities because he said, 'I'm not quite sure …' Well, I said, 'You have to turn around and come back. There's something wrong. I got a call that Allison's helicopter is down in the ocean but they says everything is all right.'"

Their arrival at the hotel started the long painful wait for information. People had questions. But there were few answers. Allison's boyfriend was a mess. "Brian said when he showed up at the hotel, he was sitting on the floor and crying his heart out. Brian said he didn't know what to say to him, or what to do for him. All he could do was cry, cry, cry."

Allison's friend and cousin Valerie Maher called her mother as she was going to work. When her mother asked if Allison had flown out that day, Valerie said yes, and her mother then told her the news about the crash. "And I'm like, what?," Valerie recalls. At first she assumed they'd all be rescued. "People were saying everyone was saved, then people were saying they couldn't find them. I didn't know what to expect. I drove back to my house and I was waiting and waiting for a call ... I was an emotional wreck."

Then Valerie's aunt called with confirmation that Allison didn't make it. "It was just total disbelief because, you know, I mean how could someone innocently as she was ..." Valerie can't finish the sentence.

Just the night before, she and Allison had been planning their next birthday party, in about six weeks' time. Valerie was older, but their birthdays were just a day apart—Allison was born on April 16; Valerie, April 17—and that year, Allison wouldn't be offshore on her birthday. They were planning to spend an evening at Yuk Yuk's comedy club and do more of what they always did when they were together. "Laughing and carrying on," Valerie says.

Hours later, with still no news, Richard was looking at the same television footage Marjorie had seen earlier of Robert Decker being lifted off a helicopter on a stretcher and being placed in an ambulance. Seeing that confirmed what he had been thinking since morning. "He had his head up and he was looking around. He thought all the people were still with him. And I said, 'My dear, Allison is gone.'"

The longer they waited that day the more their frustration grew. Robert Decker had been rescued and a search was continuing for the others, but that was all anyone was saying. Richard was becoming fed up with the lack of information from anyone in an official capacity. "They were jerking us around all day," he recalls. "Finally, it came to five o'clock and they knew they had Allison down in the morgue then but they weren't telling us. And they said, 'We're going to put you up in a hotel for tonight,' and I said, 'You're not putting me up in a hotel because I'm going to my home.' And then someone stopped me as I was going out the door and said they had Allison's body down in the morgue."

To this day, Richard believes that his family should have been told earlier in the day that Allison's body had been recovered that morning just after the crash. "They didn't want to tell us that they had bodies, because of everybody else," he says. "And there's only one girl on it, so they knew it was our daughter. And they could've taken us aside and told us." Marjorie thinks the crash was such a shock to officials that no one knew what to say to the people gathered at the hotel. "They didn't know how to tell us, I don't think."

While the confirmation of Allison's death was the worst possible news, Richard says he was relieved to hear that her body had been retrieved from the water. He talks about that moment slowly, drawing in a heavy sigh as tears fill his eyes. It's as if he is reliving that time. He pauses for a long time before saying quietly, "At least we got Allison home."

Gregory Morris

When Heather Warren picked up the telephone in the Cardiac Intensive Care Unit of the Health Sciences Centre mid-morning on March 12, she was immediately confused.

A woman from the offices of Cougar Helicopters on the other end was saying something about a helicopter crash. "Why are they calling me and telling me that a helicopter went down," Heather thought. "I didn't know what was going on because this person had called me and she said that there was trouble and the helicopter went down and that was basically that."

It took a few minutes for the news to sink in. Heather then headed to the lounge area of the unit. There was a television there, and she could see if there was anything on the news about a helicopter crash offshore. "We were watching the news and they said that there were 16 people or however many people found in a raft, so, that was wrong!" she exclaims.

As Heather stayed near the television screen, the hospital shifted into emergency mode, preparing for possible survivors. The gut-wrenching moments ticked by without any solid information. "Between emergency and my work, they were trying to figure out if Greg was one of them that came in," she says. "And every time a helicopter flew over, it was like, 'Who's that now? Who's coming in?' Because on the news they said 16 people were in a raft. And then knowing that Robert Decker was coming in, that there was someone coming in, but he wasn't mine. That was hard. That was hard."

Cougar Helicopters began to prepare for the unanswerable questions that were already coming from the media and family members. Shortly after receiving the call at work, Heather headed to the Capital Hotel, where families were gathering.

Only a few hours earlier, Wayne Morris had dropped Greg off at the airport. The father and son had a touching routine whenever Greg was heading back to the SeaRose. "I drove him to the airport and for a while he used to give me a kiss on the cheek," he says. "Now, his buddies were all out having a smoke that morning, so he said, 'Dad, we'll shake hands.' So, I shook hands with him. And I said what I always said to him, 'Now, give us a call tonight when you get a chance.'" And with that, Greg jumped out of the car and was gone to catch his flight.

Wayne headed home to wait for Marie, who had taken Ian, their grandson, to a preschool gym. After the toddler's class was over, she and Ian headed to Greg's house. As soon she reached the driveway, she sensed that something was wrong. Instead of being at their home, Wayne was in Greg's driveway. "I pulled up into the driveway at Greg's house around 11 o'clock and Wayne was parked in the car. And I thought to myself, 'What is wrong with him? Look at the face on him. I must've done something wrong,'" she says.

Wayne had been sitting in the car by himself for about half an hour. He was in such a daze over the news he had just received that he doesn't remember Marie opening the car door and speaking to him. "I was sitting home when Marie's brother called me," he remembers. "It was around 10:30

a.m. and he said, 'Do you have the news on?' And I said, 'No.' And he said, 'A chopper is gone down.' And I said, 'Jesus, Greg is on that.'"

That's why Wayne was sitting in his car in Greg's driveway—he had rushed down the road to his son's house to find his wife. Marie remembers vividly the look on his face. "He looked angry, but it wasn't anger. He was frightened," she recalls. "And when I got out of the car, he said the helicopter had gone down and I knew it must've been Greg because he was just gone out."

In Toronto, Greg's only sibling, Rick, was heading out to lunch. He was meeting up with some former work friends. Rick laid his cellphone on his desk at the office of the insurance company where he worked and for some reason didn't take it as he went through the door. An hour or so later he returned to work and was shocked when he picked up his cellphone. "There was like, I don't know, 20 missed calls and five or six different messages," Rick recalls, "and my wife was saying to give her a call at home. I thought something had happened with the kids that I had missed. And when I got a hold of her, she said something had happened to Greg's helicopter on the trip to the rig and they were trying to figure it out."

Rick rushed to his computer and started checking news sites to find out anything more than what his wife had told him. "So, I went to the *Telegram* website and the *CBC* website and at that point it was just that a chopper had gone down and they were searching for it. And there was a lot of stuff on the news that the thing was equipped with flotation and if it was a controlled landing they should be out there."

Rick left work a short time later and took the train home. He spent the entire commute searching news sites for any more information, and making arrangements to fly home. "It was just a really weird train ride," he recalls. "I called my boss and my arrangement at the time was that my boss was based in Quebec and I was the only guy based in Ontario and I told him what happened and said, 'Something happened with my brother's helicopter and

I'm going to head to Newfoundland tonight and to be honest I don't know when I am going to be back.' And he said, 'Do what you got to do, just keep us posted and take care.'"

Rick was thankful for the support he received from his company, but he arrived in Newfoundland in a fog of confusion. No one knew the location of the passengers and crew or whether they were even alive. "I can remember it just being a lot of uncertainty. One minute you think the situation was one way and an hour later you find out it's something different."

Like most of the others, Rick spent hours waiting at the hotel briefing room, hoping for good news. "My parents were in various stages of upset. So, a lot of it for me was about doing as much as I can for them. Making arrangements, getting things organized for them as much as I could. I mean, it was just a big blur."

Then came news that the helicopter had been found. "I think initially they thought they only counted eight or 10 people inside. And then we thought, like everybody else, 'Okay well, is he one of the eight or 10 who is strapped inside or is he one of the seven or eight that isn't?'"

The whirlwind of emotions was draining. "But the biggest thing for me was if he was gone, I get it—we just need to find him and bring him home and we need to say a proper goodbye. At some point you just think, 'Okay, I just want to get him, I just want to give him a proper burial and we'll put all this stuff behind us.'"

Greg's friend and workmate Sheldon Langdon was at home studying for his journeyman cook exam that morning when he received a call. It was from his brother, who also worked offshore. His sentences were short and his words tumbled out. "And he said, 'You got to stay where you're to, I'm on the way.' And I said, 'What's wrong?' And he said, 'I'll be there in a few minutes.' So, he came down and he sat down and he said, 'Listen, you need to turn the TV on. We need to watch something on TV.' And I said, 'Well, what's going on?' And he said, 'A chopper went down.' And I said, 'Well, which one is it?' And he said, 'I think it's the SeaRose.' And I stopped for a second and I said, 'Oh shit! That's the one Greg and them is on.' And he turned it on, and sure enough, it was all over the news. And I said, 'Shit, I got to get out of here. I've got to figure this out.'"

Sheldon and his brother jumped into a truck and sped off to the hotel, where they met Heather. "When Heather showed up, she looked at me and she said, 'They're gone.' And I said, 'You don't know that.' And she said, 'I can feel it. They're gone.' And I just walked in with her. She said, 'I just need you to come with me.' So, I went in there and stayed with her basically until she needed to go home."

Sheldon worked with four other people who were on the helicopter when it crashed: Allison Maher, Keith Escott, Peter Breen, and Derek Mullowney. "You know, every morning I used to get up and go back into the hotel where they had set up and I'd stay there all day until basically there was nobody left in the nighttime," he says. "And then I used to go home and I'd go back there in the morning and do the same thing for all four days, because, I don't know, I just needed to be there."

Marie says that time at the hotel seemed like it went on forever. But confirmation finally came: all the missing men were inside the helicopter. A recovery team retrieved the helicopter and brought it, and the men, back home.

Despite the sadness, there was a palpable relief. "The RCMP came down there," according to Wayne, "and we were all there and the first thing Heather asked the RCMP was, 'How did you know it was Greg's body?' And the RCMP said, 'We found his ID in his wallet.' That's how they identified him."

The Morrises had their son back home. At least one prayer was answered.

Although Heather spent much of the four days after the crash at the hotel waiting for information, while being supported by family and friends, she had two children aged four and six, Ian and Erin, to take care of. Despite the madness going on around her, and feeling an incredible amount of sadness and grief during those days and the weeks that followed, she still had to be a mother. She had to ensure that they were fed and bathed, that lunches were packed, and that there was some order and a sense of normalcy in their lives.

Marie caught a glimpse of how hard it was for the children to understand what was happening when they all went to Greg's funeral service. "I try not to think about it," she says slowly, "but when we had the service out at St. Mark's Church, Ian was sitting on my knee and they brought in the casket and Erin said to Ian—I'll never forget it—'Daddy's in that.' And he looked at me and said, 'Daddy's in that?' And then he laughed and said, 'Daddy's not in that!' It just broke my heart," she admits, her voice wavering while she tells the story, "because that's all they knew."

Like everyone else, Paddy Dyer held out hope as long as he could after the crash. That first night they were missing, with still no sign of helicopter or passengers, Paddy knew it wasn't going to turn out how anyone wanted. "I remember lying in bed that night, myself and the wife were just lying in bed and the wind was howling off the side of the house and we were saying that it don't matter what kind of survival suit they had on, they weren't making it through this kind of a thing."

Of all the heartbreak happening the day of the crash, Paddy thought most about Heather, working at the hospital and suddenly being told to prepare for a full-scale emergency, one that possibly involved her husband. "I can't even imagine what it was like for her being in there and everything going on. At that point in time, you had hope that they were still alive."

Thomas Anwyll

Brenda Anwyll arrived at work on the morning of March 12, 2009, and followed her usual routine. She logged into her computer at Coastal Pacific Xpress, a trucking company based out of Surrey, British Columbia and then made herself a cup of tea. She was about to start her day when someone at the front desk said that a man in the lobby had asked to see her.

Brenda was surprised to see Tom's boss standing in the doorway; it was a first in her 11 years at CPX. "It was kind of like, you know, when you're met with that type of situation," Brenda recalls, "where you never really know what's going on, and what comes into your head. So, it was kind of like, 'Oh, what are you doing here?' sort of thing."

What popped into her head was that it was close to payday, so he must be dropping off Tom's pay or maybe an expense claim cheque because Tom was in Newfoundland. "And then he asked if we could sit and talk somewhere privately, so we went into one of the conference rooms." That's when he broke the news to her. "He told me there had been an accident and nothing had been confirmed and they were looking for the site still. And, of course, at that point your mind just ends up going blank."

It was just after 9 a.m. in British Columbia, early afternoon in Newfoundland, and Tom's boss had few answers. "They just knew that the helicopter had gone down," she says. "So, at that time it was like, 'I can't even really tell you anything. We have faith in the fact that they've all taken their personal safety training courses and that they know what to do in that kind of a situation.' So, he just said, 'Let's just go to the house and, you know, sit and wait for any news we can find out.'"

Brenda recalls one thing for certain about that time: she was well taken care of by the people around her. "My co-workers were awesome, they went right into taking-care-of-me mode and shut down my computer for me and took all my work for the day. And we went off to his boss's house and there was his co-workers and myself and then I called a family member to come and be with me, my sister and her partner came to be with me as well and we sat and watched the news as well as waited for news on the telephone."

They spent several days together waiting for any word about Tom. Brenda was impressed by how many calls she received from the offshore oil companies, even when there was nothing new to report. "Even if it was to call to say, 'we haven't heard anything' or 'we don't know anything new,' we were definitely kept informed. I never once felt like I was being ignored or that nothing was happening. We were continually updated, we would get phone calls. And I really appreciated that."

Officials in Newfoundland offered to fly Brenda to St. John's immediately, to be with the other families that were gathering at a local hotel. She considered it, but then decided to remain close to her support system. "I talked to [Tom's] parents about it," she says. "They lived on Gabriola Island, his dad has since passed away, and I talked with them about it and I was torn about whether I would go to Newfoundland or whether I would stay home. Again, your mind was not really completely functioning at normal capacity during a time like this and for me I felt more comfortable staying at home and being surrounded by my family and my loved ones than being in a place I didn't know anyone, surrounded by people I didn't know.

"And yes, I could've probably drawn strength from them at the time, but I just felt more comfortable being at home in my own surroundings, in my own bed, and just being with my friends and family knowing that they would take care of my dogs and they would take care of me and that kind of stuff."

The next week, though, she flew to Newfoundland, accompanied by Tom's sister Susan. Brenda was finally heading to the island Tom had fallen in love with and had begged her many times to move to. "It was surreal," she recalls. "Very. Very surreal."

Brenda remembers stepping outside the airport in St. John's and being struck by the harshness of the weather, a combination of ice and rain and cold. "Way colder than I had ever experienced," she says.

But something else struck her, and she again thought of Tom's love of the island. "I went out there and it's like, 'Okay, I can see why he liked it out here so much.' It is a beautiful place, that's for sure. Just super nice people really, you know."

A counsellor was assigned to meet up with her and her sister-in-law to attend to their needs.

The two women arrived in time to attend a prayer service for victims of the crash at The Basilica Cathedral of St. John the Baptist. The iconic Roman Catholic building overlooks the city's downtown and was built to point directly at the Narrows, the entrance to St. John's harbour. More than 1,000 people, including Prime Minister Stephen Harper, Premier Danny Williams, and Newfoundland and Labrador's lieutenant-governor John Crosbie, filled every seat. Those who couldn't find a place to sit leaned against the walls, the stations of the cross barely above their heads, while others sat on the balcony stairs. It was another surreal moment for Brenda. "I did not meet any of the family members until that night of the service," she says. "Because some of them had left and had gone back to their own homes, you know, as many of them lived right in St. John's or close enough that they could go back and forth. So, it was definitely surreal and definitely something that—little bits and pieces stick in my brain but not lots of it. Not lots, that's for sure."

And then, it was time to return home to British Columbia, with Tom once again by her side. "We had him cremated [in Newfoundland], because it was far easier—that was his wish anyways. And with all the red tape of flying deceased persons and that sort of thing, it was just easier to have everything done in Newfoundland and I brought him home with me in the airplane.

"I remember not wanting—I said I'm not putting his ashes up in the baggage compartment. For takeoff and landings he was down by my feet, but for the rest of [the] time he was pretty well on my lap."

Matthew Davis

On flight days, when he had to be in the air by 9 a.m., Matt Davis always rose early. On the morning of March 12, 2009, he was out of bed by 6:30, leaving Marsha asleep, cuddled into their three-year-old son, William.

Marsha woke briefly, long enough to catch a glimpse of him as he left the bedroom, but quickly dozed off again. The night before she had suggested that he take the day off, as it was Shannon's fifth birthday, but Matt said he had only one flight and that he'd be back just after lunch to spend the rest of the day with them.

At the airport Matt called home before boarding the helicopter. He wished Shannon a happy birthday, said hello to William, and then chatted with Marsha long enough to say he'd see her in a few hours to celebrate.

Marsha's mother was visiting and at 10 a.m. she was in the kitchen baking a birthday cake. Marsha was nearby, watching Shannon open presents. The happy, picture-perfect family moment was interrupted by the ringing of the telephone. Marsha picked up the receiver and said hello. It was one of Matt's cousins calling to say she had heard from another family member about a helicopter crash offshore and she wondered if Matt was flying that morning.

It was a question asked in innocence and out of concern. But it threw Marsha into a state of shock. "I knew immediately it was Matt," she says. "I did know there was a flight that departed previous to his but when I had heard it first, in my heart I knew it was him. I just felt it was Matt."

A horrible feeling rushed through her and Marsha dropped the phone. She fell to the floor crying hysterically and screaming to her mother. "He's gone!" she cried out. Her mother couldn't figure out what she was talking about. "What? What are you saying, Marsha?" her mother kept repeating. "Matt is okay. Matt is fine in the helicopter."

But Marsha's mind had already gone to the worst possible scenario: Matt's helicopter had crashed and there was no way he had survived. "I had felt right then at that moment it was true," she says. "If Matt's helicopter went down offshore, and in my mind right at that moment there was no way he survived it, he was gone."

The house was suddenly in chaos, with the children rushing to their mother in panic. They understood enough to know that whatever was going on was frightening. "I'll never forget our daughter, Shannon's, reaction," Marsha recalls. "The fear in her little face. Her immediate run to my arms. She understood what I was saying but was afraid to say anything to me. Both my children knew what I was saying and in my arms. They may have been small but they knew then that something bad had happened and it had happened to their dad. They were scared. I was scaring them."

Neither of the children left her arms as she wept. "I didn't know what to do with myself. My mom kept saying it wasn't true and that I had to call someone to find this out for sure."

Marsha still had not heard from the company. She called a close friend whose husband worked at Cougar Helicopters with Matt. The response convinced her that her first instinct was right. "She told me to 'shut up, Marsh, don't say another thing, Adam and I are on the way.' I don't think she wanted to believe it but that was enough for me to confirm any suspicions. In my eyes this was true, this had really happened."

Marsha starting making phone calls to family members, including Matt's mother, Jeane, who was living in Ontario, about two hours from Ottawa.

Jeane had already called Matt and Marsha's house earlier to say happy birthday to Shannon. That's a ritual in the Davis family: You don't have to send a gift or a card, but on the morning of anyone's birthday, as soon as your feet hit the floor, you call them to say happy birthday. During that call Jeane and Matt's stepfather sang happy birthday to Shannon's squeals of delight as she said, "Grammy and Poppo, thank you!"

Jeane has a second phone line in her house for business calls. That phone started ringing about two hours later, just as she was walking past it. She stopped to answer and couldn't comprehend what the person was saying. "All I could hear was screaming, screaming, screaming," she says. "And I said, 'Hello? Hello? Can I help you? Can I help you? What is it, talk to me.' And it was screaming, just screaming like the most—if I tell you that it sounded like an animal having its guts cut out while it was still alive, now that's the only descriptive words that I can come up with."

Jeane put her husband on the line to see if he could figure out what the person was saying. By then, Marsha had calmed enough to explain what was going on and told him to turn on the television news. "Brian hung up and he just took me by the hand and brought me into the family room and said, 'Jeane, turn on the TV and go to NTV.' And of course, it was there right in front of me. The chopper, Cougar 491, has crashed. And, of course, everything is just a total mad blur from there on in."

They went straight to Ottawa airport to fly to St. John's, without calling ahead to book a reservation. Jeane will never forget what happened there.

She was at the Air Canada counter trying to buy two tickets and was told that there were no seats available on the next flight to St. John's. But when the staff heard why she was rushing home, a company employee pulled her and her husband aside and took them inside the security area, where passengers were waiting to board the plane. He then yelled out to the room full of strangers to get their attention. "And he said, 'Look, a lot of you have heard about Cougar 491,' and you could see the assent of people around, and he said, 'This is the pilot's mother and her husband, and they are desperately trying to get to St. John's. Is there anybody here in the crowd that would be willing to give up their seat?'"

Jeane cries as she remembers the response from the people about to get on the plane to go their own ways and meet up with their own loved ones. "I bet you there was 25 people who put up their hand and stepped forward. It was unbelievable. 'You can have my seat. Here's my ticket ... you take it,'" she recalls passenger after passenger saying to her. "They were almost fighting over whose seat we could actually have."

To have that happen in a city like Ottawa was a surprise, and a moment of relief during a time of unbearable stress.

Matt's sister Amanda was about six weeks from her due date when she received the news that Matt was missing. She was getting ready for her last day of work before going on maternity leave. At first the family was hesitant to say anything to her because she was so late in her pregnancy, but everyone worried that she'd hear about in the media, so her husband called her.

Amanda, who also lived in Ontario, decided to fly home, although she knew it was a risky time for her to travel, being so close to delivery. But Matt had been the person the family leaned on in trying times for so many years and Amanda sensed that he was telling her it was now her turn. "I could hear his voice in the back of my head," she says. "'There's nothing you could do for me, I'm gone.' You know, I could hear his voice reasoning with me because that's what he did—you know, solid thinker. 'You need to pull this family together. It's your turn now, like, to take over and take over the situation and control everybody.'"

Back at Marsha's, much of the day was spent in front of the TV waiting for word on a possible rescue. "I remember everyone having so much hope for a rescue," Marsha says. "That everyone wished they would find people in the lifeboats. I remember sitting on the floor in my living room watching the TV and I remember asking Matt's friend Adam, who was very familiar with sitting in those chopper seats, did he think Matt was gone. 'Marsh,' he said, 'if there was any way Matt would get home to you and the kids he would, but to be honest,' he said, 'I think you're right.'"

Marsha describes the week that followed as her "worst nightmare." She didn't get much sleep, and when she could, her mind was littered with ugly haunting dreams. "In the amount of sleep I did have that week I remember dreams I had about Matt being found upside down, strapped in his seat of the helicopter."

Marsha didn't have the physical or mental strength to go the hotel, where other families were gathering. Instead, she remained at home with her children, where many people visited them. "The kids and I had received so much love and support while waiting in our home," she says, "but I just remember being in this state of shock and also feeling so overwhelmed. Several times that week I remember wanting to hear the garage door of our home open, see Matt grinning as he walked in through the door and hear him sing out to Shannon and William, 'Daddy's home.' I wished for that so much."

But no amount of wishing could change the reality. "I had trouble accepting it. Accepting that my husband's life had been tragically taken from him, from us. That 16 other loved ones' lives were also taken with his. It was hard to believe. Everything we all knew at that moment, everything we had all lived and had hoped for in our lives, was permanently changed. Our family of four instantly changed to three … The world, as we knew, was suddenly destroyed. The nightmare was very much real."

Many times since the morning of March 12 Marsha's mind has raced back to the glimpse of Matt leaving their bedroom to head to work. "That was the last time I would have seen my husband," she says. "More than once since then I have wished I had called him back, clung on to him, and even begged him not to go."

She wonders why she didn't try to persuade him to arrange to be off work for Shannon's birthday. "What was supposed to be a wonderful day about Shannon turning five would bring so much pain," she says. "Matt went to work that day, like other loved ones did, and didn't return, never to come home again."

Timothy Lanouette

Kevin Lane can't recall exactly what he heard on the background news that grabbed his attention. He was sitting at his desk in Shearwater, Nova Scotia, around lunchtime on March 12 and all he remembers hearing were the words *Cougar* and *crash*. His mind quickly turned to his old friend, Tim Lanouette.

"And—I just had this fear that it was Tim," he says. "I got home and checked Facebook and his profile was gone. So, I pretty much knew. So, I started calling people. I called his family. And the person who confirmed it was his girlfriend at the time. It was one of those things where I knew for hours before somebody finally confirmed it for me."

Kevin was devastated. His wife returned home from work to comfort him. His voice cracks when he talks about that day: "I cried so hard. Joanne came from work. And we just cried on the couch thinking that I just hope that he wasn't scared. That was the—I just hope that he wasn't scared and then hearing that they gained altitude and that's, that's upsetting."

But it wasn't just emotions clouding Kevin's brain. He had spent many years working on helicopters and then flying in them while watching in awe as pilots like Tim manoeuvred the aircraft through the trickiest of winds and other tough weather conditions. He heard about Tim's words of encouragement in those final seconds of flight, as captured by the cockpit voice recorder. And he understood the split-second decisions they had to make. Tim as the first officer and second in command would have offered encouragement to Matt, the pilot, as Matt struggled to lower the helicopter down to the water. "Ultimately he would have supported the guy who had the decision. You support the person who is doing it because that's going to give you the best outcome. It makes perfect sense. I can hear Tim saying, 'You got this. You got this.' Like obviously I haven't heard the tape. I don't want to hear the tape. But I can hear him saying that, at that moment."

Having been so involved in the world of aviation through his job maintaining electronic systems on military helicopters, Kevin knew the stark reality of flying over the ocean and even landing safely on its surface. "If you ditch in the water and people start getting wet, then people are going to die pretty quick anyway," he says. "So, you know, I was thinking that as they were doing the search. And I was just thinking that if they have to search for people, then nobody's coming home. The one guy who lived—that's a miracle. Tim and I sailed. We know that you got 10 minutes in water like that. So, the reality was that I knew what happened before anyone told me. And that's not some psycho-spiritual thing. It's just reality."

Tim's old friend from the military school of music in British Columbia and his former bandmaster, Pierre de Villers, happened to be in St. John's on the day of the crash and staying at the same hotel where family members were gathering. He was in the city with a military band out of Halifax that was performing in the province. "The Stadacona band was on tour in Newfoundland when the crash happened," Pierre recalls. "And we were out playing and when we came back to the hotel there was a commotion. They had set up the command headquarters at the hotel. Then we found out it was because of this crash."

He had no idea Tim was involved in the crash. "Until—I think it was later that night or the next when I got a message from Kevin and he told me Tim was one of the pilots." Pierre couldn't believe the news. "I was devastated," he says. "I was devastated. I was shocked, really, in sadness and, like, all these feelings that come together. It was tough."

Peter Breen

After dropping her husband off at the airport on the morning of March 12, Janet Breen went home. The first thing she did when she got inside the house was call the Cougar Helicopters information line. The recording was set up to let people know whether flights were on time or delayed.

Her daughter Janet Marie worked at the airport at Provincial Airlines, and that morning she was on the early shift, which meant she started at 5 a.m. Sometime between 9 and 10 a.m. was her lunch break and she went to her parent's house to have something to eat.

Janet Marie told her mother something was going on at the airport because, as she left, there was some kind of commotion. "And I can see her now," Janet says, "sat up at the barstool at the counter having her breakfast. And she wasn't there five minutes and the next thing it comes on the radio that a Cougar helicopter had gone down and I said, 'My God, Janet Marie, thank God it's not Dad because I called and he's on weather-hold' … then I said, 'But who are those poor people?'"

Less than two minutes later, the phone rang. It was an official, but Janet doesn't recall whether the person was calling from Cougar or the airport or Peter's employer, East Coast Catering. She just remembers that she was told that the flight Peter was on had gone into the water.

"The only thing I remember after that phone call," she says, "I remember distinctly walking out the kitchen door and into the hall and banging that wall. I was on my knees and I was fisting the wall. Like, I was beside myself."

Janet Marie, the oldest daughter, felt her protective instincts kick in immediately. She knew her younger brother, Andrew, was at school and she worried that he would hear about the crash from someone there. "I got to go get Andrew," she told her mother. But her mother was afraid for her to get behind the wheel after just receiving the news about the chopper. "You're not getting in the car, you're not going!" Janet said. But 30-year-old Janet Marie stood her ground. "I was just concerned Andrew was going to hear it. I mean, he was in school and all the kids have cellphones and things. He was the baby. I was just afraid someone would see it on television and tell him and he would panic."

At St. Bon's, the school Peter had attended and where he had volunteered countless hours as an adult to help renovate, Andrew and his classmates were in the second period. Math class was held in the computer lab on one of the school's upper floors. He was trying to concentrate when someone across the room said something about a Cougar helicopter and it caught Andrew's attention. "And then it left my mind for a minute," he remembers, "and a few minutes later I thought, 'Fuck, Dad left this morning, and that's super-weird.'"

Andrew decided to leave the classroom and go to the washroom to check his cellphone. But as he stood to leave, there was a knock on the door.

The person at the door requested to see Andrew, asking him to accompany him downstairs. "And immediately then, it's like, you knew," Andrew says. "There was Mr. Ryan, a super nice man, Irish fellow, very funny, great guy, and he didn't say a word to me, he knew that I already realized what was going on. He didn't say a word the whole way down—probably four flights of stairs. And, like, the whole way down we both knew what happened. Neither of us never had to say anything. And then when I came downstairs Noelle and Janet Marie were there and it was just like you really knew then."

Noelle, who was 25, recalls arriving at the school with Janet Marie and asking to see Andrew. "It was horrible. The principal was there and I said, 'Where is Andrew?' And she was like, 'You need me to go talk to him.' And I was like, 'No, you are not going to talk to him, I am going to talk to him. Where is he?' And she wouldn't let me.'"

But Noelle didn't have to tell Andrew. When he arrived at the bottom of the stairs, she could tell by looking at him that he already knew why they were there.

Like Janet, Keith Normore was listening to the radio when word started to come out about a helicopter going down off St. John's. He was in his car and just leaving the city for the 15-minute drive to his Conception Bay South home.

Keith had been in St. John's to pick up a suit to wear to the funeral of his father-in-law, who had died the day before. When the radio announcer said that there was breaking news about a crash involving a Cougar helicopter, Keith went numb. "I turned up the radio and I was listening to it and before I realized it, I was after passing Avondale Access Road." That road is about 30 minutes past Keith's destination. "I just drove out the highway in a daze, never knew nothing till I saw Avondale and I had to turn around and go back."

His mind wandered between listening to the radio for any new information and trying to figure out who would've been on board the chopper that morning. "I mean, like, you're offshore—no matter what rigs are out there you always met everybody because you're at the airport, at the heliport, waiting to go, and you met everybody from all the other platforms. You knew everybody anyway, so if it was offshore, it was nine chances out of 10 they are buddies of yours through association."

As he rushed to get home to make some calls, all Keith could think about was how often he had flown that same route with Peter during their offshore days together. "Every time me and Peter flew," he says, "me and him always sat across from each other and nine times out of 10 it was by the big doors. And we'd say, 'B'ys, we're going to be the first out of here if something happens.' We always said that."

The last thing the passengers had to do before getting aboard the helicopter was to watch a safety video. "You had to watch the movie, you know, to tell you what to do if it happened and all that stuff. We always, always had in our minds when we got on the helicopter that it was a serious thing but we'd be making fun of the choppers and stuff, to take the tension off. And I mean, it was drilled into your head, you knew it was a high possibility, that kind of thing. You're an hour and a half flying over water. So, it was in everybody's head but like, you know, it was made a joke of or that sort of thing, I mean you say something jokingly but it was a serious matter."

Keith never did find out that day who was on the flight—partly because he was no longer working in the offshore industry but also because he was preoccupied with the death of his father-in-law and the funeral plans for the next day.

Twenty-four hours later Keith learned that his friend Peter and several other former co-workers had been on the flight. "I found out the next day at the funeral. One of my buddies came in with the names, and I said, 'You gotta be fucking kidding me?'

"I was flabbergasted. I mean, like, I could not believe it. I said there's no way in the world, and I started reading the names and it was all my whole crew that I worked with. Just gone, right? It's a hard thing to come to grips with."

He had a chilling thought about that fateful day in Marystown a year and a half earlier when he stepped off a rig and announced to his boss that he was leaving the offshore life—and his workmates—for good. "I would've been part of it obviously. I mean, our whole crew, Greg was our boss, you know, the whole thing was the same for the last few years and I know I would've been there."

On the morning Peter left to fly out to the SeaRose, his 90-year-old mother, Catherine, was in hospital. She had just had hip surgery. Peter had visited her the night before and called his sister Judy around midnight to remind her that he was flying out early and that she was needed at the hospital by 8 a.m. to help feed their mother. "And I said yes, I'll be there 8 o'clock," Judy says. "So I went on over to the hospital and I was there from eight to 10 and then Kevin's daughter came to relieve me … for the next shift. When I went out, my husband was in the car waiting for me."

As she left the hospital, Judy noticed a crowd of people buzzing around, ambulances lined up near the emergency entrance, and a reporter from the local television station, NTV, nearby. "And Jodi Cooke came out with her tripod," she recalls, "and I said they must be a doing a documentary or something."

Judy didn't pay much attention to the scene unfolding outside the Health Sciences Centre. She got in the car and started telling her husband about her morning. "I just said this is the worst two hours I ever spent. Mom was really upset and everything because she knew Pete was going out. She kept asking me, 'Do you think he's out there yet?'"

When they walked into their house, the phone was ringing with news that the helicopter had gone down. Judy called her brother Danny at the insurance company where he worked. Danny started rounding up the rest of the siblings.

Everyone gathered at Judy's house and sat around the television in hopes that they'd find out some information. "When we all got to Judy's and we were all watching this unfold on TV," Danny recalls, "we had thought that everything was going to be okay because I remember there was a picture on the TV of all the ambulances going out to the helipad and they took Robbie Decker in, as he was the first one off."

But then all the ambulances that were lined up at the heliport beside the Health Sciences Centre turned around and went back to the hospital building. Danny realized that there likely wasn't going to be good news and that they should head to the hotel, where company officials were gathering with the latest information. "When they came in and they said they never found any lifeboats, or they found them and they were empty, it was like every bit of air got sucked out of me," he says.

The brothers and sisters had another pressing issue. Across town, their mother lay in a hospital bed recovering from a broken hip. But they put off going to see her because the search was still ongoing and they weren't sure how much, or when, to tell her. On Saturday they called a priest, a family friend, and asked him to deliver the news to their mother. "And when he went in, she said, 'You're here to tell me something. It's Pete, isn't it?'" Kevin recalls. "Before he said anything."

Danny says it was eerie how she just seemed to know. Hospital staff moved her to a private room. "One of the ironies when Mom was in the hospital during those five days when we were waiting," he says, "Robbie Decker was in the room across from her with a security guard outside the door."

Back at Janet and Peter's house, people showed up throughout the day to comfort Janet. Other families were gathering at the Capital Hotel, where Cougar officials, crash investigators, and RCMP officers were on-site, but Janet couldn't go there. "People were piling into the house and I know they were all good people," she says, "but I just wanted everyone to go away. I just didn't want anyone there. I just wanted to stay in my house, by myself with nobody there."

Twenty-four-year-old Shannon was living in Oshawa, Ontario. Janet tried to reach him early on, but he was at work. It was stressful for everyone as the hours stretched on and no one could get in touch with him. Finally, when Janet did, she straight up prepared him for the worst, even though they still didn't know much. "I mean having to call Shannon in Oshawa and tell him about his dad," she says, "it's not like you could say Dad is sick, I think you should come home, but it's, like, Dad's gone, you know. But I had to be honest, when I spoke to him. I had to be honest with him and I said, I don't think they're going to find Dad."

That evening Janet and the children finally did go to the hotel in search of new information. That's when reality sank in for Noelle. "The night that it happened," she says, "I remember down at the hotel I thought, 'What if they don't find him?' It was dark, it was the middle of winter, and I was like, 'What if they don't find him? He won't get to see me get married. He won't get to see the grandkids.' Like, that's one of the first things you think of."

It took several days but word finally came that Peter's body and those of the others who were missing had been located and efforts were being made to retrieve them from the ocean and return them to their families.

Janet started planning the funeral service. Many people showed up at Caul's Funeral Home in St. John's to pay their respects. One person brought a hockey jersey that Peter had always wanted.

The story goes that, out on the rig, one of Peter's workmates often wore a Boston Bruins jersey that had Michael Ryder's name on the back. Ryder, from Bonavista, on Newfoundland's east coast, was a source of pride for many of the province's residents, especially when he was named to the famed Bruins in 2008. "How it all came about is that Pete was a diehard Boston Bruins fans," Janet says, "and he crucified this guy for that jersey. I don't know how many times he'd be saying, 'Come on, give it to me. Come on, you don't want it.' And when he was waking a guy brought the jersey to us. So it was on the casket and before he was buried I said 'should we take it home or leave it with him?' And Pete was cremated, it was what he wanted but anyway, we did put it in with him."

Andrew also remembers that jersey. "I was with my friends and Mom pulled me aside and wanted me to meet this guy," he recalls, "and we talked about sports and hockey and that Dad was a Bruins fan and he wanted Mom to have this. It was a Boston jersey with a name on the back. I remember it happening and once in a while it comes up and we always wonder who was that guy?"

Neither Andrew nor his mother could remember who had walked into the funeral home and handed her the jersey. "I'd like to thank him but I don't know who he is," she says.

That guy was Mark Frost, John Pelley's good friend and also a friend of Peter's. Mark—who, incidentally, is a Montreal Canadiens fan—brought the jersey to the funeral home and handed it to Janet. "The guy who owned the jersey was James Maye," Mark says. "He was a big Boston fan also and he and Peter used to talk often about how Boston was doing and about the team, as they were both big fans. Peter commented to him on how much he liked the jersey. He had said that he wanted to get one of them himself."

When Peter died, it was Jim's idea to bring the jersey to the funeral home. "Jim made a deal with me that if I put it on for a picture with him, he would give it to me to bring to [Peter's] wife for the casket so that Peter would get what he always wanted." Mark still has that picture of him and Jim, with Mark wearing the Boston jersey.

Peter's funeral was supposed to be held on Saturday, March 21, at the Basilica. But it was delayed for two days because of a snowstorm. That meant it would be held on a Monday, and Janet worried about the turnout. "But the church was blocked," she recalls. "The guy that runs the church told me that it was the biggest funeral that there ever was at the Basilica. There was not an empty seat. And the Basilica is a big church, there are balconies and everything. [Peter] knew everybody."

Noelle also remembers being overwhelmed by the sheer number of people in the church that day. "I remember when we were walking in, people were everywhere," she says. "People were lined off down the sides and stood up in the back."

Later, the family held a private burial. Because of Peter's life-long love of the Boston Bruins, they had the team logo put on his headstone and Janet and the children's signatures were etched in the marble. They went one step further to inject a little of Peter's humour into a solemn graveside memorial. "We played 'Time of Your Life,' the Green Day song." Janet laughs as she remembers.

It was a surreal moment that incorporated Peter's love of jokes and *Seinfeld* into their final goodbye. "On Seinfeld's last episode back when it ended in like '98," Andrew explains, "they played Green Day to conclude the whole show and Dad was a *Seinfeld* fan and that was always the song that came on the radio and he used to love it."

The family brought a small stereo to the cemetery to play the song but they couldn't get it to work. So Andrew yelled out, "We're playing this one way or another!" And being 17 and just having received his driver's licence, he jumped into the vehicle and drove it as close to the gravesite as he could. "So, we pulled the car up a little closer to the grave and opened the door and popped the CD that I had burned off in and played track 15 or whatever it was and put it on repeat."

> *Another turning point, a fork stuck in the road*
> *Time grabs you by the wrist, directs you where to go*
> *So make the best of this test, and don't ask why*
> *It's not a question, but a lesson learned in time*
> *It's something unpredictable, but in the end it's right*
> *I hope you had the time of your life*
> *For what it's worth, it was worth all the while*
> *It's something unpredictable, but in the end it's right*
> *I hope you had the time of your life*

Janet, Noelle, Janet Marie, Andrew, and Shannon, along with other family members, stood and listened as the wind carried the voice of Green Day's Billie Joe Armstrong over the headstones and through the trees. All in disbelief that they'd never again hear Peter's laugh roaring out from the den while he watched his favourite TV show. "There was a lot of tears," Janet says of the moment.

Gary Corbett

The morning of March 12, 2009, was a hectic one in the Corbett household. Gary, his wife, Ceily, and the children all had different reasons to get out the door early.

Sixteen-year-old Stacey and 14-year-old twins Chad and Chelsea were rushing to catch the school bus to their junior high and high schools. Ceily had an early medical appointment in the city. And Gary had to get to the airport on time for his flight to the Hibernia rig.

"He said goodbye to all of us," she recalls, "and told me he loved me and would 'call tonight.'"

After her appointment, Ceily went to work. Her government office at Occupational Health and Safety was located a short distance from the company offices where Gary worked. As she drove by, she thought it strange to see his truck in the parking lot, but then she remembered that he was planning to leave it there as a co-worker had offered to drive him to the airport.

Ceily had been in her office for a while when she looked up to see Gary's boss, Cal Dwyer, and his wife, Cheryl, walk in. "It didn't dawn on me that something had happened to Gary," she says, "but when Cal said to me about the helicopter, I panicked and was scared." Scared because he broke the news to her that the helicopter had gone down—but there was hope because he said it was a controlled landing or ditching and they were all trained for that kind of an incident.

Ceily says her body suddenly felt drained as she tried to digest what he was saying. "My co-workers were there and I know I couldn't grasp it, but there was hope. The ditching of the helicopter was supposedly a planned ditching and with their Basic Survival Training it was hoped that they would all be okay."

Ceily found it difficult to remain calm. She could see that Cal and Cheryl looked upset and worried. She thought about her three children and was afraid that she wouldn't get to their schools before they heard the news. "Trudy Northover, my best friend at work, took me and I headed to Frank Roberts Junior High and Queen Elizabeth High School in Conception Bay South to get the children from school," she says.

During the drive, Trudy received a call from her husband, who worked on the Hibernia rig with Gary when he was at sea. He was calling to offer some comfort based on a news report he had heard. "Ed phoned Trudy and let her know it had been reported they had been found safely. It turned out to be a wrong report. At the time, though, I was so relieved but I still felt I had to get the kids from school." She gently broke the news to the children, stressing that Gary and the others were likely all okay. "They were so upset," she recalls, "but I told them that they were sure they were all safe."

Ceily turned on the radio when she got home just in time to hear the latest development—a helicopter had landed at the hospital in St. John's carrying one person who had been on Flight 491. A rescue helicopter with just one survivor on board suggested to her that good news would not be coming.

Why did the helicopter only have one person? If there were survivors, why weren't they being airlifted to hospital? "I knew in my heart that the rest didn't make it," she says.

Then the telephone calls started and her house quickly filled up with people.

Many families were heading to the Capital Hotel, where company officials and investigators were holding briefings, but Ceily did not want to go anywhere. "I wanted to stay at home and that's what I did. The Hibernia management and Hyflodraulic Ltd. always kept me informed of everything that was happening regarding the recovery efforts," she says, "and their kindness is something I will always remember."

In the days after the accident, her house was filled with friends, family, and employees from Hibernia Management and Hyflodraulic Ltd., Gary's employer. She appreciated the support, but at times she felt overwhelmed and went to the bedroom to be alone. At those times she'd say "What would Gary do?" to help compose herself.

At one point Premier Danny Williams called to express condolences on his own behalf and on behalf of the government and the people of the province. "It was a nice gesture," Ceily says. "He asked the ages of the kids and I told him Chad and Chelsea were 14 and Stacey 16. I remember he said something like 'these are rough ages for kids, dealing with such a tragedy,' and basically to 'keep an eye on them.' I realized that the kids would need me to be as strong as possible and I was determined to do just that."

A broken leg kept Jack Walsh confined to his living room couch most days in the spring of 2009. At about mid-morning on March 12 he was watching television when a news special came on. He couldn't believe what the newsreader was saying: A Cougar helicopter had gone down off St. John's just a short time before and the passengers and crew, at that point, were unaccounted for. His mind raced, as his friend Gary was scheduled to take a flight to the offshore that morning. "I had a really good idea that that was the one," he says, "because I knew he was flying out and I knew when."

Jack spent the rest of the day watching the news, trying to glean as much information as he could. "It was a very difficult day, but we didn't really know till probably 24 hours later that there was stuff in the water, a life raft—and of course everybody was hoping. But we didn't know if there were any survivors then, but the guy who survived, Robert Decker."

For that reason, he says, "we all kept up a bit of hope"—that somehow Gary and the others might have been able to stay afloat and were somewhere on the ocean waiting to be rescued.

His sister-in-law was home from Yellowknife and, like Ceily, Jack surrounded himself with family and friends while he waited for any news on whether Gary and the others would be found.

Wade Duggan

It's an image Greg Duggan finds hard to push out of his head.

At his home in the Goulds neighbourhood of St. John's about 100 people had gathered. Some in the kitchen, some in the living room, all pacing back and forth between the house and the garage—a gathering place for Greg and his friends over the years—many in tears as they consoled each other. Others were on the telephone looking for any scrap of information to add to the news they were still trying to decipher: the helicopter with Wade, Greg's younger brother by five years, aboard had gone down in the Atlantic Ocean. No one could say whether the passengers and crew were in the water, in the lifeboat, or in the missing helicopter.

Then Greg spotted his father alone, in a bedroom. "I can still see me father kneeling down by the bed praying," he recalls, filling up. "Some things stand out in your life, right, powerful images? Well, it's the most powerful picture I can remember. He was praying that Wade was safe. And I can still see him kneeling down by the bed and praying. Tough image."

Tough image for a tough day that had started on such a positive note. A few hours before the chaos erupted, Greg was in his kitchen cooking a ham. It was boiling on the stove when a friend dropped by to get him to sign confirmation papers, as Greg was godfather to her son. He signed the papers, they chatted, and she left.

Then the telephone rang. It was another friend who said he was glad that Greg answered because he had just heard that an offshore chopper had crashed and he was worried about him. Greg, momentarily stunned, swore into the receiver. "Jesus, Wade is just gone out there!" he said. "What do you mean a chopper is gone down? Wade is flying today!'" His friend explained that one of the supply boats where he worked just left to get out to the site where the helicopter was believed to have gone down.

Greg started making telephone calls. He reached his parents, who were more than an hour's drive away at their home in Brigus South, and, after he told them all that he knew—which was very little—they headed to his house.

Greg didn't have a good feeling. "I knew he'd be calling me if he was all right."

Greg managed to reach Wade's boss at Hyflodraulic Limited, where Wade worked as a millwright. He told Greg that he had been assured that everyone was safe, that they were supposedly all in a lifeboat and waiting to be picked up. Greg saw the same reports when he turned on the television in his garage.

By then, his house was filling up with friends and family. Everyone was desperately clinging to hope as unofficial reports suggested that everyone appeared to be safe. It wasn't long before a relative pulled him aside. "He worked for the Coast Guard," Greg explains, "and he said, 'I'm going to tell you something right now,' he said, 'be prepared, because that's not what the Coast Guard is saying.'"

Greg kept that to himself. "I never said anything about that to nobody till I found out more details."

Then came word that a lifeboat had been found and that it was empty. "So, I knew then that things weren't going to be good. I knew right there and then. But when he told me to be prepared, he was obviously talking to his superiors and they were giving him word that things were not as what they were saying it was."

A good friend of Greg's, Steve Tizzard, was on his way to Walmart when he heard the news on his car radio. Steve, a radio operator on the Hibernia platform, had been working in the offshore 12 years by then and he knew Wade a little through Greg and from seeing him on the rig whenever his company sent him offshore.

Two days earlier, Steve and Greg had been sitting in Greg's garage having a morning coffee. Steve had to leave to pick up his brother, who was heading offshore that day for the first time ever. Greg told Steve that Wade was also getting ready to go to the rig in two days, and remarked, "That's different ... you and me onshore and our two brothers going offshore."

After he heard about the crash, Steve dropped his wife off at home and rushed to Greg's. He was panicking and in a state of disbelief, but he showed none of that when he arrived. "By the time I got into Greg's garage, I was trying to downplay the thought Wade could be on the aircraft," he recalls. "As I work closely with helicopters and Cougar directly, I knew I had a few people I could reach out to confidentially, but I would not be told the manifest," which is a list of names of people who would've been on board the helicopter. "One thing I did know very early that day was the life rafts were empty, which some people did not comprehend."

Hour after hour passed and there was no word of the searchers having found any sign of the helicopter or the missing men. Greg doesn't remember eating during that time. He and his wife decided to go for a drive and they stopped at the shoreline, where Greg got out of the truck. "I looked out over the ocean," he says, "and I was thinking 'Jesus, you're out there somewhere ...'

And I was sitting down having a smoke. She got me something to eat but I couldn't eat it. I was too fooled up."

Factual information was slow reaching Greg's house. Wade wasn't technically an offshore worker, as the Hibernia Management and Development Company had hired his employer to do contract work on the rig. The man in charge, Paul Sacuta, had been an offshore engineering supervisor for ExxonMobil before becoming president at Hibernia.

Greg says that when Paul realized that he and Wade's parents were at his home and left out of the loop, he and two other senior managers drove to Greg's. "He came out to my house in the Goulds," Greg says. "There was another couple of people with him, I didn't know who they were. But I knew him. I got a lot of respect for that man. He came into the house and he was kind of taken back at how much support the family had there.

"Like at one point he laid out pamphlets on the table, grief pamphlets. And father, I guess the emotions were getting the better of him, and he didn't mean anything by it, but he said, 'We don't need your pamphlets, we got family here. We got our support. We got our family here.' That was no disrespect to anyone, that was just how his emotions were coming at the time."

Paul must have understood. Instead of packing up his papers and leaving, he stayed and mingled with everyone. He watched as one person cooked a meat stew to keep the friends and relatives fed and another ran out and bought cigarettes for Greg's mother to help calm her. He saw first-hand what Wade meant to them all. "Paul Sacuta, he was the fella who was giving me all the information when stuff was on the go. A star character, he was a really good fellow with the way he conducted himself."

By the end of the first evening, everyone was exhausted but no one wanted to leave Greg's garage. When some did leave, others showed up. Some even stayed there all night, waiting on information and comforting each other.

At one point, Steve's wife called to check on him and he snapped at her in anger. "I recall her calling and telling me she and the boys were worried about me," he says. "There were many calls and messages coming in from all over asking if I was okay, and she asked when I would be coming home. My answer? 'At least I am fucking coming home.'" Steve says that he wished he could take that comment back.

The next evening Greg received the call that took away all hope. "I had to stand up in the kitchen in front of about a hundred people and tell them that it is no longer a rescue mission now, it is a recovery mission."

That realization triggered more anguish. This time, they were left wondering if Wade would ever be found. "All Mother was saying was that she hopes they find his body. She was worried about his body and the other bodies."

It took another day or so but word eventually came that the missing men had been located inside the sunken helicopter. All the bodies, Wade's included, had been successfully recovered. "It was some relief when they got his body," Greg says.

The week that followed was a long, excruciating blur for everyone. "From finding the chopper, bringing it up, the pictures of it coming in through the Narrows," Steve says. "The wakes, the funerals, the graveyards. I remember sitting on the side of the road by myself on Witless Bay Line, coming from Matt Davis's funeral and heading to Wade's wake and breaking my heart all by myself. I just needed to let it out I guess and that was the time and place. I tried to call my wife but I was making no sense at all."

Wade Drake

After spending some time on the ocean on the morning of March 12, 2009, Peter Drake was only too happy to get back to his apartment in Arnold's Cove for a rest.

He was inside for a few minutes when the telephone rang. It was Evelina, his older sister. She was relaying a telephone message she had just received—she couldn't remember who had called—but the person said there was trouble with the helicopter their brother Wade had flown on that morning. It had been forced to land in the water. "They had to ditch the helicopter but everyone is okay. That's what Evelina told me," Peter recalls. "And she said a supply boat was on the way to get them." Evelina said she'd call back if she heard anything else.

The call left Peter in a daze as he sat there waiting for another telephone call and an update.

Gertie heard the news from her babysitter. She was dropping off her son Liam so that she could go to a doctor's appointment. The sitter blurted it out innocently, not knowing that Gertie's brother had left for the offshore that morning by helicopter. "Did you hear about the chopper that went down this morning?," her sitter asked. The question struck Wade's sister like a bolt of lightning. "And I said, 'What?' And she said, 'Yeah, there's a chopper down.' I said, 'My God, Wade went out this morning!'"

At the nursing home where she worked, Wade's wife, Wanda, was settling in for her eight-hour shift shortly after dropping the children off at school. She hadn't spoken to Wade before he got on the helicopter for the flight. The workers weren't allowed to take a cellphone on the rig, so Wade would leave his in his truck, which was parked in Cougar's storage area.

Around 10 a.m. Wanda was on a coffee break chatting with her co-workers about a camping trip she was hoping to take that summer. The problem was that Wade wasn't a camper and preferred a hotel to a tent. She was telling her friends about her dilemma and wondering how she could convince Wade to buy a trailer so that they could go to a campground. "And I came out of the coffee room and sat down at my desk," she says, "and, you know, life was normal."

Then a co-worker approached. "Is Wade gone offshore today?," she asked Wanda. "This was 11 o'clockish … and I looked at the time and I said, 'He should be out there now.'" Wanda responded that she expected a call from him any minute to say that he had made it safely to the SeaRose. That's when she noticed the look on her co-worker's face.

"And I'm like, 'Why? Why?' And she didn't speak, she just took me to the TV room where this big humongous TV was … all I could remember seeing was two Cougar helicopters on this big massive TV and how there was a crash."

Wanda struggles to find the best words to describe how she felt inside at that moment. "I just went dead. I just went … I just lost … no feeling … I came back to my office and I was trying to call somebody, and I couldn't get the numbers right and when I looked up, my mom and dad was standing in my office door."

Her parents didn't know that it was Wade's helicopter, but her father was in his shed half an hour away when he heard on the radio there had been an offshore crash, and they rushed to be with Wanda, just in case. "And they were there," Wanda recalls, "and they were like, 'We don't know if it's Wade, we just know it's a helicopter, but we come anyway.'"

But in her heart and in her mind, Wanda knew there wouldn't be good news. "And I was like, 'I knows it's him.' I just thought the worse. I just had the feeling."

Wanda tried to keep working, but she couldn't concentrate. Other people received word of the crash from the company but, because of a mix-up, Wanda didn't get a telephone call. "Apparently the company was trying to get a hold of me but they were calling the wrong workplace," she says. "They were calling the hospital instead of the nursing home and so all this news was going around me and I was almost like I felt I was the last to know."

Wanda wasn't the only one confused in the moments after hearing the news. Gertie didn't know what to think or who to turn to for information after hearing about it from her babysitter. She called her brothers and sisters, and the information they were hearing was hopeful: the helicopter did go into the water but everyone appeared to be safe. They had also heard that people were gathering at the Comfort Inn, next to Cougar's headquarters. Gertie went there and, when she walked into the hotel, she knew from the sight of people crying that something serious had happened.

Still, Gertie tried not to give up hope because she knew that Wade and the other passengers on board the helicopter were wearing survival suits—which was mandatory—and if they were floating around in a lifeboat or in the water, they'd be picked up. She believed the large, orange flotation suits would offer at least a few hours' protection from the cold Atlantic Ocean.

But there was the possibility Wade wasn't going to make it, and Gertie called Peter, sobbing. Peter comforted her. "My thoughts were that if they were in the water on the chopper or if Wade was in the water, then they got no worries because Wade was going to survive," he explains. "Because he was that type. Strong. Hyper. So, I thought if anyone was going to survive, it was him. That's what I was thinking."

Wanda had the same thought. She finally found the telephone number for Cougar and called the office. "And they told me that they thought they were in life rafts. So, I held on to that little string of hope, that I thought they were in life rafts."

Wanda's parents helped her pick up the children at school so that they could go home and be together. "The TV was on in my house while I was waiting to hear news," she says, "because someone was packing a bag for me to go to St. John's ... so I just remember seeing the news with the survivor, that person on a stretcher, I remembers, and our TV was really, really big in my house too. I was really, really trying to see if it was him. Because I thought if there's anyone that's going to be on that stretcher, it's going to be Wade."

But it wasn't Wade. And no other news came for several hours. Wanda made the four-hour drive to St. John's with her parents and her girls. "I used them as my rock," she says. "I didn't hide the facts from them or hide the situation from them. I know they were like seven and 11 but we just clung to each other and just, you know, used each other to get through everything that was going on around us."

Some parents left their children at home when they went to the hotel, but Wanda could not leave her girls in Fortune. Feeling lost and disoriented, she walked into the hotel, where she didn't know a soul, holding each girl's hand tightly for her own comfort as much as theirs.

Officials involved in the search offered one tiny but telling piece of information late in the afternoon. They had located one body. That of Allison Maher. "I think it was around four o'clock that evening, they came in and said that they found a body," Gertie recalls. "Well, then it hit me—this is bad. So, then I just lost it. I thought, 'Oh my God, this is not good.' You know, waiting for someone to say they found another body. And then I was picturing all of them floating around, dead in the water."

By then, Peter, Wade's older brother, had arrived in St. John's. "I left Arnold's Cove and drove the two hours to St. John's," he says, "and I don't remember anything about the drive to St. John's....I knows I left Arnold's Cove and I knows I ended up in the Comfort Inn. I don't remember anything else."

As the hours passed, stories started circulating among the families and in the media. Some fact. Some speculation. No one knew where the blurred lines between hope and despair started and ended. Being at the hotel and surrounded by so many other people with just as many unanswered questions as he and his sisters and brothers had, and approaching each other desperately, seeking any amount of new information to cling to, Peter slowly realized that no relief or good news was coming. "When we got in there and started hearing different things, it started to sink in. And I guess I held on to that until I couldn't hang on to it anymore."

Wanda was exhausted. She was staying at the hotel with her parents and her children and the anguish was taking its toll. So was the lack of information coming from officials, who held briefing after briefing but never really said anything to assuage their grief, as far as she was concerned. "And I remember they had those meetings ... and I was just tired ... just tired of them beating around the bush and not finding them, and you have to know me, I'm a really quiet person, a total opposite of Wade and if Wade didn't like something, he didn't mind telling somebody he didn't like something where I would just say, 'That's fine.'"

It was during one of those meetings that Wanda couldn't take it anymore and a completely different side of her emerged. She even shocked herself. "And so I remember being in one of those meetings and sick of listening to them saying, 'they didn't find anything, they didn't find anything,' and the whole meeting room was filled, seemed like to me there was hundreds of people, and I stood up in front of everybody and I said that our husbands were down in the helicopter and what were they looking for, what were they waiting for? 'Go down and get them,' is what I said."

Wanda says she felt—as strange as it sounds—that Wade, with his strong, outspoken personality, was speaking through her. "I was really angry … and it was like Wade was telling me to tell them to stop looking on the surface of the water, they're not on the surface of the water … they looked and they looked … and it was like … it seemed liked nothing was getting done and I felt like they weren't finding anything, they were searching the surface of the water and something in me made me stand up and tell them to go down and look in the helicopter! It was like he was telling me to tell them to find them, to go down and get them."

The room was filled with people, most of them strangers to one another, listening in awe to Wanda's outburst. One of them, Lori Chynn, John Pelley's wife, who had been sitting quietly and nervously watching and listening, was impressed at people like Wanda who spoke up. It was Wanda's remark "Go down and get them" that jolted Lori into the reality of her husband's fate. "Something told me to speak up and set the fire," Wanda says. "I'm sure they were doing what they could. But being there from our perspective and the families were just sick and tired of hearing … no news, no news, no news. I know they were doing what they could but being, I guess, a grieving wife I couldn't listen to it anymore and I got up and I remembers bringing tears to one of the—because it was a very stressful time for everybody—to one of the TSB members. I felt really bad about it afterwards because he was upset about it as well afterwards. But it was really hard listening to them, like I knew they weren't coming back, but at that point we just needed our husbands back."

When Wanda stopped speaking, there was total silence. "I remembers it being not a sound in the room when I stood up," she says. "Not a sound. I think

I said it for everybody. All these people were strangers to me, they were people I had never met, like I did not know Heather Warren, I did not know Janet Breen, I did not know any of those wives. I did not know these people. But there were people who came to me afterwards and said to me, 'you said what I wanted to say.' Don't get me wrong—they were doing the best they could, the TSB and the RCMP and all these people, but it was so hard.… And the next morning they finally went down and they found them. They were there."

When the searchers announced that it was no longer a rescue mission but rather a recovery, Peter's heart sank. He loses his breath and struggles to hold back tears as he recalls that moment. "Oh, that stung a lot," he whispers, his voice cracking and fading at the same time.

They spent most of the next few days at the hotel waiting as search efforts turned from trying to locate and rescue the 16 to trying to recover their bodies.

Coincidentally, a friend of Peter's was one of the people at the controls of a remotely operated underwater vehicle (ROV) sent underwater to pull alongside the helicopter and beam back images of the scene inside. "Of course, I had to ask," he says. "All they could see was the orange suits. They were all up forward but they stayed in their seats. They stayed in their seats."

Saying that out loud causes Peter to tilt his head, lift his moistening eyes slightly, and stare away, lost in thought. "It still seems so surreal," he says after a while. "Even then it seemed so surreal. With everything going on. Even now it's surreal when I think about it. Because we didn't get to see his body. We never did get to see him or just touch him."

Not getting to see Wade's body just to prove to himself that it was indeed his brother haunts Peter to this day. The funeral homes urged families to have closed caskets.

Peter's greatest regret is that he didn't ask if the casket could be opened just long enough for him to see Wade one last time or even just to take a close look at his hands. "I wish they had to have opened it up," he says, "and if I could've seen his hands, I would have known it was him. Because he got the same hands that I got. The shape of them and the way that they are. Wade's hands was like my hands. If you'd see Wade's hands and see mine, you'd think they were the same. It's weird. But I wish now that I had to have asked to at least see that. There was so much we were trying to deal with. But I wish I had to see his hands. I would've known ..." His voice trails off and he starts to cry again.

Gertie understands. "They're known as the 'Drake hands,'" she explains. "The hair, their knuckles, the freckles. They have distinct hands."

She reaches out and rubs her brother's shoulder to comfort him. "It gives you closure when you can see him," she says quietly.

Burch Nash

After dropping her husband, Burch, off at the airport in St. John's, Marilyn Nash drove home, got the children off to school, and went back to bed. She was asleep when a loud bang woke her up. She looked out the window but couldn't see any activity or construction to account for such a noise.

Minutes later, the telephone rang. The number calling was Burch's workplace and she wondered why they'd be phoning when they knew he would be in the air at that time, on his way to the SeaRose.

When she answered, she knew right away that something was amiss. "They asked me who was home with me," she says, her voice breaking as she remembers the details of the call, "and I knew there was something wrong because she kept saying, 'Don't turn on the TV.'"

The woman who called also asked for her street address, which frustrated an already confused Marilyn. "And I didn't know the lady and she said, 'We're coming over, what's your address?' And I was like, saucy, and I said, 'He's your employee, then you should friggin' know where our address is to.'" Finally, the caller relented and told her what was happening at sea. Marilyn didn't know what to think, so she called Glenda, Burch's sister. "I was trying to get a hold of her because I didn't know what to do because it was only me and my dog at home and I'm sure the dog thought that I was losing it because I was going around with my dog in my arms and screaming and yelling, 'What's going on?'"

Burch's father, Harold, was in Glenda's driveway in Paradise cleaning out the back of his son-in-law's truck when he heard a scream and someone saying, "Burchy's gone! Burchy's helicopter is down!"

Harold, age 74, rushed inside. Glenda stood in the kitchen near the sink with the telephone up to her ear. "She was screeching," he recalls. "And then she told her mother and she started screeching."

Harold didn't know who was on the other end of the line, but he knew they weren't delivering good news. "'Burchy's gone,' that's what I heard. 'Burchy's helicopter is down.'" He moves his head slowly back and forth and his eyes moisten as he speaks under his breath. "My sonny boy, that was some day. It's something you never forget ..."

Harold and Burch's mother, Marjorie, were staying with Glenda and her husband, Claude, about 10 minutes down the road from Burch's home. They had been in town from their home in Fortune for some time. Glenda was fighting breast cancer and undergoing chemotherapy and her parents wanted to be with her to help out. Marjorie, age 71, had had hip replacement surgery a few weeks earlier and was in for a check-up.

After talking to Marilyn, Glenda called Claude, who had left just moments before. He was on a business call in his truck when Glenda buzzed in. "I said, 'I gotta go my wife is buzzing on the other line,'" Claude recalls. "And then Glenda was there and, oh my God, the screeching and the bawling in the background. And she was screeching and saying, 'Burchy is on the chopper and the chopper has crashed!' And she repeated it and I heard her mother in the background and I said, 'I'll be right back.' And I made a left at the stop sign and came back again. By the time I got home, my jeez, everything was up in arms."

The telephone rang a second time. This time it was Glenda's doctor, a cancer specialist at the Health Sciences Centre, with Glenda's latest test results. The scan indicated that the treatments were working. Her doctor couldn't understand why Glenda was crying after receiving such good news. "And she said, 'I'm giving you good news, Glenda, why are you crying?'" Glenda explained what was happening and the doctor tried to reassure her by saying that she knew about the crash and at the hospital they were hearing that everyone was okay.

Glenda found the mixed messages tough to handle. "That was the hard part, not knowing. Not having the information. I kept saying to Mom, 'Look, it's gone down but they say it's a good chance everybody's safe because they have life preservers and they got these suits and all this kind of stuff.'"

In the midst of all the chaos, they heard a noise in the next room just off the kitchen, a room that was empty at the time. "A picture fell in my living room, on my console table," Glenda says. "And I went in because I heard in my living room like something had fallen, so I went in and the picture is down."

It was a family photo of Glenda, Burch, and their parents that was taken at Burch's house a few years before. "And I came out and Mom said, 'what happened?' And I said, 'My picture fell down.' And you know what my mother said? She said, 'He's gone.'" An old superstition says if pictures fall off walls, then bad news has happened. Marjorie saw it as an omen, but Glenda quickly dismissed her mother's fears. "I said, 'Oh my God, no, Mom, we don't know anything. Don't jump to conclusions.'"

Later that day, at the hotel where families had gathered, when Marilyn heard the television announcer say that the lifeboat was found, but was empty, she started shaking. Her blood pressure spiked and an ambulance was called and rushed her to hospital.

As the hours ticked by and there was still no sign of the missing men, Claude became frustrated. "They were saying it was a controlled landing. Like, who came up with that? I have no idea because I think that gave everybody a lot of confidence," he says. "My thoughts of a controlled landing are that they knew they were going in and they managed to get it down, right? It's the same thing with a boat, all hands know we have a second and we have to get off, or try to get off. That's how I perceive that."

But with no sign of the helicopter and no positive word from searchers, Claude couldn't understand why officials would have told people it was a controlled landing on the water.

As the search changed from a rescue to a recovery, reality settled in. Glenda would look at her father and her heart would break for him. He had lost his father, a fisherman, to the sea when he was just two years old. His body was never found. Now, his only son was lost to the same ocean. "It went through my mind and I'm sure it goes through my father's mind," she says.

After days of anguish and pain and tears all Harold wanted was to make sure that Burch was out of the water and returned home for a proper burial.

Then, four days after the crash, the call came. "They phoned Glenda's Monday night after supper and said they had Burch's body," Marjorie says. Harold finishes her sentence, "He was the ninth one that was brought up."

Harold wanted to be sure it really was Burch's body retrieved from 500 feet down in the Atlantic Ocean, but he couldn't bring himself to go inside the funeral home to look at his son. He knew the damage that water could do to a body.

So instead, he asked Marilyn to look for the one thing that would confirm for him that his son had been found: his high school ring. Burch always wore it. The words Fortune Collegiate were engraved on the gold-plated ring. "Everything goes through your mind," he says, "and I said, 'make sure the ring is on his finger because that's how I'll know it's him.' Because, you know, down at the bottom of the ocean for four days you know, I mean you know as well as I do that …" He pauses for a long time. "They're disfigured, right?"

Harold waited outside in the car and a few minutes later Marilyn returned. "Yes, the ring is on his finger," she said to him, "and it says Fortune Collegiate."

In that moment Harold felt a sense of relief. Unlike his father's body all those decades before, Burch's had been found and brought back home. "When she came out and said he had the ring on, I was relieved," Harold explains. "You're darn right, because I knew it was him. Because there was no one that was on that helicopter that was in Fortune Collegiate. And his mother had given him his ring when he was a young boy and he still had it on his finger."

And the $20 bill his mother had given him the night before he left to get a morning coffee at Tim Hortons was still inside his pocket.

The irony of how Burch died wasn't lost on Glenda. She often thought during those days and in the days since about how her brother's life ended the way it had begun, just after his birth more than four decades earlier: in a helicopter.

The funeral was held in Marystown, a 45-minute drive down the road from Burch's hometown. After the service, Marjorie and Harold and the others followed closely behind the hearse as it travelled to Fortune, taking Burch home one last time. "I give God thanks for that," Harold says. "At least I knows where he's to."

Kenneth MacRae

Ken MacRae's daughter Michelle loves to dance.

In high school, she was drawn to the arts. A career in dancing was all she dreamed of. It wasn't a surprise that at 14 and in Grade 9 she'd be found after school in the audio-visual room of West Kings District High School. The AV room is tucked away in the basement of the building. Children gather there mid-afternoon because West Kings, in Auburn, Nova Scotia, was the only school in the Annapolis Valley that let children out at 2 p.m.

Michelle was with other theatre students, rehearsing for the school production of *Footloose*, on the afternoon of March 12, 2009. At around 4 p.m., her teacher asked to see her outside the classroom. Michelle was ecstatic. She thought the good news she was hoping for was finally about to come. "So, he called me out in the hallway," Michelle says. "And I was really excited, I was thinking, 'He's going to give me a speaking part!' because I was just in the chorus, I was a dancer."

But there would be no speaking part. Instead, she received devastating news delivered by a family friend. "One of my best friend's dad was there," she says, "and he's a padre in the military and he was wearing his full uniform and everything." He told Michelle that there had been a helicopter crash and her father was on the aircraft. Michelle's mind reeled. "I just remember walking out and up the stairs and out the doors with him and I didn't cry the whole time." She doesn't remember whether he spoke as they walked. All she remembers is his hand on her back gently guiding her outdoors and to his car; they drove to her home, about seven houses down the street.

When Michelle opened the door and walked inside, the situation became very real. "And I saw my mom and as soon as I saw my mom," Michelle pauses for a long time, as if reliving that moment, "we just hugged and cried."

Then began the long wait for information and answers. "You know, the search went on until, I think, sundown the next day and I think I was just going stir crazy and I just wanted everything to be normal. I maintained hope for a bit. I just wanted it to be normal."

For Michelle, normal meant returning to school. But her mother wouldn't allow it. "I tried to go to school the next day, I just wanted to have a sense of normal in my life, despite all the turmoil. And my mom kept everything calm and wouldn't let me leave the house."

Eventually, her mother relented and let her go to the school to pick up her homework. "So, I went in and talked to my teachers and got all my school work and they were like, 'No, don't worry. You don't have to do it. It's okay.' And I was like, 'No, I'm going to do my assignments. I'm not special. I'm not different.'"

By then everyone in the school knew about what had happened. "I remember one of my friends seeing me and gave me a big hug. But I didn't tell him and I said, 'How do you know?' But my teacher told me that everyone— my high school principal and all my teachers—had sat down and talked about it, and how to handle me and all this stuff."

It wasn't just her friends who were talking about it. The media spotlight quickly shone on her neighbourhood, down her street, and right at her house.

"So, there was news cars parked outside of our house and they parked in the neighbours' driveways," she recalls. "And our property was a three-acre property and our driveway is, like, a half-acre, it's pretty long. So, they'd park at the end of it."

All the attention became overwhelming and at one point her mother sent her and the children shopping to get their mind off everything that was going on. "My mom sent us to the mall and she gave us the car, which is a rarity. And we went to the mall and I remember the media car followed us a couple of kilometres down from the house."

Three provinces away, Michelle's sister, 22-year-old Alyssa, was at work at the Starbucks on the campus of the University of Ottawa, where she was a supervisor. She had two hours left in her shift when she received a strange telephone message from her close friend. "Diane called me at work and said 'Will is coming to pick you up,'" Alyssa says, "and it was still two hours before we close so I said, 'what's going on?' and she said, 'he'll tell you when he gets there.'" Alyssa insisted that Diane explain why she was being so mysterious. "And I said, 'don't mess with me, you can't leave somebody in suspense like that, don't mess with me, come on!'"

That's when Diane revealed that Alyssa's family had called and asked if she would go and be with Alyssa when she received the news. "And so then I went into the back of the store crying and my staff was being super supportive. I was hyperventilating and everything." She shivers as she recalls the moment. "Because you still don't know anything at that point; your dad was in a helicopter crash, they're still looking, they haven't found anything, you need to call your mom, Will's coming to pick you up."

Alyssa went to be with her brother, who also lived in Ottawa. She didn't even know her father had flown to Newfoundland the day before. "So, I spent the evening with my brother and my ex-husband," she says. "We went to one of his friend's house and just basically cried together, and waited, and cried."

The next day arrangements were made for Alyssa to fly home to Nova Scotia. She waited with Michelle and the rest of their family for news from Newfoundland. But the wait was long, and the longer it went on, the more Alyssa's mind played tricks on her. "There's even times when I made up stories in my head," she explains. "Like when you're going to bed at night and you're imagining that there's some illustrious spy movie where he had to fake his own death or some shit like that." She knew that wasn't possible, but she believes that it was her way of coping when neither searchers nor company officials had any real hope or information they could offer to the family. "Like, trying to build any imaginary principle in your head where he was still here. That it wasn't real. That it didn't happen. I think on some level that's a coping thing ... it's just blind hope on some level, regardless of whether it makes sense or not," she says.

Alyssa and Michelle's aunt, Lee-Ann Brubacher, found those days of waiting "heart-wrenching." She and other relatives sat around the living room staring at the television screen, much of the time in shock, hanging on to every word the hosts and the news reporters said about the ongoing search. "Those four days waiting to hear word and hoping against hope that his survival suit could withstand the cold North Atlantic, and as time went on and our hopes faded it was just—it just became dark."

Thousands of kilometres away in Fort McMurray, Jason Gulliver was in the middle of his workday. He was in the northern Alberta community carrying out inspections for his employer, FGG Inspections, when the dispatcher at his office called. "He said, 'I just got some bad news. The chopper Ken was on went down. We don't know anything as of yet but, you know, I just wanted to call and let you know.'"

Jason's heart sank. He was familiar with the weather off the east coast, especially in late winter, and what it meant for the chances of Ken and the others being rescued from the water. "You know, I didn't really think anything positive," he says. "You think the worst. Because it's the North Atlantic and I grew up on the east coast and I know what it's like, and, you know, those survival suits were a false sense of security."

Jason's worry was also based on his experience with cold-weather training. "I know winter survival. I trained to be a wildlife officer. I trained to work for DFO and, you know, if a guy goes overboard … if you don't get him out of that water within two minutes, hypothermia sets in and you're pretty much done anyways. So, again a false sense of security with these choppers going back and forth, you know, if they go down, there's nothing positive ever going to come out of it."

Still, like the others, Jason held out hope. "I think that job got cut short and we went back to Edmonton and waited around for word. And, of course, there was news coverage 24 hours a day. I think we were all stuck to the TVs waiting to hear something."

When word came that Ken's body and the bodies of the others had been recovered, he and some colleagues flew to Auburn. "I'll give FGG kudos for that one. They stepped up and they got flights for all the guys who knew Ken and hung out with Ken and we all went back. And that was a positive thing, I guess, out of anything. We all flew out of Edmonton and into Nova Scotia and we all went to Greenwood for the memorial service."

That service wasn't easy to attend. Jason barely spoke to anyone while he was there. "It was probably one of the hardest things I had to do, for sure. I mean, I was lost for words most of the time. There's not really much you can say or do that's going to comfort anyone in that situation. It's not like it's somebody who is terminally ill or it's old age or it's a natural cause, it's a tragic event where you just can't—you don't even know what to say to somebody."

Jason sat in the church and quietly accepted that his friend and hunting buddy was gone. Never again would they have the chance to go on another early morning trip to the bush to do something they both loved.

The Investigation

It was a total of eight days from the time searchers started looking for the helicopter and the missing 16 people until the wreckage was recovered and returned to St. John's, where investigators quickly discovered the cause of the crash.

The searchers were challenged in the hours after the helicopter went into the water: the aircraft's emergency locator transmitter wasn't sending out a distress signal and neither were the personal locator beacons worn by the missing passengers and crew. Also, it was mid-March, when weather in the North Atlantic is unpredictable at best. They could only hope that any storms or other harsh, late winter weather would remain at bay until the search and rescue, or recovery, produced results.

The search continued all day Thursday and into Friday. By 8 p.m. Friday, with no sign of any of the missing passengers and crew or the helicopter itself, the Joint Rescue Coordination Centre called off the search.

An offshore supply vessel, the *Atlantic Osprey*, owned by Husky Energy, was enlisted to help find and recover the helicopter. While sailing over the site of the last known coordinates on March 13, the day after the crash, the

Osprey's sonar detected a large object 169 metres (just over 500 feet) below the surface.

The next day, the vessel returned to the area. Aboard were investigators from the TSB as well as officials from Cougar, Sikorsky, and the RCMP. The *Osprey* was equipped with ROVs with cameras attached. The relatively small robots are connected to the vessel by cables.

Within a few hours, the ROVs confirmed that the object at the bottom of the ocean was the missing helicopter. Initially, the cameras indicated that the bodies of upwards of 10 people were inside. By late that evening, word came that all 16 missing men were inside the helicopter, still strapped in their seats.

The ROVs retrieved the bodies by lifting the seats out of the chopper, one by one. By March 17, the work was complete and the bodies transferred to the medical examiner's office in St. John's, where drowning was determined to be the cause of death.

A large crane aboard the *Osprey* with the capability of lifting up to 50 tonnes pulled the wreckage from the ocean floor and placed it in a cage, which was then raised to the surface. The recovery went well and the crew retrieved 95 per cent of the helicopter.

The wreckage was transported to St. John's, where it was sent to the airport and placed inside a provincial government hangar. There, the helicopter was dismantled and the parts laid out on the cement floor of the large building.

On the morning of March 20, eight days after the crash, the examination of the wreckage began. Investigators had a starting point. The first sign of trouble with Flight 491 came from a visual and verbal warning indicating that the aircraft was running dangerously low on oil. A similar incident had occurred in Australia less than a year earlier, involving the same make of helicopter, the S-92. That problem was eventually traced to mounting studs that had cracked off from the oil filter bowl. Investigators in St. John's first turned their attention to the helicopter's main gearbox and attached oil filter.

Within hours, they confirmed that two of the three titanium mounting studs that attached the oil filter bowl assembly to the main gearbox housing were broken. The discovery alerted those in the hangar that morning who were familiar with the incident in Australia.

In July 2008, a chopper operated by Canadian Helicopters Corporation was transporting 16 people from an offshore oil facility to Broome, in western Australia. The aircraft was 6,000 feet in the air and had been flying for 90 minutes when suddenly visual and verbal warnings indicated that the oil pressure had dropped. The crew immediately began a descent and found a suitable place to land within seven minutes, but, the captain said, had he been flying over water and there was no secondary indication that the gearbox was about to fail, he would have continued toward land at a low altitude.

Examination of the chopper in Australia revealed that two of the three studs mounted on the oil filter bowl assembly had cracked and the bowl had become partially separated, causing a total loss of oil. One of those failed studs had been repaired less than a month previously.

The knowledge of that incident eight months earlier and seeing the broken studs from the Cougar wreckage led investigators to believe that they had uncovered the cause of the crash of Flight 491.

After a safety review of the Australian incident, Sikorsky issued an "Alert Service Bulletin" the following January, six weeks before the Cougar crash. It required that the titanium studs be replaced with steel mounting studs. Operators were told that the change was to be done within 1,250 flying hours or within one year.

The TSB issued a news release the day the fractured studs were discovered on the Cougar helicopter. The statement said the Federal Aviation Administration (FAA), the agency responsible for regulating aviation in the US, would be issuing an emergency order that the titanium studs on all S-92s be replaced with steel studs before the helicopters were allowed to fly again.

Within four days, more than half of the S-92s around the world had the existing mounting studs removed and replaced. Others made the change shortly thereafter.

Twenty-three months after the accident, the TSB released its final report into the crash of Flight 491. It concluded that the helicopter initially ran into trouble when one of the titanium mounting studs that locked the oil filter bowl onto the main gearbox cracked because of fatigue. The stud, similar to a bolt, had weakened from repeated oil filter replacements and re-use of the original nuts.

The fracture in that stud put increased pressure on a second stud and eventually the second one also broke. "This led to a total loss of oil," the TSB concluded, "which 11 minutes later ultimately brought the helicopter down."

The report outlined what it called a "complex web of 16 factors" that played a role in the crash, including the overall design of the helicopter, maintenance procedures, ambiguous flight manual directions regarding massive oil loss, and pilot training.

There was also an in-depth look at the aircraft's certification. The helicopter was approved as having the capability to operate for 30 minutes after losing all lubrication from the main gearbox. The certification was granted because the possibility of such a loss was considered extremely remote. Although the Cougar pilots gave no indication that they believed the helicopter had a run-dry capability—the industry term for being able to continue operating with only trace amounts of oil—the TSB recommended that aviation regulators in North America and Europe remove the "extremely remote" provision from its rules and urged the FAA to "look at today's operating environments—Hibernia, the Arctic, the North Sea, any of these extreme locations—and decide whether even 30 minutes is enough time."

It also recommended that Transport Canada prohibit transport helicopters from flying when the seas are too rough to permit safe ditching, and that the agency require that underwater breathing devices be mandatory on flights over water where survival suits are required.

Of those four recommendations, only two were implemented by 2018: flights are postponed if rough seas prevent safe ditching and emergency underwater air supply is available on flights over water. The board submitted regular requests to the regulatory agencies for updates on the status of the other recommendations involving the extremely remote rule and the adequacy of the 30-minute run-dry time. It received answers that were not totally satisfactory to the board or, in some cases, hadn't received a reply at all. "The risks identified ... have not abated and remain significant," the board reported in March 2016.

The status of the recommendations was then labelled as dormant. The TSB no longer carries out regular inquiries into where the recommendations stand as it has concluded that "continued assessments will not likely yield further results."

While the TSB studied the cause of the crash, a public inquiry was held in the province to determine how to reduce the risk of flying to the offshore, led by retired Supreme Court judge Robert Wells. The hearings included public presentations by some grieving family members—less than a year after the crash—who expressed their concerns and sometimes their quiet anger during the sessions.

One of the early recommendations to be put in place from that inquiry involved lowering Search and Rescue response times from about 45 minutes to less than 20 minutes.

Within months, a lawsuit was launched against the manufacturer of the helicopter and its related companies on behalf of many of the families and the lone survivor. It was settled a short time later, but no details of the financial settlements have ever been released.

The Legacy

John Pelley

It's a simple enough question: How are you doing now? But before she answers, Lori Chynn takes a deep breath and a long pause. When she does speak, her words are insightful. "The pain is always there," she says. "It's like losing a limb or something. Like, you learn to manage, you learn to cope. But the hurt and the scars are always there."

It has been a long road for Lori to be able to describe the impact of the death of her husband, John Pelley. A high school counsellor and psychologist had been suddenly thrust into dealing with the kind of pain and grief students would reach out to her about.

"Now I have a deeper understanding of how your brain reacts and how people react differently. It was a real dark place and it took a long time. But little by little, having your voice heard," she explains, "it's like the kids who come to counselling to see me, you know, sometimes it's just somebody listening." Lori realized that she wasn't just experiencing the mental effects of grief; it was also physical and she wasn't eating or sleeping properly. "For almost 15 years before that, I was used to being on the other side. It's given me a different view of what the other side is like. And it's a very dark place to be. The whole situation has made me a better counsellor, a better psychologist, to be honest with you."

Having her voice heard is important to Lori. In the months after the crash, hers became a familiar public voice in a quest for improved safety for flights travelling to the offshore. She spoke on radio. She went on supper-hour television news programs. She was interviewed by newspapers. And when the government of Newfoundland and Labrador appointed a former Supreme Court judge to oversee an inquiry into finding ways to make helicopter transportation safer for offshore workers, Lori made a presentation at the public hearings.

That was just 11 months after John's death. Her words, she testified, were guided by thoughts of John and what he would have done had he been in her position. "You see, my husband, a very proud, intelligent, and articulate man, was known for speaking up for what he believed in," she told the inquiry. "John gives me the strength to be here today."

Lori's comments were reflective and thoughtful as she told the inquiry about her husband's passion for life and his love of the outdoors, especially salmon fishing, and how she and John led a private and low-key lifestyle in Deer Lake. She talked about his public death and how dealing with the constant reminder of the tragedy through the daily news was difficult. She criticized the decision not to replace the titanium mounting studs as soon as the problem was identified. "In my opinion, the decision to fly the helicopters before waiting to replace the studs was a reactive tactic, not a proactive stance," she said. "I'm sure we are all aware that with knowledge comes responsibility."

There was hardly a sound or movement in the room during her presentation except for the shuffling of papers and the whirring of computers and recording equipment as she questioned why her husband and the other passengers weren't told about the mechanical issues with the S-92 helicopter. She insisted that workers have the right to know that kind of relevant information before they make the decision to fly offshore. "Given John's aversion for flying," she said, "I strongly feel that if he was provided with the information regarding the problems with the helicopter studs, he would have opted not to fly on Flight 491 on March 12, 2009."

Like the other family members of victims who made presentations, Lori's message brought the sometimes very technical, legal sessions down to a personal level that wasn't lost on anyone in the room. "We all have been robbed," she said. "I feel in my heart that this tragedy was preventable. Even though John was a brave and strong man, I fear of what his last moments of that fateful flight were. You see, my husband possessed incredible instincts. I'm sure that he knew what his fate was to be. I just hope and pray that he did not suffer and that his death, along with the deaths of his friends and colleagues, will not be in vain."

Ten years later, Lori says it wasn't her intention to become the voice of concern. But it was the only way she could try to make sense of what happened. She believes that John would have sought out answers that same way had he been in her situation. "It's like I just had to find out more. And that's my type of personality. The more reflecting I do, that's where we were similar. We were very stubborn people who were like, 'No, I have to get to the bottom of this. This doesn't make sense. Why, why, why?' And when I spoke there, it was like floodgates opened up. It was amazing. It was cathartic. It was like, 'Oh my God, I'm ready to take this on.'"

Lori didn't try to speak for anyone but herself. She wanted to explain to the room full of legal, transportation, and offshore oil experts the pain she felt at losing her life partner. "I'm sure there's people offshore and people involved in the helicopter industry who thought I was crazy and didn't know what I was talking about, but I do know what it is like to lose somebody and lose the person that I love the most and never, ever, envisioned being without. It was an awful, awful thing that I would never want anybody to have to go through. I mean, it was a nightmare. People say that when stuff like this happens, but I mean it is. It's this …" she breathes deeply and sighs heavily again while searching for the right words. "It's this dark, dark place."

Shane Fudge, John's buddy from nursing school days, who then joined him working in the offshore, still misses their friendship. He's sure he's not the only one who feels that way. "He had so many different interests," he says. "He was very musically talented, so he had a great group of friends there and he was into sports so he had another group of friends there. And fishing, things like that—so all of the groups and individuals that he hung around with, he always kept in contact, so I think we all felt the same way. Everybody that met him, he made everyone feel close to him and he respected everyone's interest, no matter what."

When he thinks of John today—10 years later—he can still see his face and hear his voice: "Our conversations are still fresh and I don't think I'll ever forget him. He definitely had a positive and profound effect on my life and that's how I want to remember him."

And as for Mark Frost, the friend so jolted by John's death that he sat down and turned his heartbreak into a song, his view on life has changed since the crash. He stopped working at sea, partly because, when the crash happened, he saw how it destroyed the life John and Lori had planned together. "John and Lori had modelled their life around putting a foundation down first," he says. "But it's just unfortunate the way it happened it never got played out that way. To me, it just struck a chord with me. John was 41 when he died. Now I'm at that age. It just really made me feel that you couldn't waste time putting money away for the future. And spending time offshore and building up money is nice but you never can know when something will happen."

Mark felt that he needed to spend more time at home with his family. And in addition to that, he and his wife had a second child, making it harder for him to leave for three weeks at a time. But he hasn't left the oil industry. In fact, his job now focuses on safety in the offshore. After the accident, Mark became involved with a task force that examined when it would be safe for helicopters to start flying offshore again. Those flights had been put on hold after the crash.

Mark was also asked to be part of the Wells inquiry. He started taking safety courses; that work became important to him because it meant that he could make a difference for offshore workers in the future. "I felt really strongly about that," he explains. "If John was going to die, and all the other guys too, I want to make sure that there needs to be something good come out of it. It can't be for nothing. We lost those guys and we have to do something to make sure it doesn't happen again. And you know for their sake and their memory to show that these people died to make it better for everyone else. And I think we did that."

Mark says that people still complain about certain aspects of offshore travel, but much has changed in the decade since the crash. "The suits have got a lot better. The training has got a lot better. The search and rescue response times have got a lot better. The equipment that they have is a lot better. The procedures is a lot better. The pilot's training is a lot better. It's good to see that that happened. And I was proud to see that happen."

To nurture the memory of his good friend, Mark often turns to Facebook. In some cases, individual Facebook pages—such as John's—are still online. The pictures and conversations from when they were alive are visible at the click of a mouse. Mark knows some might think that morbid, but he finds it comforting: "I like the living memorial thing where it's something that's always there, that used to be part of them, that they had and you can see what they wrote, see what people wrote to them."

Mark knows that Lori also often monitors John's Facebook page: "To me, when I go on there, I feel I'm speaking to him and to her," he reflects, "because

I know she can read it and she writes on it sometimes. And I know that ... well, I feel that he can to. It just feels like ... I mean, I know he's not going to write me back but, I don't know, it feels like ... it feels like it's a way I can say something to him sometimes. A connection. And I just enjoy reading what Lori wrote. Or what his brother wrote. Or his mom. I'm glad it's there. I hope it don't go away."

And there's another reason Mark likes John's Facebook page: the reminders and other surprises that often just appear out of nowhere. "Like, the other day, a memory just popped up," he says. "Facebook prompts you sometimes with, you know, '10 years ago this happened ...' and one popped up of me and John and Greg at that golf tournament. Oddly enough, I was playing golf the same day and it was the only time I golfed this year, and the memory popped up that morning. And, I don't know, that's just like a nice little thing sometimes. Even though I could've went back and looked at that picture anytime, it's kind of nice to have it prompt you like that and remind you of an anniversary sometimes."

Stories like that make Lori feel good. She has learned much more about John since he died. She knew that he was a good nurse but she didn't realize his humility and how much people respected him. "John was a thinker," she explains. "When it came to his work, he was very methodical. The doctors, I remember, told me when I was in that dreary hotel for those five days about John's work and how much it was valued. And you know, during that time and thereafter, I'd keep hearing stories and people coming up to me and saying, 'John saved my life. You know, if John didn't get me off the rig when I got there' or whatever, so there were stories that came out after. I mean, I still hear stories now. Corner Brook is a small place and he worked at the hospital. I'll meet people and they are coming up to me and saying, 'You're John Pelley's wife ...' And even at the school people come up to me and say 'John diagnosed me and treated me for something.'"

Lori has created several scholarships in John's memory. One, through the nursing school in Corner Brook, a 30-minute drive from her home in Deer Lake, is awarded to someone interested in studying trauma in nursing. Scholarships have also been set up at Elwood High School in their hometown of Deer Lake. "I thought it would be really nice to put one there. So, his rec hockey team approached me and said they'd like to have a memorial hockey tournament every year and donate money to the scholarship. So, what I do now is I just give them the money I was going to put in and right now we have a nice trust built up and every October they have a memorial tournament that lasts two days ... and the monies raised, we usually give out anywhere from one to three $750 scholarships."

Lori says that it's possibly the largest monetary scholarship at the school, and she's proud that it benefits students about to graduate from high school. "That's a nice little bit of money to go towards their tuition," she says proudly, "or their books or their residence or whatever. So, we've been able to do some good things in his memory and his legacy."

That stadium in Deer Lake where they hung out as teenagers all those years ago—John the hockey player, Lori the young figure skater—now has a bench in the lobby in his name. Lori often drops by to see the young children sitting on the bench. "And it's nice because it's used and it's taken care of. You'll see kids waiting for their parents or sitting down and having a snack, or just hanging out and talking with their friends and it makes me feel ..." She pauses while trying to find the right word and then simply says, "Yeah, it's nice. The smell of the Hodder. I used to always say, 'Oh goodness, that's the best smell ever!' It takes you back, it's good memories."

Lori travels to St. John's every spring on the anniversary of John's death to attend the annual memorial service. But she also travels there to visit the fence where Cougar Helicopters was located. Over the years it has become a makeshift memorial where family and friends place flowers in the days leading up to the anniversary of the crash. A few years back there was a vicious spring windstorm on the day of the anniversary and she was standing at the fence struggling to put up a wreath when Fred Hutton, host of *NTV Evening News,* approached her. "He gets out of his vehicle and helps me put the wreath on and he asked me 'Why do you come here?' And I don't know, it's something we had started the first year and it seems like it's where I need to be. And we stay there for just a few minutes to put the wreath on. It's what I need to do. It's part of my healing. That's my thing because that is the last place he was, really."

Lori sometimes listens to the "beautiful song" Mark wrote in memory of John. She put some of the lyrics on a small plaque near John's grave. The words on his headstone convey how he lived, not how he died. Over the years, Lori has become good friends with Mark's wife. Lori is now working at a different high school but still counselling and guiding young people.

Inasmuch as she can, Lori has started living again. "I'm doing well," she says. "It's taken a long time for me to get here. After the inquiry, I made some decisions to do what I had to do to heal, to have a voice, and to give John a voice. That has made me a stronger person. I went back to work and that was very important to me. We didn't have children, unfortunately, so I had time to do what I had to do. It's given me a different perspective on life. John was the type of person who lived his life to the fullest, and you can ask anybody that.

"I think ... that's where I am. I'm just trying to make the best of each day and try to be grateful for what we had. It's something that's with me forever and it'll always be there. It makes me sad but at the same time, he was a beautiful person and just talking about him makes me smile."

Allison Maher

On a warm summer day, Marjorie Maher is in her kitchen in Aquaforte. She picks up the kettle as steam rises from the spout and prepares to pour a cup of tea. She and Richard are ready to sit down and share stories and memories of Allison. But before the boiling water even splashes into the cup, there's another rush of anguish and Marjorie sits down. Her fingertips rub her eyelids, trying to stop the tears. "I said I wouldn't do this," she says, referring to the crying. "But it's hard ..." Her words barely leave her lips.

Allison's presence in her childhood home is as strong today as it was before the crash. Perhaps even stronger. Her drawings and photographs of her are framed and hanging on the living room and kitchen walls. Her drawings are in almost every room, on the refrigerator, and in the large photo album the family created in her memory.

As Marjorie composes herself, Richard jumps in and talks about his daughter and her beautiful green eyes, auburn hair, and love of laughing. But he too tears up just saying her name. And as he looks around the room at all the pictures, Richard also cries, his sobs heavy as he touches the photo albums filled with her pictures and her drawings. "And that's all they are," he says. "Just pictures. Nothing left. But that's it. The two of them could be gone. Jesus. Brian could be gone too."

Richard shakes his head as he reveals that he came close to losing his only son to an oil-related tragedy. "He almost got killed in Alberta on the oil rig. He was up on the second floor of the drilling platform and he got caught in the drill. And he was going around and around. And they say no one comes out of that."

Brian, only 20 years old, became tangled in a large piece of machinery. "The only thing that saved his life is that the safety harness burst," Richard says. "That was because he was a big fellow. If he was a small fellow, he would've been killed. His shoulder got hauled out of its socket and it threw him off the platform, off the second storey down onto the ground, and he was in hospital for a few days. He was lucky he only got a shoulder injury, but the people there said usually if you got caught in that drill you don't get out."

Brian is nearing 40 now and still working in the offshore industry. He is sometimes sent out to work on rigs for three weeks at a time. "He's doing okay now," Marjorie says. "He had a rough time too. He knows he had to go on, and that's it."

Allison's boyfriend has moved on with his life. Marjorie and Richard think about him often and about how much he and Allison cared for each other and the fun they fit into their short time together.

Allison's friends have also gone on with their lives. But they always contact Marjorie and Richard during special moments of the year: her birthday, Christmas, and on the anniversary of the crash.

Valerie Maher still finds it difficult to believe that her childhood friend is gone, and has been for 10 years. Allison made such a difference in people's lives in the short time she was alive that Valerie wonders how much more she could have done in the past decade. "She could be a mom. I could be a godmother to her child. It was unfortunate what happened, because the Cougar incident took a very precious person from all of our lives and from society itself. I'm sure she could've and would've been a huge impact on a lot of different people and just made such a bonus to society. You know, she was always there to help everyone, always there to be a friend and always there to listen. Allison is stamped on the hearts of many and it's sad that she is no longer with us."

A few years ago, Marjorie's friend Carol Ann O'Neill—who chairs a local artists' co-operative—was visiting, and she took special notice of Allison's drawings around the house. "Oh, I loved it," Carol Ann recalls. "I just saw it and I thought with the art exhibit we do, I said, 'Marge, I think we need to print some of her work,' because I knew there must be a lot of people who would like to have it. And lots of people were interested." There was so much interest that most of the pieces Marjorie and Richard made available sold at the annual art exhibit and sale held on Newfoundland's southern shore, where Marjorie and Richard live. Allison's work has become a regular part of the yearly art show.

A few miles down the road from the Maher house in Aquaforte is a grotto known locally as Mass Rock. It's located behind a local Roman Catholic church in the community of Renews. A string of statues and wooden crosses are built around a small, winding trail and running brook. Allison's parents have placed a memorial and plaque there in her name, near some stone angels and a water fountain that lights up at night. Little knick-knacks, all items that meant something to Allison, are all around it. A small flowerpot filled with daisies, two black wooden cats, a plastic rabbit, and a bright red and black ladybug drawn on a round rock. Marjorie says since Allison's memorial was put there the grotto has become even more popular.

Marjorie hadn't known Allison was considering changing jobs shortly before the accident. "She was kind of thinking about giving it up, her friends told us after," she says. "She never said anything to us. But she used to phone me sometimes in the daytime and I think she was kind of trying to tell me that she was going to be giving it up."

According to Valerie, part of the reason that Allison wanted to get away from working offshore was because she didn't feel safe flying over the ocean, especially when it came to the survival suits workers had to wear during the helicopter flights. "The thing was she used to always complain about the suits, where she was so short," Valerie recalls. "She always used to say, 'My God, that suit don't fit right. You know, like if we ever crashed, jeez, that would never save anyone anyway.'"

Valerie finds it eerie to think about now but she believes Allison had a premonition that something would eventually happen. "It's almost like she had predicted what would take place. About six to eight months before the crash, myself and my friend Marlene went and had our fortunes told. And we went to Allison's house that evening and were telling her about it and gave her the guy's number and she looked at us and said, 'What if I don't have a future? What if there's nothing?' And you know, I think about these things now."

Marjorie also remembers things that meant little before Allison's death but give her pause for thought now. In particular, she remembers the evening before the flight. She was at home watching television and for some reason she couldn't stop thinking about Allison. "I was right restless. A funny old feeling came over me and I was right anxious. So, we were sitting down watching television and I couldn't content myself at all. I don't know what way I got. But you know, it's a funny thing—I was here in the kitchen and I wanted to phone her. I was going to phone her. So, I went over to the phone and it was about 10 o'clock that night."

Marjorie cries as she tells the rest of the story. "And I went to pick up the phone and it was like something pushed me away from the phone. And I went right down and I went to bed. And I slept the whole night."

And then there's Allison's black cat, Skylar. When Allison went to sea for three weeks, Marjorie and Richard would take Skylar to their house. The night before she returned, they'd bring the cat back to her home in Mount Pearl so that she would be waiting in the window when Allison returned the next day. After Allison died, her parents took Skylar in for good.

Whenever someone opens a door, Skylar bolts toward it, in a rush to get outside. But one night, a strange thing happened. "I put on a pair of pyjamas that belonged to Allison and the cat was in the kitchen and the front door was open, and she was running to get out the door, but when she passed me, she just stopped," Marjorie says. "And she came back and started smelling the pyjamas. The only way I could content her was to bring her downstairs where I had some blankets belonging to Allison. And the poor thing was so confused, she was smelling Allison but she couldn't find her."

Skylar is now about 15 years old and Richard believes there are still times when the cat "is walking around like she's looking for Allison."

Marjorie also thinks about Alison's knee pain. It had been troubling her for some time and Richard convinced her to see a doctor about it. "You could hear it cracking. The doctor said, 'You can't work like that. You've got to stay off work.' And she said, 'No, I can't stay off work.'" The morning of the flight, the pain was bothering her. But Marjorie says Allison persisted in going to sea. "Her boyfriend didn't really want her to go out because her knee was hurting. But she was so determined and so strong, and that's the way she was. And he said he woke up and she was asleep and he said, 'I hope she stays asleep.' And he was hoping and hoping she hadn't had [the alarm] set, but by jingles he said, she had the clock alarmed and she was up and she was going."

Richard wonders if Allison had taken the doctor's advice whether she would have been at home resting her leg on March 12 instead of flying to the rig. The what-ifs are haunting and the anger is still strong, especially for

Richard. As far as he's concerned, he says repeatedly, "Allison would be alive today if Search and Rescue had to be in St. John's."

But despite the lingering questions, the couple focus on the positive and remember how many people loved their daughter as much as they did. They keep a huge collection of notes and emails and condolences people sent to them. Most knew Allison. Many didn't. But they just reached out to say they were sorry to hear about her death. "We could sit down for hours and read this," Marjorie says. "Every now and then I picks it up and reads some of it. Some people had poems written about her. People that didn't even know her."

Richard also finds the collection comforting. "I don't know how many thousands of mass cards we had." Marjorie finishes his thought: "Oh my God, we had a huge, huge, huge gift bag. Holy heavens! It was the biggest funeral we've ever seen on the southern shore. There were people who couldn't even get into the church."

Allison's sunny personality led to the emotional outpouring, Richard says. "Wherever she went, she made friends because she was always jovial. She was always teasing people to make them laugh."

Allison's house in Mount Pearl was eventually sold. Some days though, Marjorie and Richard drive down her street, past where she lived. "We often drive by the house, just for a spin and just to have a look at it," Marjorie says. "Her grandmother went down one time and saw a black cat in the window and couldn't believe it!"

They think about Allison's love of animals, the focus of many of her drawings. Cats, dogs, horses. Especially ladybugs. Marjorie says that as a child Allison was obsessed with the tiny beetle that is considered to be a sign of good luck. "When she was a little girl, a ladybug would come on the window.... And she'd get a dropper and she'd go in and put little drops of Kool-Aid on the window for the ladybugs and they'd drink it. And when she'd be going off to school, she'd say, 'Now Mom, don't you touch the ladybugs today!'

And I'd say, 'I won't touch it!' So, now every now and then someone in the family sees a ladybug and gives us a call and says, 'Oh my, Allison is here today.'"

Of all the pictures and drawings and memories Richard and Marjorie have of their daughter one tiny square piece of paper is especially dear, and one that has gotten them through many tough times. It's a short, handwritten description Allison once penned about herself. They keep it close by, to remember how lucky they were to have her for a daughter.

> *I am a pretty simple girl.*
> *I like the simple things in life.*
> *And just like having fun with friends and family.*

As Richard talks about how Allison saw herself as a simple spirit, he stops mid-sentence and points straight ahead. "Well, look at that," he exclaims.

A brightly coloured ladybug slowly makes its way across the kitchen window.

Gregory Morris

Ten years. That translates into roughly 3,650 days. For some, the loss of the people on Cougar Flight 491 is something they've lived and breathed every day of the past decade. Some still can't talk about it openly. Others cope with the grief through daily rituals.

Like Wayne Morris's morning visit to Greg's gravesite in the cemetery in Outer Cove. "I'm down there every morning," he explains. "I just stops there and looks at the grave and the headstone. Throw him a few kisses. And then I'm gone again. The only time I can't get up there is in the winter time. If it's plowed, I'll go up by his headstone."

It's become habit but it's also a routine that helps him cope with the loss of his firstborn. "If I don't get down there, it's like my day is not the same. I looks at Greg's picture on the headstone and Thunder beside him. The big dog he had. We raised it but he owned it."

Thunder died several years before Greg and the pet was so loved that Greg kept Thunder's ashes in his parent's home. When Greg died, the family decided they'd place some of the ashes with him. On his headstone alongside the picture of Greg and Thunder are his favourites team logos—the Montreal Canadiens on one side, the Michigan Wolverines on the other. The phrase "Go Habs Go" is between the logos.

Marie understands her husband's reasons for going to the cemetery every day, but she doesn't often accompany him. "I'm the opposite," she says. "I can't go there. Wayne and I used to go there before Greg was there to look at all the relatives and I didn't mind it at all. But I just haven't been able to go there. It's just too real for me to think that he's up there." The few times she has gone, she has a hard time after she leaves.

As she watches Greg's son, Ian, grow, Marie's mind sometimes tricks her. Like when she's sitting in the stands watching him play hockey, she'll find herself slipping back to a time when Greg was that age and he would race up and down the ice chasing the puck. She went to all of his games. "When I go to Ian's hockey games and he's going up the ice on a breakaway, and Heather is sitting next to me, I'll say, 'Go Greg go!' because he's just like Greg on the ice. And that's the only time I call him Greg. When he plays hockey, with the hockey equipment on and the moves he makes, he's just like him."

Marie isn't aware she is yelling out Greg's name until Heather nudges her. "And Heather will say, 'You're calling him Greg again.' And I'll say, 'Oh my God, I'm not even aware of it!'"

Ian is like his father. Tall. Good looking. Into sports. Not just hockey, but basketball, soccer, softball. When Marie sees him excel at sports, she is sometimes overwhelmed with sadness. "He's got a lot of trophies," she says. "His bedroom wall is full of them. That kills me because he's a good little hockey player and he's a good ball player and Greg got to see none of that, you know. He would've loved that, to see him scoring and that."

Moments from the past have taken on a new meaning. Like the times Marie would take Thunder for a walk and she'd pass by Greg and Heather's home, a short distance from her own. "Every time I walked down with the dog, Thunder," she says, "and Greg would be out cutting the grass, I would always think of that song, 'If Anything Happened to You.'" She had no idea why the lyrics of the song by the Ennis Sisters would go through her mind at those times.

If anything happened to you,
If my worst fear should ever come true,
I'd have no reason to carry on through,
If anything happened to you.
So promise me you will take care,
It's a wicked old world out there;
I'd be devastated, be broken and blue,
If anything happened to you.

The words would play over and over in Marie's head. "And I don't know why but every time I'd pass by and whether he'd be out or even if he wasn't out and I knew he was home, I used to think … I used to see that helicopter and I'd worry about him."

For years, Marie had wanted a picture of her Greg and Rick with their wives and children. They each had two children at the time. But the timing never worked out, until about seven months before the crash. Rick and his family happened to make it home that summer. "I wanted to get the whole family together and I had a job to do it," she says. "I was after them for ages. And then they were all home for some reason. And none of them wanted to go get the picture that morning because they all had something on the go. One of the kids got down there and screeched and cried because they didn't want to get their picture taken. We got her straightened away and then one of the other kids started to cry and I said, 'We're getting that picture taken, I don't care!'"

They finally got the picture taken and, looking at it now, there is no indication of how much work it was to get everyone in sync. She laughs now when she thinks about that day. But she is grateful to see the family portrait hanging on her living room wall.

Rick often shows his three children pictures of Greg. Madison and Michael have little to no memory of him, as they were so young at the time of his death. Matthew was born two years after the accident. "I've got some pictures and stuff up," he says, "so I just try to make sure when the anniversary comes around that we talk about it. And there's a service every year and we put a little thing in the paper every year and we just try to remind them of who he was and the kind of person he was. And in our case Matthew's middle name is Gregory ..." Rick's voice breaks as he says his brother's name out loud, and he starts crying. It takes a few seconds before he can continue. "So we have something for him when he gets older to learn what that means, to be named after him that way. We thought it would be nice to do that."

The pictures Rick has around the house of Greg showcase his personality. "I think the one thing is that in all the pictures we have of him and the kids, he's always smiling. Big sense of humour. Big personality ... we just want to remind them that he was a good man who was just taken from us too soon." The tears and the memories weaken his voice, and he struggles to finish his sentences. "He was just a really good guy. He didn't have any enemies. People liked being around him. He had a great sense of humour. Very social. Very gregarious, you know ... That's missed."

While Wayne copes by visiting the cemetery often, Rick put his energy into helping with the Cougar Flight 491 memorial erected by the government of Newfoundland and Labrador and the City of St. John's.

The memorial, unveiled in the fall of 2014, is located just a few metres from the shores of Quidi Vidi Lake in the city's east end. A spiral-shaped, stainless steel sculpture symbolizes the early visions of a flying machine sketched by Leonardo da Vinci in the 15th century. A light shines up through the middle and the names of the 17 who died are etched on the circular wings of the memorial that rise into the air.

The artwork also includes the names of six men who died in another offshore tragedy, a little-known helicopter crash that happened on March 13, 1985. That chopper went down shortly after lifting off from an offshore rig in Placentia Bay, taking the lives of Captain Gary Freeman Fowlow, First Officer Frank Kearney, Brian Garbett, Art Smith, Bernie Murphy, and Jim Wilson. They were on a 20-minute flight from the oil rig Bowdrill I to St. John's, when the helicopter crashed less than 1,500 metres from the rig.

Twenty-four years apart, only one day separates the anniversaries of these two crashes. "When all this went down, you just sort of realize how precarious all this stuff is," Rick explains. "I think you just take it for granted that nothing is going to happen. Afterwards, when we started working on the memorial, I met one of the ladies whose husband died in the other helicopter incident in the '80s. I didn't even know that that had happened. I mean, as far as I knew, this was the safest way to get people back and forth. And nothing had ever happened and nothing ever would. But you just sort of realize that in the case of this thing it was a 50-cent bolt that sheared through that caused all this stuff. And then you talk to these ladies from the '80s and you know it felt like their husbands had been forgotten because it was so long ago. But I think when we started to work on the memorial it allowed them to feel like they had a little bit of a voice."

Similarly, the memorial to the loss of Cougar Flight 491 helped give Rick a voice. "For me, knowing that they were going to do something. I mean, I wanted to be a part of it. Again, I'm not there. I was home for about a month all together when it happened … it was a good way to still be involved in that process and have a say and have some comfort that what they were going to do would be respectful and appropriate and it was something that he would approve of, if that's the right word."

While that larger memorial pays tribute to all those who died that day, smaller reminders of Greg can be found at Quidi Vidi Lake. His name is still in the record books for his rowing victory at the annual Quidi Vidi Regatta. Just a few hundred metres from the memorial, a park bench, put there by Heather, faces the water. Greg's name is engraved on the bench.

And at the playground in the community of Outer Cove, next door to the school Greg went to as a child, is another small plaque bearing his name. Some of the playground equipment was placed there in his memory.

Paddy Dyer still mourns, too. "He was my best friend. He still is," he says. "I still got a picture of him on my fridge to this day. The two of us stood up at my wedding. I miss him. I still miss him. I remember saying to my wife that we're going to save all the newspapers from the days after the crash and I still got them. I saved all the *Telegram* newspapers because, if the time ever came that Greg's children wanted to read about it, I said I'd have all the newspapers from that time. So, I still got them."

A few years back Paddy's daughter had to write an assignment for her junior high class. Greg was her godfather and she wrote her paper on what happened with the Cougar helicopter. Paddy dug out those old newspapers to help her. "I remember looking at all those newspapers and it was just like it was happening all over again, like the emotions, just everything opened up and, God, I was crying. They say time heals all wounds but I don't believe that because the wound is there and it just opens back up again."

Paddy has the same feeling when he attends the yearly memorial service in St. John's. "It's like the first day that it happened," he says. "I find it wild because the wound is there and it opens up every time that you go to the service or when you look at the articles. Wounds are just scarred over, they never heal."

For years, Greg played recreational hockey in the Avalon East Senior Hockey League. His childhood friend, Mike Ozon, played on the Outer Cove team with him. They had met in Grade 4 at St. Francis of Assisi school the year Mike's family moved to Logy Bay from Labrador, and they stayed friends right into adulthood, continuing to play hockey together. A few times they even travelled to Montreal so that Greg could see his favourite NHL team in action.

"Greg was the most fun person," Mike says. "He had a great smile, a big radiant smile. He was always joking with us and he was always there for a good time. He was the leader of the pack when it came to having fun, that's for sure." Mike and Greg stood for Paddy at his wedding.

After Greg's death, the leader of their rec team created a player-of-the-game award in Greg's memory. They don't hand out a trophy or any kind of a mounted plaque, but instead they give the winner a simple stainless steel soup ladle. "This spoon is representative of Greg being a cook and stuff," Mike says, "so we said in Greg's honour we'd give this spoon to the player of the game. We just toss it over to him. And they hang on to it till the next game."

The team began awarding the 8- to 10-inch-long silver dipping spoon the first year after Greg's death. It has been handed out after every single game the team has played since its creation. "After every game, we give out the spoon. Usually, I will just designate someone—and it's all for fun games—and sometimes whoever has the spoon from the week before, we just leave it to them to give it to whoever."

The spoon award has become legendary within the six-team league, especially with the older players, but Mike says new players often look at it, puzzled. "Some of the young guys now who didn't quite know Greg, the first time we gave out the spoon they were looking at us like, 'What's this all about?' So, we had to explain Greg was one of us who played on the team and he passed away in the Cougar crash."

Mike says it's his way to remember an old friend who was taken way too soon. "It seems like a day doesn't go by when I think of him. Even to this day, the gang of us are always texting each other and talking about Greg and just all the funny stuff he'd do and say, and we'd say, 'If Morris was here now …' He was one of them great people in the world who all of a sudden is gone and you miss him."

Sheldon Langdon—who worked closely with Greg in the galley on board the SeaRose—rarely discusses how he feels about what happened and its effect on him. When he does open up, he is pensive. "When I went back to work after the crash, when I went back to the rig, on days, I was the only one left from our crew. It wasn't very good. Even now, it's kind of strange. I find since the crash I haven't been going to the TV room as often. I don't know, it just feels different. I don't enjoy it the same. I don't know how to explain it really. It's like something is missing."

It took time for Sheldon to accept that it could have been him on that helicopter if it wasn't for Greg's kindness in assigning himself to head out to sea and giving Sheldon a chance to stay home a little longer with his family. "That was rough for a little while," he reflects. "It's not a good feeling. At first, I didn't know if I'd be able to go back to work, but then I said, 'Well, you know, I got a family that I need to provide for and I know Greg wouldn't be very happy if I gave it up and put them in financial … not hardship but at least a different way of life.' So, I felt I had to go back. I felt I needed to really. But I mean, the first couple of hitches I went out there I was like, 'I don't know if I can do this.' It's gotten better, but even now, it's … I don't know, it's weird."

Like Greg's father's routine of visiting his son at the cemetery every day, Sheldon has his way of dealing with the loss when he is aboard the rig. His voice quivers and he cries a little as he describes it. "On the SeaRose, Greg had this chair that he used to sit in and that was the only chair he'd sit in. And Peter had a chair he'd sit in," he says, referring to Peter Breen, "and it was the only chair he'd sit in. And the catering crew sits at the same table. But I haven't sat in either of those chairs in eight years." He pauses, as if picturing himself standing over Greg's chair but not being able to bring himself to sit on it. "Even if all the caterers sit at the one table and they are the only two chairs available, I won't sit in them. It feels weird."

Sheldon misses Greg's laugh. He misses the music always being on when Greg was around. He misses Greg's feeble attempts at singing. But what he misses most is watching hockey games with him in the TV room on the rig. "We'd be up until 11:30, quarter to 12 in the nighttime watching the hockey games," he says. "And if he had to be at work late at night doing inventory in the office, I'd go down and give him a hand and watch the last couple of periods of the hockey game together.... We got a good group of people there now, but I don't know ... it's just not the same."

Early in Greg's career, when he worked aboard the Henry Goodrich, he befriended a young 20-year-old who was new to the offshore oil world and didn't know anyone on the drill rig. That was in June 2000, and Ambrose Griffiths has never forgotten how Greg made him feel. "It was my first time offshore," Ambrose says, "and maybe he noticed that I needed a friend, and I guess that's the reason we hit it off. For the first while offshore it was hard for me to adjust and he basically kept my mind off it. He had good spirits and he kept everything alive, you know. And to have someone like Greg there that's easy to get along with and keeps everyone entertained to keep your mind off it ... it's almost like you knew him forever, you know. And he was just so easy to get along with and he was a great laugh." He and Greg worked together for five years on that rig, and after work, they'd hang out, either at the gym or in the TV room.

The crash shook up Ambrose for a long time and he eventually left the offshore. He still has a photo of Greg and his family on his refrigerator. It has been there for years. It was taken at St. John's airport and, in the photo, Greg is walking alongside the wire fence heading toward the arrivals area of Cougar Helicopters, still wearing his bright orange survival suit with the hood bunched up around his shoulders and neck. Heather and the children are on the other side of the fence and Ian and Erin look excited at seeing their father. It's summer. Ian has a T-shirt, shorts, and a ballcap on and Erin is wearing a cute orange polka-dot dress. Greg has a huge grin on his face. His arm is stretched out and he is waving his hand at the children and Heather. That picture still moves Ambrose. "I just think about all the good times we had," he reflects, "and the good person Greg was. He was very family-oriented, and Heather and the kids were utmost important to him."

A few years after the crash, Ambrose's son was born and he named him after Greg: Kian Gregory Griffiths. "Greg is not someone I will ever forget, you know, but I just wanted to have his name in my family. It was just something about Greg. There's always that one person that you connect with and have a good friendship. When I first went offshore the friendship that we developed in such a short time ... he was an exceptional person, b'y. I'm still in contact with his wife and you know I still do like to talk about Greg. Hard to believe 10 years has passed."

Heather has the original of the photo that Ambrose keeps on his refrigerator. It's in a brown and black wooden frame and hangs on the wall in her and Greg's home. It's one of the first things anyone notices after walking in the house.

Heather is much stronger today. "I went to counselling for five years and that helped," she says. "I don't usually cry. I haven't cried in a long time. I just think I'm doing good for the kids. That's the most important thing."

Despite the passage of time, which doesn't always make things easier to accept, but rather blurs the details, making them less painful, she wishes she could see Greg again, stand inches from him to see the change in his facial characteristics as he neared 50. "He was a great husband and father who loved every aspect of his life," she says. "Besides his personality, he was very handsome and, as he got older, he became even more handsome. I wish I could see him now."

Ian and Erin are now teenagers and Ian, according to Heather, has Greg's traits. She believes he is going to be a heartbreaker just like his father, and that makes her feel good. She sees traits in Erin too that reflect Greg, but Erin is more like her mother. The more Heather talks about her family, the slower the words come, as if she is looking into the sky imagining what turns their lives would have taken had fate not intervened. After a long pause, her voice trails off and her words almost disappear into the air as she talks about how tough it has been trying to balance grieving over the loss of her life partner with trying to keep life as normal as possible for two growing children.

Greg's mother, Marie, is like the children's second mother and she has been a godsend, according to Heather. But Heather doesn't want to put too much strain on Marie and Wayne, who are in their 70s, so she bears much of the weight of parenting herself. "I think I've done a pretty good job, but sometimes I just wish someone would say 'Hey, you're doing a good job,'" she says, her voice wavering and dropping to a whisper. "Just to hear it because it's a struggle, right?"

Heather was 29 when she met Greg. Married at 32. Children by 35. "We never got to our 10th year," she says. "He died when he was 40. I'm totally thankful for what we had. But Greg was the love of my life. I loved and still love him dearly."

Thomas Anwyll

Brenda Anwyll was in a strange headspace in the days and weeks after she returned home to British Columbia with her husband's ashes. At times she accepted what happened. Other times she couldn't believe he was gone. "For the longest time, I would sometimes joke that it wasn't really Tom in his box," she says, "that he ended up getting picked up by some Portuguese fishing vessel and he didn't speak Portuguese and they didn't speak English and they were having a beer on some ferry somewhere, or some fishing boat somewhere. It was, I guess, just my way of coping with things. You know the reality in the front of your mind but in the back of your mind you want this different outcome."

She no longer works at Coastal Pacific Xpress, the trucking company in Surrey where she was in March 2009. She worked there for 11 years but while she was on leave after Tom's death the trucking industry took a downturn. Brenda returned to work part-time but as the company struggled, she decided she'd leave the job, as a way of helping at least one co-worker. "They were going to do this restructuring and they were going to lay some people off," she explains, "and I asked them if they'd consider buying me out rather than laying somebody off who actually needed their job. Because of the lawsuit, of course, I have an income and I didn't want someone to not have an income. So I thought, you know, that would be the right thing to do."

Being at home has given Brenda a chance to pursue two projects in memory of Tom. The first was dear to his heart: building a favourite car of his, the Austin automobile made in England in the late 1940s and early 1950s. Over the years he had assembled pieces of different cars with the idea that one day he would bring them all together to create his very own Austin, marketed back then as having a top speed of 110 kilometres an hour. Tom wanted to put in a much larger engine to give it added power.

"It was a long-term project," Brenda says. "It was a 1948 Austin of England, called an Austin A40 and it has a 392 blown Hemi in it, 700 horsepower. So, it's a little tiny car with 700 horsepower. It's scary!" She laughs. "He had bought several cars and basically pulled them apart and pieced them together and he was making this car. He built the whole chassis for it and the suspension and shortened the wheelbase so it would fit this little tiny car."

Tom had worked on the car for years in his spare time. When he'd get back home after being on the road for work, he'd spend much of his time tinkering at it. And it was almost road ready in the spring of 2009. "The motor was working before he left, and, you know, he had the body all there in pieces and together." A hint of melancholy slips into Brenda's voice as she talks about how close Tom came to finishing the project. "And I think his idea was to just drive it, looking the way it was, you know, not painted, with a little bit of rust here and there and he thought it would be kind of cool to drive it like that for a while."

Tom had even planned what colour he would eventually paint it. "It's not called candy apple red, it's just called candy red. It's very deep and you can almost see the layers of red and silver in there. It's very, very pretty. Re-sale red, we used to joke around because red cars apparently sell like crazy. But that was supposed to be his keeper car."

Brenda decided she'd try to finish the project. Friends helped her paint the car and they installed the windows, but she knew she'd never take such a powerful vehicle out on the road. So when one of Tom's friends—also a lover of old cars and racing machines—approached her to buy it, she had an idea. "The idea was that we would take it to different car shows for a year and put a poster up that, you know, said this was the car that Tom built and kind of explained what happened and how this car came about."

Brenda agreed to sell it on the condition that he keep it and take it to car shows. "And he said, 'Yep, yep, yep. I will do that.' So he purchased it off of me and finished it and got it out there on the road. I finished it to a certain point and he did some fine tuning on it and added a few things to it and it is out there and it is acknowledged whenever he goes to a car show with it, that this is 'The car that Tom built,' as he puts it and so that is out there." It definitely attracts attention. "He goes to as many car shows as he can through the nice summer months. And he still has it to this day. He still has that car and he takes it out to car shows and he lets people know that this is the car that Tom built."

The other love in Brenda and Tom's life was their pets, including the French bulldogs with their scrunched-up faces that Tom loved so much. Brenda created an award that is handed out by the French bulldog club she is involved with. "I have a trophy that is handed out once a year to the dog that wins best puppy. We have a special French bulldog show once a year that our club puts on and for that particular show, I donate the trophy and the dog's name gets engraved on Tom's trophy. And everybody knows it's Tom's trophy." People look forward to claiming the Thomas Anwyll Perpetual Memorial Trophy: "It's amazing the feedback I have from people and what people say after they've won it. The last lady that won it, her dog got best puppy and she started to cry and I'm like, 'Congratulations, congratulations!' And I go, 'I guess you're so happy!' And she said, 'What makes me the happiest is that my dog won Tom's trophy.' And I'm like, that makes me cry! Apparently, it's quite sought after, so that makes me feel good."

The fact that Brenda and Tom did not have children is bittersweet: "I've talked to people on both sides of the coin and in some ways it's heartbreaking and in other ways I didn't have to deal with myself grieving as well as children grieving. So, you know, in that aspect, part of me says I kind of got off easy in that way. But at the same time, I don't have a part of him to keep his name going."

As Brenda talks about Tom, she wells up and her voice softens to a whisper: "I remember telling his mom—because his mom, she really took it very hard and she still takes it very hard—but I said to her that I have to appreciate what I had, not what I don't have."

Brenda pauses for a long time, as if trying to put their life and Tom's death in perspective. She casts her mind back to the young man she met at a small-town racetrack all those years ago who impressed her with his dry sense of humour, his happy attitude, and his big, strong arms, and she finds her voice again. "And so, you know, the 24 years I had him in my life, I appreciate that. He was my best friend."

And as for that dream car of his, that 1948 Austin A40 with its 700 horsepower Hemi engine and deep candy red colour, it is still on the road travelling the drag-racing circuit in Tom's name, following nearly the same route Tom did when he made his way around the racetracks of British Columbia and the northern US states of Washington and Oregon. "I'm not going to beat around the bush, I get emotional when I see it," Brenda sighs. "And I'll have my little cry. But it's nice to see it out there for sure."

Matthew Davis

Through the 10 years since Matt Davis died, his memory has been kept alive.

He's there in the conversations Marsha and the children have about him every day.

He's there in the Gerald Squires portrait that hangs in her living room, of Matt dressed sharply in his pilot's uniform, standing in the great outdoors he loved so much, a helicopter in the background.

And he's there in the picture that hangs in his mother's kitchen in Kingston, Ontario. She starts every day with a peck on his cheek and a "good morning!" "I'm his mom ... I refuse to let go of him," Jeane says. "He's part of me. He's always going to be part of me."

Many people remember Matt as the strong, caring family man he became, but in Jeane's mind he'll always be the little boy standing in his crib; the three- or four-year-old running into the house crying, "Mommy, I hurt my knee, I fell on the crunkity," because his tiny mouth couldn't yet get around the word concrete; the child at nursery school who saw that one child had more candy than anyone else so he made sure they were shared equally.

Those memories help her cope, but Jeane still thinks about how she lost Matt's father when he was so young, and then Matt. "God in his infinite wisdom for some reason," she says, "just wasn't satisfied to take my beautiful, beautiful husband at the age of 38, he had to come back and take my beautiful son at the age of 34. And I often go about my day thinking, 'What did I do? What am I paying for? What happened? Somewhere along the way wasn't it enough for him to take one of my men, did he have to take two?'"

Jeane is often asked how she can keep going, how she can continue to stay so strong. Her answer is simple: "My only answer is—what choice does anybody have? You have no choice. So you just keep on going. And you keep smiling. And you keep talking to the ones that have left you." And she does talk to Matt. Some mornings she heads out the door for one reason or another only to realize she has rushed past his picture in the kitchen without saying good morning. She whips back inside and gently touches his face or chest and says, "Sorry, love, I forgot to kiss you good morning."

The picture is of a uniformed Matt standing next to a Sikorsky helicopter. Jeane enjoys looking at that one in particular, but there are many others that make her smile, including one of him, with a big, proud grin on his face, standing beside George Bush Sr.

The former US president often flew to Labrador to go salmon fishing. Matt met him a couple of times when he was part of the flight crew that transported Bush in and out of the remote lakes in the Big Land. Matt is standing next to Bush, who is wearing a fly vest and looking relaxed and ready to hit the river. Matt is wearing a shirt, tie, and sport coat. Jeane laughs. "And the story that Matthew said was that, 'Oh my gosh, Mom, they were going to take a picture of me and George Bush and I told them, 'Oh my gosh no, you can't take a picture of me and Mr. Bush like this. My mother would kill me. Hold on a second.' And he said, 'I ran in and put on a shirt and tie and my sports jacket and ran back out and stood by him and said, 'Now sir, now you can take the picture. My Mom would be happy.'"

Jeane is the first to admit that she is biased, being Matt's mother and all, but, she says, Matt was perfect. She finds it helps to put her feelings on paper, in poems about him, including one she wrote about the photograph on her kitchen wall.

The Photograph

I miss my son each morning
I talk to him through the day
He looks back at me, says Mom you're crazy
And I realize it's only delay …
The realization I have him no more
To hold and hug so tight
And for him to joke and tease me
And to tell me, Mom, everything will be alright
My one and only precious boy
His father through and through

The outdoors was his life, and to soar above it all
Was his dream come true
His sisters he loved to tease
The wife he chose was special
Shannon and William were his miracles
And to Matthew, life was what you made it, with those you loved.
Mom

Matt's sister Amanda still finds it difficult to talk about what he meant to her. "I lost my best friend," she says. Amanda was seven and a half months pregnant at the time of the crash. She now believes that being occupied with the pregnancy helped her get through the stress of that time. When the baby was born, Amanda knew what his name would be. "So his name is Matthew Robert. He goes by Bobby, but his legal name is Matthew." She and her husband often talk to him and his sister about how he got his name and how much their Uncle Matt meant to the family.

"Unfortunately, he's a statistic," Amanda laments, "but he's saving lives from what happened. And you know what, if he could've chose how to go, it may not have been as tragic, but he died doing what he loved. How many people can say that? I mean it's not the best scenario in what happened obviously but he died doing what he loved and he lived every moment of his life like that and that gives me some peace."

Matt's baby sister, Amy, becomes teary-eyed when she thinks of how his children are going through exactly what Matt and his sisters faced when their father died. The three sisters feel they have a responsibility to help pass on Matt's legacy to his children, just as he passed on his father's to them.

Matt's older sister, PJ, agrees. "Wherever and whoever he encountered, Matt will be remembered as a solid person," she says, "one who never compromised his own integrity for the sake of saving face. I think he inherited that from Dad. He had a pure heart and was kind and this shone through when I had the chance to see him with Shannon and Will."

Scott Parsons often thinks about his childhood days when he and Matt and other cousins and friends would spend their time outdoors, roaming around and exploring the woods of Holyrood. Scott and a few other close friends remember Matt through a very personal memorial. It's in the woods, at the edge of a small lake in a remote area of central Newfoundland. Two weeks before the crash, Scott, Matt, and the others were on a week-long snowmobile trip to a cabin area called Devil's Lake. One afternoon Matt decided to stay at the camp while everyone else went out for a few hours of snowmobiling.

"And we said, 'Well, we won't be gone too long,'" Scott recalls. "So, we went out and did a little run for an hour or two and when we came back Matt had several holes cut in the ice, he had a campfire over in the woods, he had the lines set, and he was fishing. He had a pot of tea on the fire and we all came back and he was sat back in the snowbank with the kettle boiling and the fish going and where he had the fire was right in a little peninsula out on this lake at the cabin."

It was a scene of someone who was happy to be in the outdoors, a moment that stayed with all of them. A year later, when the group returned to the area for their annual winter snowmobile trip—for the first time without Matt— they decided to recreate the moment and turn it into a memorial to him. They call it Matt's Cafe. "We erected a solar light up on the tree. We put a nice sign up there that says Matt's Cafe on it with the solar light above it." They go there around mid-February every year, about the time Matt last joined them in 2009. They light a fire, pour shots of Fireball Whiskey—Matt's favourite drink out on the ice, as it kept him warm—and throw it in the fire for him. Then, the reminiscing starts and they sit around and tell stories about Matt. "He was just a great soul, he was just a fun guy, and I miss him," Scott says.

Marsha's sister Janis also thinks of Matt often. She's the one who pranked him by pretending she was pregnant one April Fool's Day and watched in glee as Matt pranced around saying he was happy and excited and he couldn't wait to share the news with his wife, Marsha. When she revealed it was a made-up story, Matt vowed to get her back.

Janis believes that he did—from beyond the grave, but in a good way. "Fast-forward a few years after the accident," she says, "I decided to play this trick on my mother and sister on April Fool's … again. They, of course, believed me, and reacted the same as Matt, happy and excited! But after 10 minutes in, I couldn't help but start laughing and had to tell them how I had tricked them with the same story as Matt!"

But this is where Matt may have had his revenge, Janis says. "Only to find out a week later this time, I'm actually six weeks pregnant! The joke was on me! Part of me would like to believe some way, somehow Matt had a hand in that. That it was his way of getting back at me for pranking him. And if so, Matt managed to gift me with one of the best April Fool's pranks ever! It makes me smile every April Fool's to this day."

Janis wishes her children could have known their Uncle Matt. "I will be forever thankful for his memories. We often talk about Matt stories, and love seeing him come through the personalities of Shannon and William. His big smile—William. His big opinions—Shannon. And his caring heart from both. I will always cherish the memories and smile at his unforgettable Matthew Davis ways," she says.

Marsha's loss also runs deep but on a whole different level. "I think of Matt every day," she says. "Mostly thinking about the happy memories of us. The little things that pop up in our day-to-day life to remind me of him."

Most of that, Marsha says, is because of William and Shannon. They don't have many memories of their father—William was about to turn three at the time of the crash, Shannon turned five that day—but Matt's DNA is part of them and, as they've become teenagers, that's now unmistakable. "There are things about Shannon and William that remind me of Matt every day," she explains. "It could be a smile that William gives that reminds me of him, or how both Shannon and William's smiles make those cute little dimples appear, and how William has the same chubby chipmunk cheeks. Could be looking into my daughter's eyes and see Matt looking back at me. Or how William's hair is so thick like Matt's was. How easy those cowlicks make his hair grow in a same direction Matt wore his."

Their mannerisms are pleasant reminders of Matt. "William pulling at his pants and fixing his shirt like Matt did or how strong Shannon's opinions can be when she feels passionate about a certain topic," she explains. "Shannon's use of words can sound so much like Matt. It is as if Matt were here expressing them himself." And Shannon and William also have an amazing talent to draw, just like their father.

Marsha can't explain the hurt, the sadness, and the tears that came with losing Matt. She finds late winter and early spring the hardest. The weeks leading up to the anniversary of his death and the month following still cause anxiety. "Perhaps because of all the highs and lows I know I will experience from that day alone," she says. "The high, of course, is celebrating Shannon's birthday and the low, Matt's death and everything surrounding it. I try now to think of March 12 as a day to celebrate the life Matt had lived and to be happy to have shared a big part of that life with him—March 12 is our little girl's birthday."

Getting to that point hasn't been easy. The first year after Matt's death was a blur. It is tough to grieve. Even tougher when surrounded by small children who need constant attention and nourishing. "I literally would get up every day, go through the motions of daily living, mostly just for Shannon and William, the best way I could. Shannon and William gave me a purpose."

Thanks to incredible support from her family and friends, Marsha believes she is finally healing. "I smile now most days when I think of Matt. We talk about Matt every day in our family. Most of the tears cried are often happy tears for me. Tears from laughing at the great memories I can share with the kids." That's not to say that she doesn't have moments when she longs for all that she and the children have lost. "Little moments where I cry because Matt has missed out on knowing his children and for Shannon and William being robbed of growing up having their amazing dad," she says. "Most of the memories they will have of their dad are ones I pass on to them about how great of a dad Matt was, how great of a person he was, from myself, our family and friends. Matt had instilled so many positive attitudes in me that I have and will continue to pass along to our children, so that our children can know and learn from his beliefs."

Marsha can already see that Shannon and William treasure the memories she shares with them about their father, and those their young minds have retained. Shannon remembers her father teaching her how to cast a fishing rod and William remembers them bumping their knuckles together as they'd pass in the hall, with Matt saying, "Nucks, little dude."

"That is what I would like for Matt's legacy to be," Marsha says. "The love he had for his family and the passion he had for being a pilot. I want Matt to stand out to Shannon and William as a proud family man, a proud father. That he loved them so unconditionally, as I do. I know Shannon and William know this now but I want them to remember years from now they had a wonderful dad who loved them both so very much."

Another daily reminder always makes them smile: when they step outside their house and walk to the end of the street, they see a road sign that says "Capt. Matthew Davis Drive."

Matt's children will find comfort in knowing how he handled the monumental task he was handed on the morning of March 12, 2009. "Matt was the captain in command that day who did the very best he could do, in a situation that was out of his control. I believe my husband acted professionally," Marsha says. "However, the outcome was inevitable. There was no one in the world that wanted more than anything to get everyone aboard that flight home that day. I know he did everything possible when he was handed the impossible. In my eyes, that makes him a hero."

Timothy Lanouette

Kevin Lane is still in Shearwater, Nova Scotia. But he is no longer in the military. No longer sailing to far-off ports aboard Navy vessels and ensuring that the aircraft they carry are wired properly. "Yeah, I'm a civilian now and the world is a different place for me," he says. "I've just about seven years out now. And so, I'm sort of acclimatizing to becoming like a normal human again." He explains: "I always felt owned by the military. When I got out, I decided to do something where I was the boss, not because I needed to be in control but I just didn't want to be owned. And I wanted to do something entirely different. Now, I'm helping people feel confident instead of making people earn their confidence, which was more my job in the military."

Kevin is a full-time photographer. He often thinks of his time with Tim and how their friendship developed because of Tim's ability to make people feel confident. "I mean, this sounds so ridiculous because you're talking about someone who has passed and it can be seen as you're glorifying somebody, but he really changed my life. I used to play guitar in front of my family and I couldn't open my mouth to sing," Kevin explains. "I was terrified to sing. But because of Tim I ended up being the lead singer in this Big Johnson band, and then on to Stereotype and a few other bands and I've sang in clubs all over the place and Halifax and I don't hesitate to sing in front of people now. And so, I have to be thankful that he came in to the avionics room that day on HMCS *Provider* and said, 'Want to play some music together?'"

Tim taught him how two people from two totally different worlds—that of the officer who pilots the aircraft and the technician who helps keep it running efficiently—can find common ground. "He humanized the pilots," he says. "It was bizarre to me how much he and I had in common even though our lives were completely different. You know, he was a pilot, he was fairly well off, and he had kids and the things that he did—everything that he did he was extremely skilled at. I really wish I would've known him long enough to see him learn something. I guess the S-92 is sort of an example of him learning something. But I would've liked to have seen that up close because I never saw Tim in a situation where he wasn't an expert. He helped me relate to pilots, which helped me later in my career quite a bit to think of officers as human."

Now that Kevin knows again what life is like outside of the military, he wishes that he could talk to Tim about it. In the military it's expected that a member lay his or her life on the line for others, without question. But he wonders why Tim, as a civilian, would want to do that. "I would've liked to have Tim's input on my reality now. I would've liked to have known him now because he got out first and he was still doing this thing, this flying." Kevin pauses, searching for the right word as he tries to explain what he means. "You know, he was putting his life at risk to fly to an oil rig. I just … that's a weird thing and I really wish I could have … I could have talked to him more about that in context. He was just so excited to be flying a new aircraft. And to be doing something that was fun. He said it was fun, it was a lot more relaxed than the military. And, I guess, I feel robbed."

Tim Lanouette was the real deal. "I really don't like it when somebody has passed away and, all of a sudden, they become a saint," Kevin explains. "And everything they did was great. I've been frustrated with that attitude amongst people a number of times. Flight safety has been such a big deal for my career that every time something happens we look at all the minutiae. What things went wrong and how do we make these things safe? But this is different. This is my friend. And you know there's always Facebook posts every year, but very few people talk about the people they were. It's really easy to idolize people and I'm just not sure all the stories that I hear about people are true. But you know, Tim—what would be the worst thing I could say about Tim? Is there a bad thing I could say about him? I never really saw him do anything wrong. Tim was really a great guy. I miss him. And that's a genuine thing. He was a very good friend."

Pierre de Villers has also left the military. He retired in 2016. Now, he lives in New Brunswick and divides his time between sailing, diving, and playing in bands. He also thinks of Tim often, and he uses a simple explanation for how he remembers him: "I always think of him as one of the good guys. In the forces there's good guys and there's not-so-good guys. And he was one of the good guys."

Peter Breen

Danny Breen was standing at a bar in Gander enjoying an early evening drink with some friends. He was attending a municipalities conference and had just finished a long day of meetings, when the bartender walked over. "That gentleman over there just bought you that," she said, as she laid a beer on the bar in front of him. Danny looked across the room but didn't recognize the person she pointed to. Shortly after, the stranger approached the St. John's politician directly. "And he came over to me and said, 'I knew your brother and I just wanted to buy you a beer.'"

Incidents like that have happened frequently in the years since Peter died. "Not a week goes by that I'm out somewhere and somebody will come up to me and say, 'Danny boy, I remember your brother Pete.' And these are all different people. And people that I never knew, and they'd say, 'I knew your brother Pete; boy we were good friends. I just wanted to give you and your family our condolences.' And that's still today."

And that's not all. In 2011 when the Boston Bruins won hockey's most coveted trophy, "somebody came in with a little Stanley Cup and attached it to the headstone," Danny explains. "The day after they won, that little Stanley Cup ... one of those you get in beer boxes ... appeared on Pete's headstone." He can't think of many people who had that impact on others. "He was a very selfless person. He put everybody ahead of himself, especially his family."

Danny and his brother Kevin, the siblings who went into politics, joke about the advantage of having Peter as their brother come election time. Not only did he help them by walking through entire neighbourhoods dropping candidate flyers into mailboxes, his name was often the topic of conversation as the two knocked on doors. And they weren't the ones bringing up Peter's name. "The first time I ran," Danny says, "I don't know how many times I met people at the door who would say, 'I know your brother.' And it was constant. It's incredible. It wasn't 'I remember him' or 'I remember that face,' they would bring it out to you that he made a mark on people when he met them. He made an impression." Kevin agrees and starts to cry when he tries to explain what he remembers most about his younger brother. "His goodness," he says, "that's all ... I think of him all the time."

On the first anniversary of Peter's death, a small mass was held for him at St. Patrick's Mercy Home, a long-term-care facility in the city. His sister Judy says Robert Decker, the lone survivor, showed up that day. "He carried up a candle. He was very gracious," she says, adding that Robert made sure to spend time with their mother. "He went over to Mom and Mom was speaking really low then because she was 91, and he leaned over, and she said, 'I'm praying for you all the time and I'm so happy you're alive, I'm so glad you're doing okay.'" Judy still fills up about the touching moment.

Peter's brothers and sisters have lingering questions about the crash: how it could have happened and why the problem with the studs in the oil filter assembly hadn't been addressed earlier. "The day after, or the day of the accident, they grounded everything for so long," Judy says. "Well, they should've did that when they knew there was a problem. Everything should've been grounded then, rather than later."

Focusing on that gets them nowhere, they know. Instead, they try to think about how much Peter meant to them. If Danny has one regret about his brother's life, it's that he didn't get to see his grandchildren. "That bothers me," he says. "Because if you seen Pete around kids and what he's done with his kids and what he did for his kids, you know, Pete would be walking his daughters and sons everywhere, you'd see him all over the place and to see him not have a chance to see his grandkids … I'm not a bitter person … but I am a little bitter that he never got to experience that because it would have meant so much to him."

Peter's wife, Janet, and their children also have moments of anger over the crash. Not all the time, but sitting around the kitchen table talking about Peter, it inevitably comes up.

Janet: "Not all the time, but I still get angry when I think about it."

Noelle: "I'm 100 per cent still angry."

Janet: "For that little bolt and for how much it cost, and even if it had cost $1 million or $5, it should have never happened. It shouldn't have."

Noelle: "And that's the issue. And that's why, in my opinion, that the anger is still with everybody. Because it was preventable. It was an accident, but it wasn't. Somebody fucked up."

Janet: "I mean, if somebody dies because they have cancer, it's sad, or however they die it's sad. But this should never have happened."

Janet Marie: "It shouldn't have. And at the time I still worked at the airport and I had pilots come to me and I had maintenance people come to me and telling me this was preventable and it should not have happened. And this helicopter should never have taken off."

Peter did not mention any concerns he might've had about flying to the rigs to Janet in their years together. But a few months before the accident, he did say something that she often recalls. They were in the kitchen and Peter was cooking, as he loved to do while he was at home. Suddenly he said, "If anything ever happens to me on one of those choppers, make sure you're well looked after." Janet tried to hush him up, not wanting to hear any such talk. "And I said, 'Give it up!' And I kinda laughed and said, 'Give it up, you're freaking me out!'"

But Peter persisted. "No, this is not a joke. I'm really serious," he said. "I'm just saying, if anything happens to me on one of those choppers, just make sure you're well looked after. And down the road, if you meet someone, just make sure he's nice and even though the kids would be older, make sure he's nice to them too."

Janet dismissed what he was saying. But after the accident, she wondered if he was nervous about something and trying to tell her, but didn't want to scare her.

Janet's world darkened in the weeks and months after Peter's death. She wouldn't put a coat on because she thought she didn't deserve to be warm, as he had spent all those days on the ocean floor.

She wouldn't buy herself a Tim Hortons' coffee, which she did several times a day before his death, because she felt she shouldn't have one if Peter couldn't have one.

She couldn't pick up his life insurance cheque because she felt that Peter had worked so hard all his life that it wasn't right for her to receive this money. Despite repeated calls from the company and even pressure from her mother, she just couldn't. At one point, she even lied to a company official, saying that she was sick, as a way of avoiding going there to get the cheque. Eventually, she capitulated. But it tore her apart inside. "And I still feel like that," she says. "I mean it really bothers me. I walked into the office and I got it and I walked out and I gotta tell you, I got into that car and I screeched. I felt like ... I don't know what the word is, but I felt that I had this money, this cheque in my hand that I don't deserve this. It's terrible. Like, it's terrible."

For the longest time Janet went to Peter's grave every day, until her doctor said it was unhealthy. "I spent so much time in there that my doctor said 'you have to stop going to the cemetery.' I went there every single day and I stayed for quite some time. I would even be in there when it was dusk and my poor mother would be frightened to death, she'd say, 'Janet, you can't be going in there.'"

That burden of grief is heavy. Janet still has Peter's toothbrush, the one he used that morning. His shoes are next to hers on a rack in the closet. His pants and clothes are in the closets too and his wallet, still holding his ID and other cards, is on the table beside her bed. "I spent many, many nights here in tears, but nobody knows," Janet says ruefully. "It's a really rough life. And I've had people say to me, 'You know, Janet, it's been almost nine years you should be over it.' And I don't get mad, I just very politely say, 'Listen, you walk in my shoes for two seconds and then you say that to me.' This is rough. It's really hard."

And, Janet says, it is getting harder. She says that if someone had told her that she'd be a widow in her mid-50s, she would have said they were crazy. "Everybody is different, I guess, but I feel I'm going backwards. I feel I'm getting worse as the years go on, in regards to being upset and sad. I don't think I'm as good now as I was five years ago. I find it's really getting difficult. Like you miss him, of course you always miss him. That's never going to change. But it's just like … ah, stupid things. Like, why me? Like, why did this have to happen? And I'm sure everybody says that, you know. I mean it's horrible. You know you're never going to see him again. It's horrible."

Many times she just wants to be left alone. But it's during those moments that family strength lifts her up, and she relies on her children, who understand what she has gone through and is still going through. "Someone said it's not something you are going to get over," her daughter Noelle explains, "but it's a new normal that you adjust to. And that has stuck with me since, literally, like the words were coming out of her mouth and it was ingraining to my brain. This is our life, this is our new normal."

After Peter's remains were cremated, each of the children received a locket or memory case with some of his ashes. Andrew still has two pairs of his father's boots that he often wears. They all feel that their father is still with them, and some of them, like Noelle and her mother, see signs they can't explain.

According to superstition, finding a dime after the death of a loved one is a message of encouragement from the person who has passed. Noelle wasn't a believer until the strangest thing happened to her. "We were at the airport the day after the crash," she explains. "And I am not one to have cash on me, but when we came out of the airport there was a dime right there on my front seat in the car. And I'm like, 'Where the hell did that come from?' I believe something because we have all found dimes in some weird spots. I can't see how it got there."

Janet recounts a similar experience. "When we lived on Eastbourne Crescent, she always used to tell me about the dimes. I knew she was finding them but figured they were just falling out of people's pockets, or whatever. But I was getting in bed on Eastbourne Crescent one night and I'll never forget it, I pulled down the covers and I can't say dead centre but almost dead centre of that bed was a dime. And everybody knows I never have five cents on me. Everything is debit and credit. So, I thought, jeez, this is kind of weird. I didn't make a real big deal of it. So then, two years later I moved to this new house and I go upstairs and, so help me God, not a word of a lie, I pulled down the sheets and almost dead centre in the bed in this house there was a dime."

Such a strange occurrence has become a running joke with Noelle's children. "I still to this day find them everywhere and it's kind of a joke when my husband finds one or the girls find one, they'll say, 'Look, Poppy left another dime.'"

Noelle and Janet Marie have since married and both have children. Like Danny, Janet wishes Peter was around to watch them grow up. "He wanted grandkids so bad," Janet says. "And he never did get to meet them. Like, it's not fair."

Knowing Peter wouldn't be around to witness the big moments in their lives has played on Noelle's mind for years. "He didn't see us get married either. That bothered me. That was a big thing." But Andrew, on the other hand, tries to put it into perspective. "I look at other families that have kids that were literally infants and don't have a memory at all," he says. "At least we were old enough to have something."

Janet couldn't see it that way for the longest time. "I remember saying to Andrew a long time ago when this happened, 'You know what, I wish you were little.' And he said why? And I said, 'Because if you were little, you'd have no memory of it.' And he said, 'Mom, I'd rather be the age I am because I knew my dad for 17 years.'"

Janet wanted to create a memorial to Peter but she couldn't think of what exactly she wanted to do. Then one day it hit her. "Pete loved the Regatta and he always walked around Quidi Vidi Lake. I'm sure every day when he was home when there's good weather, you know, that was just something he always did. So, I said I wonder if I could get a bench there?"

Before long a bench bearing his name was placed near the boathouse alongside the lake. It's adjacent to the one put there by Greg Morris's wife, Heather. Peter wasn't a rower like his father—who also has a bench in his name at the lake just a few feet away—but he loved the area.

As for Andrew, it appears that he inherited his father's sense of humour. He too has watched *Seinfeld* episodes hundreds of times each. "Like, I still watch it literally all the time, to this day, whether I put it on in the morning when I'm getting ready, or whatever." And he and his sisters often say "Serenity now" aloud when things get stressful.

That life-sized portrait of Kramer the children gave their father all those years ago, the one that towered over his TV while he sat there shaking with laughter over the comedy show? It's now in Janet Marie's house. Sometimes when she walks by it, she smiles and thinks about the joy it brought her father.

Keith Normore has not returned to the offshore. He considered it after the crash; his trade was in demand and the money was tempting. But it was a fleeting thought, dismissed after he mentioned it to his young daughter. "I said, 'What do you think about that?' And she said, 'I really don't want you to go out there. I don't want something to happen to you too.'"

But there's another reason Keith hasn't returned to a job on the rigs. Not only did he lose some of his best buds, like Peter and Derek Mullowney, he also believed it wasn't safe to be flying offshore. "You knew it was going to happen, you knew one of these days it was going to happen. And it will happen again," he predicts, "because, I mean, the stuff we used to see, it was unbelievable."

Keith recalls one time when he and Peter were boarding a chopper to fly home from one of the rigs. They were sitting across from each other and, as final preparations were being made before departure, they noticed oil dripping from a panel. They sent word to the pilot, who shut down the engine to check it out. Someone removed the panel, wiped away the oil with a rag, tightened something, and then gave the pilot the thumbs-up to take off. It was scary, Keith states, but that didn't matter to the workers, who just wanted to get off the rig and fly the 90 minutes to be at home with their families.

Keith still misses working with Peter offshore, especially his sense of humour. "When it would be really rough offshore and the rig would be rolling around, he'd be rubbing his hands together and he'd be saying, 'Oh, the sea is angry, my friend! The sea is angry.' It was always something to be taking the edge off and make you feel better, or to give you a chuckle to get your mind off it."

Peter is never far from Keith's mind. "Oh my God, I gotta tell you, it's like I'm still there, b'y. It's unbelievable. I still can't believe it's 10 years later. I can still hear his laughing voice and I can see him as plain as day. It's just certain things that happens every day that he pops into your mind because he was such … well, I knew him for 16 years, I basically lived with him for almost six years in Come By Chance and then nine and a half years offshore. I mean, they're your family for six months of the year. And then we were together even on our days off. So, there's so much stuff that we'd done and laughed at and made fun of and all that stuff, there's hardly anything that can happen today that you don't think of him."

And Keith also thinks about how hard the last decade must have been on Peter's family and how it still must be tough today. "Janet and the kids, that was Peter's life. That's all he talked about. He was a family man, 100 per cent. Definitely. He was just a loveable fellow, that was it. There's no other way to say it."

Gary Corbett

Ten years have passed since that evening in March 2009 when Gary Corbett popped into Jack Walsh's home to bring him supper and to check on his friend who was laid up with a broken leg. Gary was heading out to sea the next morning and he wanted to make sure that Jack didn't need anything before he left.

Jack remembers the pork chop dinner with all the fixings, the trip Gary made to the pharmacy to pick up painkillers for him, and then moving Jack's truck from the driveway into a sheltered area. He cries a little when he thinks about that night and how life changed the next morning. "We were best friends," he says through the tears, "and he wanted to—he just wanted to say 'I'll see you in a couple of weeks.' And that's the last thing he said to me: I'll see you in a couple of weeks."

Jack still goes on fishing trips. His trip mates now are his 89-year-old father-in-law and Roger, Gary's brother. Standing at the edge of the water, the fly rod held tightly in his hands and the thin, strong line whipping back and forth over his head before splashing down on top of the water, Jack doesn't feel far from Gary. Almost like his old friend is beside him.

"I can kinda feel his presence," Jack says. "I feel at peace in there in the woods and Gary comes to mind a lot. It just brings me back to all the places where we used to go trouting because we were always together trouting. So, you know, every time I'm trouting I kind of feel him there. It's a nice feeling to have."

Jack has never missed the Cougar Memorial Service held every year on March 12. He keeps pictures of Gary around his house and he has kept in touch with Ceily, Gary's wife, over the years. He also keeps in touch with Gary's children and has enjoyed watching them grow into young adults. "Ceily and the kids, Stacey, Chad and Chelsea," he fills up just saying their names, "will always be close, special people to me. When I'm around his kids ... I see children that are raised well and decent like him."

Jack has a partner now, Linda Warford, who has gotten to know Ceily and meets her for a coffee every now and then. Linda never met Gary, however, "I feel like I know Gary because Jack talks about him all the time," she says. "He'll smile when he talks about their times together and you know it's so obvious to me that they had such a solid, solid friendship and ... like Jack said, he will always be part of our lives."

Jack longs for a friendship like the one he had with Gary. "I really miss that. I haven't had it since, like, a friend with Gary's qualities. And I'm going to be 65 coming up, so it's going to be hard to find that, you know, again. It's like losing a piece of you, kind of." That boiling pot he and Gary made for a ball team so many years ago during a night of invention and imbibing in the shed is still in use. "My brother has it now, he still plays ball and he is using the same pot ... there had to be a couple of repairs over the years but it's still the same pot that we made."

For Ceily, gathering the strength to talk about the loss of her husband has been a huge hurdle. "It isn't easy for me to do, but I hope I can do justice to the life of a much-loved husband and dad." Many things, moments, still play through her mind.

It breaks her heart to think about Gary's last words to their son, Chad. "The last thing he said was 'when I get back, we're going on a fishing trip.'"

It breaks her heart that he was so close to giving up going to the offshore. "He hated being out there," she says. "The last time he completed his Basic Survival Training he told me he wouldn't renew it anymore and he was just going to work from the office or shop."

It breaks her heart that Gary wasn't even supposed to be on Cougar Flight 491. He was flying out to the Hibernia a day earlier than originally planned to get a head start before his co-workers were to join him the next day.

It also breaks her heart when she thinks that the one thing Gary feared—a chopper crash into the ocean, something he believed was inevitable and not survivable—was what took his life. "The one thing he hated about going offshore was the helicopter ride. He hated flying over the water. When I think of the crash, I wonder what he was feeling and the fear he felt. It haunts me to this day and I put it to the back of my mind."

In the months following the tragedy, Ceily went to some of the meetings officials held with families, including one in which the TSB released the results of its investigation. "They showed a computer animation of what they believed happened at sea," she recalls. "This, to me, was the hardest thing to watch and the most haunting. That meeting was very emotional and I had to be there. I had to know ... what the Transportation Safety Board thought exactly happened that day."

Ceily harboured her own anger—at both Sikorsky, the helicopter manufacturer, and Cougar Helicopters for not dealing with the problem sooner—but she refused to let that anger overcome her.

If any good came from that day, it's the awards created in Gary's honour. Gary graduated from Queen Elizabeth High School in Foxtrap in Conception Bay South in 1979. His three children attended and graduated from the same school. Now, each year the company he worked for, Hyflodraulic Limited, sponsors two scholarships in his memory. They are awarded annually to graduating students—one to a female and one to a male—who are in the Technology/Skilled Trades Program. The winners must display a keen interest and a positive attitude, with a high regard for safe work practices, and an aptitude for continuous learning.

Ceily is thankful to the company for making the awards available. "Each year two of the kids and a representative from Hyflodraulic Ltd. present the awards, a cheque and a plaque," she says. "There is a beautiful plaque at the school and it is engraved every year with the names of the recipients. We wanted to do something to remember Gary and felt this was fitting. I feel he'd be very proud that these scholarships are ongoing at Queen Elizabeth's Awards Ceremony every fall."

Ceily has learned in the last decade about her own strength. "One thing people have often said to me is, 'you're so strong.' I have never considered myself to be strong but I do realize that when you face a terrible ordeal strength will shine through." A network of support enveloped her and the children, but Ceily says she has learned to rely on herself, not just others. "My focus has been my kids—and that has helped me get through many tough times. I've relied on my friends, my family, my faith, and the community as a whole. They all helped get us through this horrific time," she says, "but, after a couple of weeks, we had to step up. I needed to get the children back to school and move forward with some normalcy, although our lives would never be normal, a new normal had to set in. I've learned that people are overall good and willing to help me when I need it and I have a strong network to call on when I need them."

The toughest time after the crash, Ceily says, was when everyone else went back to their own lives. "As time went on and the house wasn't full with people anymore ... we had to pick up the pieces and make the decisions and steps to move forward and make Gary proud."

The children are grown up now, but Ceily still thinks about what they missed. "The loss that our family and all the other families suffered that day has changed our lives forever," she says. "As the years pass we put one foot ahead of the other and move forward. That is what Gary would have wanted for us. We'll always love and miss Gary and I'll always wonder 'what if' but as the years pass our memories bring smiles of happier times and we try not to think about the crash as much. For my part, every time I see a Cougar helicopter fly overhead, I shudder, but I'll always say a quick prayer that they arrive safely at their destination."

As for how she's doing herself, Ceily says, "When I think about the last decade, I can't believe we survived it. I look at Stacey, Chad, and Chelsea with a great sense of pride and then I get sad thinking about what Gary has missed: the driving lessons, the report cards, the graduations, and I hope that somehow, somewhere he is watching and I know he would be very proud also. I think of the times I've needed him and how I've had to make so many decisions without him. I think of the several times since the accident that I've had one-sided conversations with Gary and how I feel better afterwards—a sense of peace. I know in my heart he would be proud of us all. Our lives were devastated that day, along with the lives of so many other families, but time has eased the pain."

She accepts that the pain will always be present, but now when they sit around and talk about Gary, it's about everything but how his life ended. "We smile and remember the good times, the laughter, and the wonderful memories of a loving dad, husband, son, and brother who died much too young. Gary was always safety oriented but that day on March 12, 2009, safety was out of his control. I don't want the crash of Cougar Flight 491 to be why Gary is remembered. I want him to be remembered for him—the man he was and the man he could have been."

Wade Duggan

After his brother, Wade, lost his life in the helicopter crash, Greg Duggan took time away from his job as a driller on the Hibernia platform. His friends and co-workers who were still working on the rigs travelled by supply boat, as all flights to the offshore were cancelled after the crash.

When the helicopters were cleared to fly again, workers were given a choice of travelling by air or by sea. By then, Greg was already at Hibernia, having sailed out to the platform before flights resumed.

When it was time for him to return home for his three-week break, a senior platform manager called Greg into his office. "Now, you're going back on the boat, so you'll be going out on Tuesday morning," he told Greg. But Greg simply asked how long before the chopper would be leaving that morning. He just looked at Greg. "Why, you'd actually get on the chopper again?" he asked. Greg nodded. "Whatever takes me home first, man." The platform manager shook his head. "By Jesus, you got guts," he said.

With that, Greg walked out of the office, up a flight of stairs, and onto the helideck. He didn't know that a short distance away a group of workers was watching Greg from an office. His friend Steve Tizzard was one of them. "There were probably a dozen people watching the helicopter on the helideck," Steve says. "As we just watched silently and Greg took to the stairs and walked towards the aircraft, I said to the guys, 'If he can do it, I guess we can too, guys.'"

The men fell in line behind Greg. One by one they walked toward the chopper. "There's fellas that came behind me that was petrified," Greg recalls, "but they went because I went."

Greg's action sent a strong message to the others, but that wasn't his intent. "I did it because I wanted to get home. The people at home needed me more than I needed to be stuck on the rig. But don't tell me that flight wasn't wild. I mean, you're sitting down there, you're thinking ... you're thinking," he pauses, momentarily lost in thought. "I wouldn't want to go through that again. My knees were knocking, I can guarantee you that."

Greg considered leaving the offshore after Wade's death. His parents had already lost one son and he knew that they worried about the possibility of losing their only other child. It played on his mind. "All the time," he says, "all the time. Mother is petrified."

But life doesn't stop for grieving, and Greg stayed with the job for the same reason he and others went into offshore work in the first place: the money. He had been going back and forth for 10 years and the big paycheque allowed him the lifestyle he wanted for his family.

After two decades offshore, Greg has many good friends on the rig he enjoys being around. He often jokes that he knows more about some of them than he knows about his wife, considering the frequent 3 a.m. conversations he's had with fellow drillers.

Greg still questions why Wade paid the ultimate price, especially since his younger brother worked mostly onshore and wasn't even supposed to be on the flight that day. "I struggle with, 'Okay, why wasn't it me?' I mean, I was at it myself. I had a full-time job. I was taking way more flights than he ever was. He didn't fly that often. And he is the one who died and I'm still living. I'm still going back and forth, you know what I mean?"

In the months after Wade's death, Greg was approached by a fellow rig worker, Jonny Andrews, who asked if he thought that Wade would have approved of an annual hockey tournament in his name. Greg assured him that he absolutely would have and went straight to his father with the suggestion.

Tears fill Kevin's eyes when he talks about the idea. "So, Greg phoned me one night and said, 'Father, we're gonna do this now in Wade's name: The Wade Duggan Memorial Fund.' Jeez, I said, it's unreal. God, yes, yes, yes! I'll help wherever I can. But I didn't have to help because the boys offshore did it and they are still doing it. Jonny Andrews, Steve Tizzard, and a whole lot of the boys. There's a whole bunch of them."

Jonny had been involved in rec hockey for a long time and some of the players included his offshore buddies. One night after a game, about six months after the crash, they were sitting in the dressing room drinking beer and the conversation came around to organizing an annual tournament strictly for offshore workers. Between all the rigs and platforms operating in the offshore at the time—such as Hibernia, SeaRose, Terra Nova, Henry Goodrich, Glomar, West Aquarius—and all the companies that service the industry, they figured there would be enough interest.

Someone mentioned turning it into a fundraiser, suggesting that they use some of the money to pay for the stadium rental and give the rest to a charity. Another player's comment made Jonny think. "Brian Hawkins came up with the idea that we should take the money and give it to minor hockey players who needs it," he says. "Because he grew up in Amherst Cove on the southern shore, a little small community, and he had next to nothing. He loved playing hockey but he could never afford it."

That reminded Jonny of his own years in minor hockey growing up in

Corner Brook, on Newfoundland's west coast. He was a goalie, which meant his equipment was considerably more expensive than the other players'. "I remember hearing my parents having conversations about how much everything costs …" He pauses as he remembers those times. "I don't know, it was just something I remember hearing as a child. I kept playing street hockey with friends and stuff and someone could be a really good street hockey player and someone would come up to them and say, 'Jeez, you're a really good street hockey player, you should play ice hockey. How come you don't play?' And sometimes you'd hear that line coming back, 'No, I can't afford it.'"

Jonny and the others worked on a plan for the hockey tournament. "Our mission statement is to help remove the statement, 'No, I can't afford it.' And then we were like, 'yeah that's what we'll do.' The money we raise from the tournament we'll take it and sponsor kids who needs it to play hockey. And so the next time we skated together we talked about it a bit more and I thought about Wade and I said, 'Boys, you know, we might be able to name the tournament the Wade Duggan Tournament and if Greg and his family will allow it we'll keep his memory alive.'"

They received the family's blessing, and the first annual tournament was held at the Goulds arena in 2011.

Only six teams registered, but they raised $7,400 to sponsor a few children in minor hockey. So many players and teams registered in subsequent years that the event was expanded to two tournaments. "We've been raising anywhere from $40,000 to $50,000 a year, from both of them," Jonny says. "The most kids we helped was 43 one year. And for 2018, it was 35. It's pretty awesome."

Another reason for the fundraiser's success is support from companies working in the offshore oil industry. Greg says that much of that support in the early years came from Paul Sacuta, the former head of Hibernia and a senior engineer at ExxonMobil who went to Greg's house after the crash to personally ensure that the family was kept up to date on the search.

Greg says Paul even drove an hour and a half to his parent's home on the southern shore the following Christmas Eve to bring his mother flowers and to have coffee with her. Paul died of cancer in 2013. "Before he passed away, he called me and Steve Tizzard out to a meeting," Greg recalls, "and he told us, 'Boys, I'm dying, but you got my commitment for this hockey tournament, you got Exxon's support as long as you're running it.' He told us that. And that tells you the type of person he was. He was a class act."

Along with the memorial tournament, Steve Tizzard also worked on another fundraiser connected to Cougar Flight 491. He and his wife, Kelli, sold hats and patches with the 491 logo on them. "We sold over $97,000 worth in a month. We paid our bills and gave over $66,000 to the kids left behind. For the families whose loved one didn't have kids we gave them an equal share for a charity of their choice."

The fundraisers, Steve says, have helped him and others get through some tough times after the crash. He sought professional help a few years after the accident to help with his anxiety over flying. March 12 is still a very difficult day. When Steve attends the memorial service and looks at all the children in the church pews, he sees their fathers' eyes in some of them and it catapults him right back to that day. "I still certainly struggle," he says. "I look around the rig and see so many young people, fresh faces. Some of them don't know what we went through out here and what we fought for so everyone could be safe. When I get in the chopper, I am content it's a safe aircraft, as safe as any helicopter can be. That doesn't mean I don't say a prayer before we take off and when we land."

The hockey tournament brings Steve peace. "The tournament is one big positive in a huge sea of negatives … at the rink is what it's all about, there is not an enemy there, we are all brothers and sisters that week. We are all there for one purpose, for one person, and it's pretty damn special. I think of the guys often, believe it or not, perhaps too much sometimes. Allison as well. Everyone in that helicopter that day made my life safer."

The tournament is also important to Jonny, who is in his early 40s and has three children. He has left the offshore. He still works in the oil industry supplying fuel, but his job is on land now. He got to know Wade well during his time at Hibernia, as they watched more than a few hockey games, especially when they worked the nightshift together. But his questions about the crash remain with him. "It never should've happened," he says. "They knew there were faulty studs on that gearbox and they sent out a notification to change them within six or eight or 12 months or a certain amount of hours, so they could've just pulled all the choppers in at the time and said 'we are not flying until it's all done.'"

After the flights resumed, Jonny, still working on Hibernia, found it frightening to fly to the platform. "I remembers this one ride in particular coming home in probably 2015 or '16, and it was a white-knuckler. Like, everyone on the chopper was frightened to death. The pilot said there was an engine problem and they were idling down. Everyone was nervous as anything. Normally, you relax and sleep the whole way but they had an issue with this chopper. And it was pretty much after then that I said to the wife that I'm going. I came in tense, the whole time I came in I was thinking about the kids."

These days Jonny's and Greg's email inboxes are filled with heartfelt words from families grateful for the opportunity the memorial fund provides for their children. The letters can be overwhelming. They redact the names and often share the comments with other offshore workers to reaffirm the impact of what they are doing. "For example, I got an email from the mom of a young fellow we have been sponsoring for years," Greg says. "It says, 'Thank you so much! Can you believe this is his last year playing? I had no income since August 10, so without you he would not be playing hockey. I am going to start training October 31st at a call centre. Jobs for my age aren't easy to come by.' So that's one lady. A single parent. His mother says without this he wouldn't be able to play."

Organizing the tournament is time-consuming, especially in the spring when games and schedules and presentations have to be arranged and again in the fall when Greg and others have to sift through applications and arrange accounts with sports stores to cover children's hockey expenses. It's a lot of work for someone with a young family and who is away from home for three weeks at a time.

At moments, the demands of the tournament collide with the reality of what Greg's family has gone through—Wade's public death, the constant reminders of the details of the crash, and the news stories that air on the radio and TV without any notice—and it takes a toll. "It's hard reliving it all the time," he says. "This accident is always going to be in the limelight. I mean you got the Ocean Ranger and you got the 491. Every year, the last 30, 40 years the Ocean Ranger is remembered. It's always brought up in the news, you know what I mean. It's a big accident for Newfoundland as a whole, high profile. It changed the province."

But then he reads the emails and realizes how many children are benefitting from what's being done in Wade's memory. "The thing about the hockey, I don't care if they ever go to the NHL or anything like that, but if it keeps one kid out of trouble, it's worth it to me. It's worth it."

Kevin loves to talk about the Wade Duggan Memorial Fund. He takes in almost every game when the event is held at the Goulds arena. He sometimes wears Wade's black leather jacket to the arena, a jacket that still has the Buckingham Castors logo on it, the team Wade played with in Quebec the first time he left the province for hockey in the mid-1990s. As Kevin watches the rig workers whip up and down the ice, he thinks about the years Wade spent on that very sheet of ice as a minor league player chasing his dream of a hockey career. "He would have made it into the NHL," Kevin laments.

Greg has a little girl now, the Duggans' only grandchild. Greg and his wife wanted children for years but had not been successful. One night, a few weeks after the crash, Greg was in the kitchen looking at Wade's picture on the windowsill. His wife had placed a small angel figurine next to it, with a little card that included a quotation.

It was the middle of the night and Greg was the only one up, missing his brother. "So, I was looking at the picture and it caught my eye," he says. "And you know what it said on that card? It said, 'A quiet strength will bring you grace.'" He doesn't know why it resonated with him but he rushed into the bedroom and woke up his wife. "I said, 'Gertie, it's all going to work out, we're going to have a little girl.' And she said, 'What are you getting on with, three o'clock in the morning?' And I said, 'I'm telling you, I got a sign or something, I don't know what happened, but I'm telling you right now, we're going to have a girl and when she comes along, we'll call her Grace if that happens.' And she said, 'If that happens, you can call her what you want!'"

Little Grace was born a year and a few months later. Nine years old she, like Wade, loves hockey. She plays in a minor hockey league for girls, and in the stands for just about every game is her grandfather. "Oh, yeah, I loves it. Loves it," says Kevin, beaming from his seat, as he watches her skate up the ice. "She loves it more too, right? She loves to see me here. I don't think she'd go on the ice if I wasn't here. She hears all about Wade, talks about him all the time right, and I'll say to her, 'B'y, you got to be like Uncle Wade, get out on the ice and get going,' and she kind of enjoys that, you know, she knows I'm here watching. I'll be here when she's on the ice, that's for sure."

It nags at Greg that Wade didn't get to meet Grace or watch her grow up and see her interest in hockey. "I mean, he is spoke about to her all the time," he says. "We got pictures all over the house. You come into my garage, there's a spot on the wall there. Nine pictures of Wade in a collage of pictures, and his hockey stick is over the pictures and two Toronto Maple Leafs flags over that. That's on my wall since the week he died."

Greg and Wade spent many evenings in that garage, having a beer and chatting about the day and how the Leafs were doing. "Little things I can remember ... he said to me one day about two weeks before he died, I was a lot bigger then, I was 100 pounds bigger, he said, 'You got to lose some weight. I don't want to lose me brother.' Two weeks later he was dead. And after he died I started to think about what he said ... little things in life he said to me ... so I went on a diet after he died and lost 100 pounds. That's what he wanted me to do, so that's what I did."

Grace's parents have told her the story of her name. She was so proud that she recounted it to her classmates. She even talks about him like he is alive. "Up in her bedroom over her bed is Wade's obituary picture. He's looking down over her bed all the time. He'll never be forgotten. I mean, time makes it easier, we're used to living now without him, yes, and time heals everything, but you don't forget. I don't. I still have my moments out in the garage by myself, out there in the morning sitting down looking at his picture and all of a sudden you start to fill up, you know what I mean?

"He would probably have kids by now, and I got one little girl. And she got no cousins, no aunts, no uncles on our side. It's just me now. I got no other brothers or sisters. It was just me and him. And I know how much he would've loved her and being around her and watching her with hockey. I thinks about how much Grace would have benefitted from meeting Wade. That's what I thinks about. I do cherish the good times and all that, but I do think about what could have been. How much different Mother and Father's life would have been. I lost me brother, yes, but Mother and Father lost their son. No one is supposed to bury their son, right?"

He especially thinks about his father, Kevin, who had such a deep connection with Wade because of their love of hockey. His parents like to spend time in Kevin's boyhood home of Grates Cove, on the tip of the Bay de Verde Peninsula. Greg says his father and some others put up a small memorial to Wade behind the old Catholic church—where services are now only held on special occasions, such as when a long-time member of the community passes away—that consists of a small cross about 3 feet by 3 feet, a statue of the Virgin Mary, and a picture of Wade. "He'd go down there, and he'd sit down there and that was his spot to go," Greg says. "And he'd sit down there for an hour. At the first of it, he'd also spend a lot of time at the graveyard, but my little girl occupies a lot of his time now, like that was the light that came along when we needed it to, in that sort of way."

Kevin agrees. "Let me tell you something," he says, "when he went, when his light went out, her bright light came in. And it's like the wife always says, she's the bright light of the family now." Still, his son never leaves his mind and memories of Wade are everywhere and in everything he does. They are in the wrenches and other carpentry tools that Wade used. He comes to mind every time Kevin picks up his hammer. And he is in his mind every time hockey comes on television or when he is at the arena watching Grace as she learns the sport. "You ease off, yes, you ease off but you never forget. You never forget. Especially coming to a place like this, I was there and watched him ... that all comes back to you, it don't leave you. It never, never leaves you."

For a long time Kevin couldn't talk openly about Wade or what happened to him. But now, it's different. "Now, I can sit here and talk all night about it," he says. "We know Wade is gone, but he enjoyed himself when he was on the earth, because I made sure of that. He did what he could in a short period of time, you know, and he had a good job, made a lot of money and a lot of people didn't get to 32, you know. Now, 32 is not very much but—yeah, I can talk about it now, I must say. I don't know what does it, what it is but the more you talks, the better it is. That's what I find."

And when Kevin talks about his younger son, it's not only about his hockey abilities; he talks about Wade's personality, how he liked to joke, and how he lit up a room when he walked into it.

Kevin remembers one story about a trip Wade made to Halifax with his boss at Hyflodraulics. When Wade and his boss walked into a bar, the band stopped mid-tune and the singer yelled for Wade to come up on stage. The band were from Bay Bulls, just a half hour up the road from Wade's hometown of Brigus South. "I mean, that's personality there, right?" he laughs. "He could reach out to anybody. He could talk all day to people."

Greg still travels to and from the rigs by helicopter, and Kevin sighs heavily as he says that all he can do is trust and pray that safety has improved. "You have to be okay with it, you know what I'm saying? I mean he has a livelihood, a little girl out there in hockey, big bills like all of them."

Greg heads down the southern shore frequently to his hometown to see his folks and to swing by the cemetery to visit with Wade. "I goes to the graveyard, I go sit down and have a coffee, just up on top of the hill in the graveyard."

During those times he forgets about the hockey tournament, about the stresses of his job at sea, and about the helicopter flight that changed everything in his world.

Instead, he just thinks about his little brother and the times they shared with their parents. The four of them, one close and happy family. "B'y, I misses him," he says quietly. "I still do ... I still do."

Wade Drake

The first snowfall. That's what gets to Peter Drake.

When fall is over and enough snowflakes accumulate on the frozen ground to create a smooth layer of crisp snow, that's when he feels the deepest sadness about the loss of his brother, Wade.

"Sure, you move on with your life and there's days perhaps that you don't think of him and you probably feel a little bit guilty," Peter laments. "But one of the worst times for me for really missing him is the first snowfall. The first snowfall hits me hard every … every year. Because we both loved being on the Skidoos and stuff like that. If he was on the rig and I was home after the first snowfall, then the phone would ring. He'd want to know if it was any good to take the Skidoo out when he gets home."

Peter often thinks about the long painful days at the hotel in St. John's after the crash. "How we got through it in a way was our family. We had our family there. We were all there hoping for the same thing. Because if you were alone, how much worse would it have been?" Just as often, though, he thinks back to that snowmobiling trip to the west coast in February 2009, when he and Wade and a bunch of friends, including John Pelley, went on their final adventure together. Much of it is captured in video and pictures and burned to a DVD that Peter has watched more than once.

In one picture, Wade is on a snowmobile as it lifts into the air about 3 metres off the ground and at about a 45 degree angle. There is nothing but snowdrifts and small chunks of snow rising up behind the big machine like a mass of swirling clouds. In another, Wade is in the cabin wearing oven mitts as he holds up a large pan of fried fish he just pulled off a hot stove. His grin is so wide that it shows just about every tooth.

And in one video, John Pelley sits at the kitchen table strumming a guitar. On the table is a binder filled with sheets of paper bearing the words to the songs he sings. It is late evening and the lights are low. A TV is on in one corner of the room. A hockey game is on the screen, but the sound is off. Wade is sitting back looking comfortable in an old chesterfield chair, a beer in his hand and one of his legs rising up and down to the beat of the music while his foot taps the floor. John's voice is deep and strong, and there's hardly a sound from the others as he sings "I Died in Vain," a traditional folk song of heartbreak and forsaken love. Many know it as "The Butcher Boy."

In London city where I did dwell
A butcher boy, I loved right well
He courted me, my life away
But now with me, he will not stay
I wish, I wish, I wish in vain
I wish I was a maid again
A maid again I ne'er will be
'Til cherries grow on an apple tree
At every word she dropped a tear

And at every line cried "Willie dear
Oh, what a foolish girl was I
To be led astray by a butcher boy."

A smile crosses Wade's face and he chuckles as John changes that last line to include Wade.

What a foolish girl was I
To fall in love with a Fortune boy.

In those moments, just two weeks before his death, Wade is in his element. "I think back so often now," Peter says. "Wade spent so many years going on those kinds of trips to the west coast with different groups of friends. But he was adamant that year that I go. So he set it up, him and John and I went. It was a beautiful trip. … What a trip. Was it meant to be? It had to be meant to be."

Gertie thinks about what could have been for Wade. "He's still never far from my mind," she says. "When I sit down and think about Wade, I'm like, 'Damn!'" She pauses for a long time before continuing. "Because, you know, he had so much left to do and he was so full of life. And his girls are doing things now like graduating and one day they'll be getting married and he won't be there."

Gertie attends the memorials held in St. John's in March every year. But Peter hasn't gone to the last few. Instead, he goes to the west coast for a snowmobile trip. He jokes that Wade would prefer a week of skidooing and partying it up in a cabin to a melancholy church service. "The cabin trip is the same time of year as the memorial," he says. "And I said, 'If Wade was here, what would he say?' And he would say, 'You're f'ing crazy if you're going in there and not going on your Skidoo trip!'"

Gertie seeks comfort from a short quotation—she doesn't know who wrote it—that makes her think of Wade's approach to life: *Remember me with smiles and laughter, for that is how I will remember you all.* "That's him." Gertie nods her head as she says the words. "You can't help but remember Wade with a smile. It hurts, but you gotta smile because he always made you laugh. If you went in somewhere where he was too and he didn't make you laugh, then there is something wrong with you."

Gertie uses Wade's own style of humour to sum up his over-the-top personality, his love of life, and his desire to be around happy people and focus on having fun times. "He'd be so pissed off if he knew he was dead," she declares and she bursts out laughing. It was the kind of joke her brother would have cracked.

Laughter is also slowly returning to Wanda's life. For the longest time after her husband's death, it didn't come at all. She returned to work but the anguish took its toll, especially when she returned home at the end of the day to an empty house. She cries so hard when she thinks of the time after the crash that she can hardly get her words out. "I don't even know how I'm still alive actually. Like, I thought I couldn't live without him. That's how I always felt. He was always taking care of me. And after the crash, I didn't ... I couldn't ... I just didn't think I could ever live without him."

Wanda was used to being without Wade for long periods of time, but this was different. She found it tough to do even the simplest household chores. She'd get home from work and lie on her bed. All she could think was that the life she and the children knew was all gone now, snatched away in the blink of an eye. She says she never ever in her scariest dreams considered that the helicopter he was flying in was unsafe. "I didn't worry about him about going out there. I did not worry about him out there," she emphasizes. "I really thought they had his back. I didn't worry. You know what I worried more about? Him leaving this house and driving to St. John's. Because he used to leave in the nighttime."

But she has persevered and, slowly, Wanda found the same strength she mustered up that day at the hotel when she confronted investigators and search organizers. She did it because of Taylor and Jenna-Wade, who were growing up fast and needed her. "I felt I had to tell myself that I'm not letting this get the best of me. And I kept having to say that to myself, that I'm not letting this take me away. And from that time on really, I guess, I had to stand on my own two feet after that. I had to be the strong person. I had to take care of myself and my girls."

For Wanda, the healing had begun. Through the grief and the struggle to comprehend what had happened, she realized she needed a career change. She left her nursing-home job after more than two decades and started her own photography business. "Life takes you in different places and you don't expect to go there," she explains. "I like capturing memories for others, I guess." The new career allowed her to set her own hours.

Wade never saw the television broadcast from that audition back in the winter of 2009 when he took Jenna-Wade and Taylor to St. John's to sing. The show didn't air until two months after his death. He would have been happy to know his girls' love of music continued to grow as they grew up.

Garth Brooks was one of Wade's favourite singers. Wade would often sing the country music singer's songs around the house, especially one of his biggest hits, "The Dance." Wanda says whenever she and the children hear those songs now they think of Wade. Several times they've heard a Garth Brooks song right when they needed it the most. Some years after Wade's death, Wanda took the children to one of Brooks's concerts. The show was happy and moving and sad. As they listened to Wade's favourite entertainer, standing on the stage in front of them singing all of Wade's favourite songs, they felt that Wade was sitting there beside them.

Music had become such an important part of the children's lives because of their father that they asked their mother if she would create a music award in his memory at their school, Lake Academy in Fortune. Wanda loved the idea. The write-up about the Wade J. Drake Memorial Music Award says the award "was created in memory of Wade at the request of his daughters who wanted to remember him in a special way for his praise and encouragement for the love of music in their lives.... Through his daughters' love of music, Wade had developed an interest as well to play guitar and had hoped one day to sing and play along with his daughters."

Each year, the award is given to a Grade 7 student who loves music. The student receives a plaque, which includes a write-up about Wade, and a cheque for $100. "I do it so he's remembered and people will know who he was. And, I guess, so he's always remembered by people who never knew him. I just needed to do something so that people will remember."

There's also another memorial in Wade's name in Fortune: The Wade Drake & Burch Nash Family Park. The small south coast town of 1,400 suffered a tremendous loss in the Cougar crash, losing Wade and Burch Nash. So, the town, the province, and corporate and private sponsors created the open space as a way to remember them. The park opened in 2012, and at the ribbon-cutting ceremony Taylor and Jenna-Wade sang a song called "I Miss You," in memory of their father.

The recreational area has a playground with swings and slides, seesaws, and merry-go-rounds. There are picnic tables and a small field where children can kick around a ball. There are benches and trees in which people can dedicate plaques in memory of others. A red crushed-stone trail meanders around the perimeter of the park and to the left of the entrance an oversized gazebo-style storyboard sheltered beneath a grey shingled roof tells the story of Wade, Burch Nash, and Cougar Flight 491.

The park and the music award are tangible ways for Wanda and her family to share how much he meant. The girls are still musical and Jenna-Wade, who has learned to play guitar, sometimes picks up her father's guitar. "We got to try to put pieces back together and try to have a life again," Wanda says. "We still misses him every day. And when occasions come, birthdays and graduations, you know, it's the knife down through you again. I guess it's part of life. You loses someone, it's part of life. But it don't make it any easier."

As Wanda copes with her loss, she often thinks about what others in a similar situation are going through. "My heart goes out to anyone who's got to feel the way that we feel, really. From all of our perspectives, I think we're all still trying to get somewhere and trying to … we're still working on it, you know. I don't think there's any getting better from what happened to Wade, I don't think that's the right words for it, but we're still working it out."

Burch Nash

The dream was always the same. He was in a helicopter that was falling out of the sky. Straight down into the ocean, leaving him drowning. Burch Nash woke up every time he had the nightmare, with one agonizing thought: that searchers would find his body and bring him back home to Fortune.

The terrifying dream became so frequent in the eight to 10 months before the crash that Burch privately asked friends what it meant to have a recurring dream. They asked him what he was dreaming about, and he told them. He went to church in hopes that he could "get in with the Lord," as he believed it would help ensure that his body would be recovered.

But Burch did not share his premonition or worries with his wife, Marilyn. She knew about the dream but when she'd press him for details of what awakened him two and three times a night, causing him to jump out of bed and then spend the rest of the hours tossing and turning, he'd pass it off as "foolishness." She found out what had been waking him only in the days following his death.

Marilyn told that story to a hushed room at the offshore helicopter safety inquiry. "A few nights after the funeral I was at our friend's home and there were several people there," she told the crowded, but quiet, room. "And I just said, 'now I'll never know Burch's dream,' and all my friends' eyes dropped."

That's when her friends told her what had been clouding Burch's mind. "My heart broke even more, if that was even possible," she testified. "All I could think was how he had to feel every single time that he stepped on that chopper. He had to wonder if today was the day. I truly believe the minute they turned around that Burch knew this was it, this is the end. I cannot even begin to imagine feeling that way. The fear must have been unbearable. My husband was a very brave man, but I know that he had to be very scared that morning."

With her daughters Alicia and Alexandria sitting with her and Allison nearby in the inquiry room, Marilyn talked about the morning of March 12, 11 months earlier, of having to break the news to her and Burch's three girls, who were 20, 15, and 14. "Getting the call that dreadful morning was the most difficult thing we have ever had to face. Telling your children that their dad will not be coming home was absolutely heartbreaking. Just to see the look in their eyes tore my heart out."

And then Marilyn took aim at the companies. "How could this happen? Why did our husbands and our daughter have to die? They all died because some people decided that this inexpensive part could wait, and they didn't even bother to inspect those bolts before they left for the offshore. Wouldn't you think that knowing there was a problem with the bolts in the gearbox, that it would make a point of checking to make sure everything was okay?" She continued her condemnation by telling the inquiry that her life ended on March 12 when Burch died; all 17 people who lost their lives that morning "should be here."

Alicia, a university student at the time, cried and struggled to get the words out as she told her story. "I lost my supporter, my protector, and my best friend," she said. "It feels like only yesterday he came into my room to give me a goodbye hug and told me to make him proud. Little did I know those would be the last words I'd hear him say."

Marilyn poured her heart out at the inquiry for one reason. "Well, you know, I just had to get it out there because I didn't want anyone to have to deal with what we dealt with," she explains. "I mean, I felt bad enough for me, but it's my kids that I really felt for. For the sake of something so inexpensive and easy to repair … I mean, it's people's lives and you know a lot of them men are scared of it. Because everyone that came to the funeral home, I know that I wasn't in my proper mind, but I know that I spoke to a lot of them men and asked how they felt and I had a lot of people tell me they kissed the ground when they walked off the helicopter. They were just so grateful to get off it."

Alicia is married now and has her own children, a boy and a girl. Connor Burch is five and Kennedy Rae four. Burch's mother, Marjorie, has packed up two large boxes of Burch's things, a collection that includes his trophies and medals, his boxing gloves, his hockey sweater, a baseball, and a small wooden yellow dory and an airplane that Burch played with when he was a child, and plans to give it to Connor so that he too can enjoy his grandfather's things. She wants him to have those things so he'll know more about who he was named after.

In their home in Ontario, Alicia placed a portrait of her father in Kennedy's bedroom on her dresser. She put it there after Kennedy walked into the room one day carrying the big framed picture and saying, "Poppy Burch just told me to put that picture in my room so I can talk to him all the time and say good night." Marilyn often hears Kennedy in her room talking and when she goes in and asks who she is talking to, Kennedy says, "Oh, Poppy, he's being so silly today!"

It's out of the mouths of babes, but Marilyn says it comforts her to think that he is watching over them.

In 2018 Alexandria had a baby girl, Penelope Nash Hare, who would have been Burch's third grandchild. They call her Ellie. In one newborn photo she is wrapped in a quilt handmade from Burch's shirts.

It's unfair that Burch did not see any of that, Marilyn bemoans: not the grandchildren, not the loving relationships his children are in, not the graduations. But they all keep his memory and legacy alive by talking about him constantly and by telling their children stories about their grandfather. "He made a big impact on everybody, he was so happy-go-lucky," Marilyn says.

Glenda agrees. "One thing for sure," she says, "Burch's kids will never let their children grow up without knowing who their grandfather was and what he stood for and how much he loved them." Glenda laments no longer having her brother around. Even just to pick up the telephone to call him for a chat. Before Burch's death, she and her husband, Claude, and their families got together for barbeques or to go sailing, and on long weekends they'd often book a cabin just to be together. Burch's parents travelled from Fortune to see them all on the weekends. And other times Burch just hung out at Glenda and Claude's house. "He'd come over and we'd sit down and watch the game or whatever and have a sociable beer or whatever," Claude says. "A lot of what I miss is that we were all close together. His kids was here. His father and mother was here. They could come in anytime at all, and we might not get together for three weeks again while he was gone but when he was around, we were going to be doing something on the weekend. And then all of a sudden— gone! That was all taken away from us. Just like that."

Claude is thankful, though, for having had someone like Burch in his life. "He was a real family guy. The kids loved him," he says. "His wife and kids were everything. He came in one time you know, they were going to a hockey game—that was when the St. John's Maple Leafs were here—and he took the two or three kids to the stadium and they had to dress up and paint their faces and they won fans of the game! And I can see them there now, Alex with her

Maple Leafs T-shirt on, one side of her face one colour and another side of her face another colour ... but that's him and the girls, they were like it all the time."

Glenda and Burch grew even closer in the years before his death, after Burch and his family moved nearby. "Like every brother and sister, we had arguments. But the one thing I never had was the proper chance to say goodbye. It's not like he was sick and you know that he was going to die or something, but I never had the proper chance. That I resent. Big time. But you know things happen and we have no control. But I'm glad that we had, you know, the really good childhood years and the adult years that we stayed together."

Glenda appreciates the memorial park created in the town of Fortune in memory of Burch and Wade Drake. When she heard that it included a playground for children, an area to play soccer, benches and picnic tables all surrounded by trees, and a walking trail, the word *awesome* ran through her mind. "The park is like just a place of solitude," she explains. "It's just that inner peace and knowing the two men were awesome dads and for the kids to enjoy it: it's good, it's comforting." She dabs her eyes as she speaks about the park and the reason it was built. "Good can come out of bad. Oh my God, can it ever."

Every summer, the Senior's Club in Fortune holds a family fun day at the park. It was originally all about the children, with everything that they would enjoy: cookies, chips, bars, pop, and music. But in the last few years more adults show up. "Someone makes sandwiches and they have a good old mug-up in the park." It is another way, she says, for people to learn about her brother and know who Burch was. What makes the community park extra special is where it was built. "When they put the park there, I couldn't get over it. I thought, 'Oh my God!' It was built right on the property where Burchy used to go to school. It was where our old school, Haddon Academy, used to be. That's where we went for our elementary school years, before Fortune Collegiate. For a lot of people in the community, what better place to put a park."

Burch's mother and father now live down the road from their old home in Fortune in a senior's cottage, a tiny two-bedroom bungalow they've filled with physical reminders of Burch.

His obituary is pinned to the refrigerator door. Pictures of him are on most walls. In one photo, Burch, wearing dark sunglasses and a red bandanna around his head, is sitting on his beloved Yamaha motorbike, the one he bought only after getting his mother's approval. Included is a tiny picture inset of Marjorie with Burch standing over her, his arms wrapped tightly around his mother's head and shoulders and smiles on both their faces. Below the picture is a poem. *He is gone. You can shed tears that he is gone or you can smile because he lived* are the opening lines.

The motorcycle now belongs to his daughter Alexandria. It's in her garage and she says it isn't going anywhere. Allison has his snowmobile.

Down the hall in one of the rooms are two pillows on a bed, both with Burch's face embroidered on the material. Sports trophies he earned as a child are on the nearby bureau. In the living room, a digital picture frame flashes photos of Burch and his family, and in every one someone has their arms around him or he has his arms around them.

Harold and Marjorie's days are filled with thoughts of their son, the memories floating in and out of their minds as often as the ocean tide just outside their door and down the road comes and goes. Harold flicks through one of the many photo albums they have of the children. "Daddy's little helper" is written above one photo and, in it, a young Burch is outdoors chopping wood with his father. Alongside another picture is a patch of Burch's curly blond hair from that time when he was six or seven and had his first haircut.

Harold and Marjorie sometimes drive past the house in which they raised the children—where they lived for 48 years—and as Marjorie looks at the gravel laneway, she still pictures Burch and the other children playing hockey. His hockey stick from those years is in the porch closet just inside the cottage's front door.

Harold still pictures his little boy fishing for trout along the banks of Fortune Brook, looking up at him with his tiny voice saying, "Daddy, sing me 'Aunt Martha's Sheep!,'" the song Burch loved when he was a child.

Their days now include a ritual that helps them cope with the unbelievable heartbreak of losing their only son. They get up in the morning, have breakfast, and head out the door. After a short drive, they are at the graveyard, where they tidy up around Burch's headstone. The plot is meticulous, surrounded by red roses, yellow lilies, and solar lights. After she finishes straightening up some of the flowers, Marjorie leans down and kisses the picture of Burch on the headstone. "I always gives him a kiss," she says. "It just helps me start the day off. And I always says a prayer, The Lord's Prayer."

Before getting back into the car, they stand and stare mournfully at his grave. "That's where he's resting to," Marjorie says wistfully. "Yep, that's where he's resting to," Harold repeats as he draws a deep breath. "I come visit every morning and visit him every afternoon. It makes me feel good then."

Then they drive down the road, stopping this time at the community park. Pictures of Burch and Wade Drake adorn the large marble memorial at the entrance. As Harold walks by, he pauses and stares for a moment. "It's the same way with the park," he says. "He's there and I got to touch him every time, I goes over and I rubs his face. Every day. I don't know why but I just got to do it. And then when I do, it's like everything feels okay." They sit and watch the children and listen to their voices as they run around jumping and racing back and forth from the swings to the slide to the seesaw. "It's always full of kids." Harold smiles. "It's nice when you see it. The kids has good fun and they enjoys themselves, and that's all that matters."

When they return home about an hour or so later, Harold heads to his 8 foot by 10 foot shed in the backyard. It's filled with tools that line the shelves or hang off the wall. On the back wall hangs a plaque-mounted picture of Burch, which includes a write-up about his life. "And there he is there," Harold says, as he steps in to the small metal shed. "That's my boy there. I even got him out in the shed with me. I comes out here often, twice and three times every day." When he sits there alone, Harold remembers his son. "He was a real character. It makes no difference what people was or who they was, he was still nice to everybody. Got along with everybody." He enjoys reading the words on the side of the picture that are taken from Burch's obituary. They describe an amazing husband, father, son, and brother, a great athlete and sportsman. A man who liked long bike rides with his buddies when he wasn't offshore, and who enjoyed Saturday nights watching hockey or playing cards when he was working at sea with the people who were his other family. A man who lived each day to its fullest and looked forward to the next. A man who will be remembered for his devious smile and his favourite phrase: "If you can't convince them, confuse them." Harold chuckles as he says that line out loud.

Harold doesn't take his eyes off his son's face as his laugh fades. "But he was my friend," he says, his voice suddenly low and melancholy, his eyes filling with tears. "He meant a lot to us. He didn't mean a lot, he meant everything."

In their 80s now, Harold knows time is catching up to him and Marjorie. "I'll be alongside of him someday, I pray to God that I will. So that we'll be all together; me, him, his mother, and our dear Glenda."

After a while he heads back inside the cottage, where Marjorie is serving up a lunch of goulash, Burch's favourite meal. "You don't get over it," she explains of their lives now and their daily routine. "You just live through it. You don't forget it. You just live through it."

After they finish eating, she lays the dishes in the sink, letting the water and dish liquid wash over them. They move into the living room to rest for a while, Marjorie on the couch, Harold in his beige cloth lazy-boy chair. Leaning back, he says, "I was too young to understand it when I lost my dad," he says, "but I'm older now and I lost Burchy, and I think, I'm almost sure, he thought the same thing of me and his mother. We were something else to him."

Marjorie tries to explain the many trips to the cemetery and park. "If we don't go in there, the day never started, and it never ends if we don't do it at night. One thing I'm thankful for is that we got his body. I don't know what we'd be like if we hadn't got his body. I don't know how we'd cope with it."

In a few hours, they'll be up and on the go again, reaching for their coats and heading out the door. They'll get in the car and Harold will back out of the driveway, and turn toward the road that leads to the cemetery.

Kenneth MacRae

In the immediate years after her father's death, when she was still a teenager, Michelle MacRae considered the crash from every angle. She needed to learn every detail. "I read every article released, really," she says. "I'd read everything. And maybe Grade 10 or Grade 11, I started really searching. I went to boarding school and I would sit there in my room for hours and just read articles. And I would just read them all. Like, every single one. Especially if it was a new piece of information. Just to get, I don't know, a different perspective."

Michelle even wrote a one-person play a year after the crash. Not about the flight itself but about hearing the news and its effect on her and her family. This time she was given a speaking role, as she had wanted when she was in Grade 9, but this one she gave to herself. The 20-minute monologue opened by playing the black box tapes from the cockpit. "Everyone takes inspiration from what happened in different ways and at the time mine was in theatre," Michelle explains. "I wrote it and I performed it at a school in front of a lot of people."

Seven years after her father's death, Michelle decided she wanted to live in Newfoundland. She had been attending university in Nova Scotia but transferred to Memorial University of Newfoundland. When people asked her why she was moving to St. John's, she told them a lie. "I tell very, very few people about the reason I really came here," she says. "MUN has cheap tuition," she'd say to anyone who asked. But her real reason for moving to the city was to see the last place her father was, to see where he died. She didn't know much about the province before moving. She had visited only once before, with her mother to attend one of the memorial services in the first two years after the crash.

Michelle realized that she wanted to spend time in the place where the heartbreak of the crash meant something important to the residents and hadn't been forgotten. "I think it was a different experience being in Nova Scotia versus being here," she explains. "There you just didn't have that sense of community about what happened. You know, I was the girl in high school whose dad died. And here, it was just perceived differently. People understood differently about what was going on. It's a very profound thing here. It's something everyone remembers."

Michelle believes that many people in the province know someone, or of someone, who was directly affected because of the number of Newfoundlanders who died in the crash. "So, it's really a different environment to be in. I don't know if it gave me closure, but I definitely came here looking for that. Looking for a sense of community." Within one month of moving to St. John's in August 2016, Michelle was hired by a local spa and worked with a young woman named Allison. "So, I worked with Allison from October through till March. And that month I went to my manager … I normally work every Sunday, but I had asked her if I could have Sunday, the 12th, off."

"Why do you want that day off?" her boss asked. Michelle told her the secret she had shared with only a few since moving to Newfoundland seven months earlier. "I was like, 'it's for my dad's memorial service.' And I just gave her the lowdown and she was like, 'Oh, Allison Nash's dad was in that too.'" A co-worker, someone she walked by every workday was living with the same grief. Michelle couldn't believe it. The news that Michelle's father had also died in the Cougar crash quickly reached Allison's ears and Allison soon approached her about it. "She just came up to me and said, 'Oh my God, your dad was in this too!' And we talked about it and we hugged, and we cried." Every time they'd pass each other in the hallway after that, Michelle thought about their fathers and assumed that Allison did too. It was the assurance she was looking for that moving to Newfoundland was a good idea, that the memory of the crash in the province was very present and very real as she suspected.

About a year after the crash, Michelle's sister, 23-year-old Alyssa, was still at the University of Ottawa, studying Human Resources, working as a supervisor at the Starbucks coffee shop in the campus food court, when her manager asked her to prepare a presentation to other managers on health and safety. The manager knew that Alyssa was passionate about that area of her studies.

Alyssa decided to present the business, financial, and personal side of health and safety in the workplace. No one in the training room knew that her father had died a year earlier in a helicopter crash off Newfoundland. After she outlined some research, she said she wanted to focus on a specific example of an accident in the workplace. "And I laid out what happened with the crash," Alyssa says. She based it on what was in the news and what was on the TSB's website. "I didn't want it to be biased when I presented that component. And I talked about—what's the business case? What's the financial impact? What was the impact on the community and all those kinds of things. And then they said, 'what was the personal impact,' and I put the picture up of the 17 people who were lost. And I didn't want to get into other families' business, but that was the impact—17 lives were lost and 18 families were changed forever."

Then, with the course participants still unaware of her personal connection to the Cougar crash, Alyssa said, "Let's talk about my personal impact," and she put a picture of her own family up on the screen. "I said, 'Let's talk about the impact on families,' and I showed his picture, and I said, 'So, this is my dad.'" The room was totally quiet. "There was dead silence. Dead silence. I mean, those last five slides I was, by the end of it, I was shaking, physically shaking. But I got through it. I was very proud of myself for getting through it without completely losing it."

Many of Alyssa's co-workers thanked her for such a powerful presentation. She left the room that day hoping that she had made a difference for others working in the field of health and safety. "I'm hoping if you change just one person, if you've impacted just one person to change how they think about health and safety, then it mattered."

At one point during her studies, Alyssa almost failed a course because the details about the crash were in a textbook that was required reading. "And like a dumbass, trying to be a good student," she says, "I read ahead, right around mid-term time. So, I was reading the chapter we would have been doing after mid-terms—this was a Health and Safety class in university as part of my Human Resources degree—and the accident was in my textbook, and I just lost it."

Alyssa's first visit to Newfoundland wasn't until 2018 and even then it was a last-minute decision prompted by Michelle, who asked her to attend the annual memorial service. As her plane touched down in St. John's, Alyssa couldn't hold back her tears. "The plane was landing, and I just thought to myself, it's like maybe I'm crossing the same airspace that he did. And I started—I was glad I was in the back of the plane, so nobody could see me—I was crying because—and it's in part probably why I wanted to go to the helicopter pad, because that's somewhere he was. It's some morbid thought of like the last time he was alive, he might've been flying here."

The church was about 80 per cent full for the memorial service and, as she sat in the pew, all Alyssa could think about was the young children sitting in front of her. Many of them looked to be eight or nine years old, she figured, and wouldn't have known their father or uncle who was lost. That thought bothered her and reminded her of Michelle's age when their father died. "Michelle was 14," she says, "and I find a lot of my grieving has been more for her sometimes than for me because I'm like, 'I'm 22, I'm an adult, I can handle it, I can get through it.' He was there for my graduation, he was there for all my awkward teenage years shit, but he wasn't there for Michelle. I was so angry that he got taken away from her."

The last time Alyssa saw her father was the Thanksgiving before the crash. They didn't go hunting that trip. Instead they went for a quiet walk on a trail. "In some respects, it makes you value the people in your life and the impact they have on it and not to take any of it for granted."

Alyssa cherishes her relationship with her father and sums it up by saying that he was "an anchor." But a decade after his death, there are days when he doesn't cross her mind, and that frightens her. "I think with the passage of time it scares you more that you think of them less ... and it's not a bad thing, you're just moving on with life. You'll always remember them, but you start to forget the way that they looked, or you forget the sound of their voice, and that tears the shit out of you because it's not what you want ... because you don't want to forget them. And then I think on some level, I don't know when you're going to be done saying goodbye."

Ken's sister-in-law Lee-Ann Brubacher can't help but laugh at the mention of Ken's name when she tells stories about their political arguments and how neither would give an inch on accepting the other's views, or when she talks about the times he taught her the rules and subtleties of poker. She misses his silly jokes, but mostly laments what his death did to his family. "It was a terrible loss," she says. "He had so much love for his family and his kids. All of them were deeply, deeply scarred by the loss of their dad. And I think Michelle and Alyssa are very much their father's daughters ... Their openness and their kindness and their humour and their beaming smiles and it's interesting because Alyssa is not his natural born daughter. She's his stepdaughter. But, yet they are just so much alike. It's amazing how much she was influenced by Ken and rightly so. If anyone was awesome to be influenced by, it was being influenced by Ken.

"The love that we all had for Ken, it deeply affected me, there is not a day goes by that I don't think of him. I'm sure there isn't. He was just such a nice, good person, a lot of fun and I miss him—I miss his friendship deeply."

Jason Gulliver also still remembers Ken often. Especially since his friend had only recently retired from the military, in his mid-40s. "He had a whole family. He just semi-retired. He had plans. He had just bought a new rifle and he was looking at buying a Buell motorcycle at the time, so he would have something to ride around where he was living with the trails."

Jason still hunts every November at the same spot in the Alberta bush. "I can see spots where he would sit in the morning when he'd go hunting. And you go up, and you say, 'Yup, that's where Kenny would go when you drop him off in the morning.' It seems like it was like last year. I don't think it goes away. I guarantee if you found 50 names, or 50 people that knew Ken MacRae, they would probably all say the exact same thing. He was the nicest guy you could ever meet. I don't think he ever had a bad word to say about anybody. So easy to get along with."

By mid-to-late December winter has settled in over St. John's. At Quidi Vidi Lake, thick rolls of clouds tumble across the sky as walkers trudge through the snowy path around the lake. Most seem oblivious to the small memorial across from the boathouse. Its silver stainless steel blends in with the snow. Ice-covered bushes and a few tall, thin trees surround the monument but do little to slow the cold wind.

During the warmer months the bushes and trees spring to life. By summer, thick green ferns and yellow, white, and purple daisies sprout up along the sides of a walkway of large flat rocks that lead to the sculpture. Wooden benches form a circle around it, and in the middle of a busy city it is a peaceful place where people can sit and stare at the memorial and the water, and perhaps contemplate loss and legacy.

On this day, that beauty is all but hidden under the blanket of snow. No one notices as Michelle walks toward a lone wooden bench a few metres off to the side. She moves slowly, trying not to slip on the ice underneath her feet. It's cold enough for two scarves. Both are wrapped around her shoulders and neck and bunched into the collar of her black knee-length winter coat.

Michelle has never been here before. She's only seen the tribute to the people of Cougar Flight 491 in pictures. But on this day, just two days before Christmas, she is ready to see it.

She sits on the bench and stares for a long time. Almost like her mind is revisiting ghosts of years past. She pushes back her long, thick black hair and suddenly the tears flow, her words barely decipherable between heavy sobs. "He left on the 11th and I remember hugging him in the driveway," she weeps. "I don't think I said I love you. I hugged him in the driveway and he left and drove to the airport."

The memory of that moment has blurred, but what happened the next morning hasn't. "And the next morning everyone was still asleep," she pauses to inhale a deep breath, "and I was heading to school because school started at like eight and we got out at two. And I checked the voicemails and he had left a voicemail at like 6:30. And then I talked to him on the phone, and I didn't say I love you at that time. I was in a rush just to get to school. I told him Mom was asleep, so she couldn't talk. So, I was the last one to talk with him. And ah, I just went to school and went about my day." The flood of tears continues. "I just wish I told him that I loved him. That's all."

After a few minutes she gets up from the bench and walks over to the memorial. A large black crow squawks from the tree above. A police siren wails a street or two away. Her eyes—big and dark like her father's—search up and down and around the long thin piece of stainless steel until she spots his name.

Ken MacRae.

She moves her hand up and down and over each letter, then laughs slightly, still sniffling. "I think it's funny that they wrote Ken instead of Kenneth. His name is Kenneth." She notices other shortened names. Tom, not Thomas. Tim, not Timothy. "I guess they did the names like that," she says, making small talk. "But people did call him Ken. He hated when people called him Kenny though. There's a friend of the family and they always called him Kenny and he hated it."

She keeps staring at the memorial as if trying to decide what she thinks of it. "It's different than I thought," she says. "I have only seen a picture of his name on it. But it's nice. I like it."

Michelle studies archeology in university, a field that tries to unearth the past and make sense of it—much the same as she does when she attempts to put his death and the last decade in perspective. "I think it's made me a better person. I just try to live my life every day in a way that he would be proud of. And I think that his legacy and his memory lives on in how we live and my duty on this earth is to respect that and respect his memory."

Michelle, now in her mid-20s, focuses on what she had. "I'm really fortunate for the time I got to spend with him. He was an amazing man. He was an amazing father. Even if it was only 14 years, I'm glad that I got that. A lot of people don't even have that. At least I had a father who was present and an amazing influence in my life for that short period of time."

And with that, Michelle turns to leave. She has seen what she came to see. It's still very cold, but the sky is starting to clear as she turns and heads back toward the road.

The Survivor

Does anyone know where the love of God goes,

when the waves turn the minutes to hours?

—Gordon Lightfoot, "The Wreck of the *Edmund Fitzgerald*"

Robert Decker, 27

Robert Decker left his job as an offshore weather and ice specialist after the crash of Cougar Flight 491.

He vowed that he would never work in that field again. Robert went into real estate, selling homes and properties in the St. John's area.

One of the more puzzling questions about the crash is, how could he have possibly survived? A young man who suffered massive body injuries, including a ruptured vertebra, a broken sternum, and a broken ankle, who swallowed a large amount of seawater after the chopper struck the water and started to come apart, and whose core body temperature dropped to such a dangerous level that he passed out just after his rescuer, Ian Wheeler, reached him in the extremely cold Atlantic Ocean. Robert doesn't remember anything about his rescue from that point on.

The man who oversaw the public inquiry into offshore helicopter safety called Robert's survival "miraculous." The 27-year-old was wearing a survival suit that was one size too big for him, according to the TSB. Although he had put it on properly, it was a size large. For his build, it should have been a medium. In the one hour and 20 minutes Robert was floating and bouncing around in the North Atlantic, the inside of the suit had become wet and his body temperature had dropped considerably.

The human body's normal temperature is 37°C. A document from Transport Canada that outlines how to survive in cold water says cardiac arrest resulting in death happens sometime after a body's core temperature drops below 24°C. By the time rescuers reached Robert, his body temperature had dropped to 29.8°C and he had an irregular heart rate.

In the winter of 2009, eight months after the crash, Robert testified at the inquiry. His lawyer coached him through the details of the morning of March 12: his arrival at the airport, the flight, the crash, and the rescue. Robert then took a short break before reading a prepared statement that he had written.

"I don't think that anyone will ever know why it was that I survived this disaster and the others did not. There probably is no good reason, just luck. What I do know is that I came incredibly close to losing my life also.

"There are several things that might have made some difference to my survival. I don't know whether they would have made a difference for anyone else or not. The first thing, I guess, I was relatively young, healthy, and fit at the time of the crash. Another is that maybe the fact that I braced myself against the seat in front of me reduced the force against my chest with the helicopter hitting the water. That might have left me with a little more air in my lungs.

"Also, when I regained consciousness in the submerged helicopter cabin, I know that I stayed calm and I didn't panic. I was able to concentrate in getting out of the helicopter and to the surface as quickly as possible. Many people know that I have been sailing in small boats, mostly on Conception Bay, since I was quite young, and I've taught sailing at the Royal Newfoundland Yacht Club. Many times I have been thrown into the cold sea water from an overturned boat. I think that that experience meant that when the helicopter suddenly filled with icy water, I could react instinctively without having to consciously plan what I had to do. It was like a reflex to take a breath and to hold it and just stay calm until I could get to the surface.

"As good as the training is, a couple days of controlled immersion in that pool every few years is not enough to allow anyone to develop the instinctive reactions that they need to have a chance of escaping a helicopter crash like Cougar 491.

"Other things were just luck. I was seated next to a window. The helicopter sank with the port side down. I was on the starboard side so that the open window next to me was above me when I released my seatbelt and the buoyancy of my suit probably helped carry me through it. Every second counted and small things like that made a very big difference.

"I know that many family members of the 16 passengers are here today or are listening to the broadcast. I don't know what else I can say to you other than just to tell my story as I've done here today. It could just as easily have been someone else who survived and me that did not.

"I have already privately thanked the Cougar crew that came to my rescue on March 12th, but I want to publicly thank them again here today.

"I hope that this Inquiry does make offshore travel by helicopter safer. I will not be flying offshore any more, but others continue to do it every day and they deserve to be able to do it safely. Training to escape from a crashed helicopter is important. Having good survival suits is important, and having search and rescue capacity nearby is important. But all those things are what you need after there's been a crash into the ocean.

"If we really want to make offshore helicopter travel safe, what we have to do is to make sure that every helicopter does not crash. The best way to keep every offshore worker safe is to keep every helicopter in the air where it belongs.

"Safety starts with the helicopter and I think everything else is secondary."

Appendix